TALKING TO THE SKY

a memoir

Aimee Mayo

Little Blue Typewriter Press

Talking to the Sky is a work of nonfiction. Some names and identifying details have been changed.

Published in the United States of America by Little Blue Typewriter Press

The Library of Congress has established a Cataloging-in-Publication record for this title.

TalkingtotheSky.com

Subjects:
1. Mayo, Aimee / 2. Memoir —Biography
3. Family — dysfunctional relationships
4. Southern—Rural conditions —Alabama — Nashville
5. Coming-of-age — Heroes Journey / 6. Music — Songwriting
7. Addiction / 8. Abuse
9. Mental Illness / 10. Survival and Self Invention

Paperback
978-0-578-84977-5

Hardback
978-0-578-75756-8

E-book
978-0-578-75754-4

Printed in the United States of America

For Chris, you are my everything!

Levi, Oscar and Lola— I love you too much!

Acknowledgements

The list is a little long, but I've been writing this book since before there was an iPhone, so a lot of people have helped me along the way.

Chris Lindsey, thank you for being my best friend, first reader, and my psychiatrist when I needed it. You're my mirror and sounding board. I'm so grateful that I get to spend my life with you. I love you!

Levi, Oscar, and Lola (it's hard to say anything without somebody getting jealous, but here goes...) Levi, you remind me so much of my dad, you got all the best parts. You've got the biggest heart and the best hugs ever. Oscar — "Doc Oc" you're still my guru and the funniest person I know. Thank you for making me laugh every day. Lola, you're my soulful sidekick and sweetest surprise. I learn so much from you.

You guys have asked me "when's this book coming out" for most of your lives. You're what pushed me across the finish line. The realization that you watched me work on something for so long and the thought of it never coming out was more heartbreaking than the fear of letting it go. I hope seeing the struggle it has been for me, proves to you that you can do ANYTHING if you believe, work your butt off and never give up!

Mom, there are so many wonderful things about you that didn't make it into the memoir. Thank you for always encouraging me. You are such an incredible mom, and I love you more than you will ever know! Dad, you were the biggest dreamer I've ever known.

Cory, I'm glad you were my seatmate on this insane rocket ride. You blow my mind with your talent. Thanks for sharing memories and saying, "I don't give a shit what you write about me."

Uncle Kelly, you've always been like a brother to me. You're the most thoughtful and loving person I've ever known. All of those wishes we made under that meteor shower came true. (FYI Uncle Kelly's art gallery—Gallery 202 in Franklin, TN—sells his and my mom's art.)

Aunt Debbie— you're an American treasure! We always say everybody needs an Aunt Debbie. I love you!

Truman, I'm glad you're in my family.

Bart Herbison, thank you for telling me in that smokey, authoritative voice, "Aimee, it's one of the best books I've ever read, and I read A LOT." That phone call is what made me decide to put the book on Kickstarter. Troy Verges, thank you! You loved the book in 2008 and always encouraged me. Thank you to Leah, Beth, Vanessa, Laurie and Cathi, and all of my family and friends in Gadsden, Alabama. I love you!

Melissa Mathews, Tyler Dunson, and Lisa Bolt thank you all so much for everything. Julian, thank you for learning how to make an audiobook with me. You rocked it!

Extra special thanks to Kenny Chesney, Keith Urban, Tim McGraw, Jamey Johnson, Brantley Gilbert, Sarah Buxton, Martina McBride, Tom Bukovac, and Dallas Davidson.

Thank you to Taylor and Andrea Swift for one of the best lessons I've ever learned to believe in my dream the way I see it and to be willing to walk away if it ain't right.

Thank you to Rodrigo Corral for the badass cover. My expectations were ridiculous, and you and Dasha exceeded them all. I want to thank Dee Downey Pruitt, Lee Linton, Alice, MB Roberts, Courtney Greenhalgh, Joan Rogers and David. Jennifer Medina, thank you for the clarity in confusion. You were a superhero fixing all those indentations. Dana Perino, you're a diamond that shines so bright on everyone around you. Thank you for cheering me on! Thank you to Kristin Barlowe and Jon Morgan for the photo, and thank you to Lorrie Turk for the lashes and pretty make-up!

Tanya Farrell. You're an answered prayer- I'm so glad you're guiding and helping me get this book out into the world.

Thank you Christopher Schelling for answering a hundred texts just because you're awesome! You're who gave me the best advice anyone did about writing this book — trust your instinct.

I'm almost positive that I'm forgetting people, who I really need to thank, so thank you! I'm so grateful to everyone who backed my memoir on Kickstarter — you made this book real. All your names (I hope it's all your names) are listed at the end. Love and infinite blessings. Aimee

Author's Note

To you—this book took 15 years of my life and I know I never shut up about that. I think because I'm trying to justify it to myself—especially when I don't even know why I wrote it. Through the years, I've had a dozen editors try to fix it, and every time I hated how they changed it. So, the book isn't perfect, the punctuation is still kind of messed up, but it is my heart on paper. After years of confusion, I decided to just tell it like a talk. Thank you for picking it up. I hope you're why I wrote it.

Some names and identifying details have been changed.

Contents

Chapter One

———

WILD WORLD

Blue Horses

THE ONLY CHILDHOOD CHRISTMAS I REMEMBER is the one that never came. I was eight years old the night the phone call came that exploded like a bomb in my grandmother's kitchen. I sat in my mother's parents' cramped living room, finishing up Daddy's present—a paint-by-numbers portrait of blue horses. I knew Daddy loved horses because every time he got any money, we went to the track. We celebrated my little brother Cory's second birthday there and stayed until the sun came up.

"Happy-go-lucky!" Maw Maw hollered. I didn't have to look up from my cardboard canvas to know she had solved the puzzle before anyone on the TV show got close. She was the queen of Wheel of Fortune.

It felt like Christmas at their house—the two taxidermy deer head on the back wall were wearing Santa Claus hats and all the grandkids' stockings hung from the gun rack. "Gimme a beer," Paw Paw said from his La-Z-Boy. He always sat there like a sleepy old shark, waiting to bite somebody's head off—grumbling at anyone who made a noise, blasting the police scanner (he called it "the radio") as it filled the air with bursts of static, high-pitched hissing, and broken voices like it had Tourette's. In map-dots like Hokes Bluff, Alabama, the scanner was big entertainment, a small-town, real-time reality show.

Jumping up, I grabbed his empty can and headed to the "The Crusher" that hung on the wall in the kitchen. I tossed the can in and jerked the lever—it crunched like a fat roach. As I opened the back door to sling it out onto the screened-in porch, I was stunned for a moment by the surreal beauty of iridescent icicles hanging from the rafters above and hundreds of cans like little silver nuggets encased in ice and glittering in the milky-blue moonlight.

I grabbed an ice-cold Budweiser from the fridge, poured a little salt on the lid the way Paw Paw liked it, and popped the top. I placed it on his side table. Budweiser will be the smell that evokes my childhood quicker than Play-Doh, Crayola crayons, or Elmer's glue.

"Weekends and slolidays," he slurred, "that's when the loons come out." He came at me, wriggling his hands in a spooky pantomime, then caught himself being silly and resumed his tough-guy demeanor.

My grandmother leaned in, looking at the old cabinet TV like it was a secret door. She took a deep drag on her Benson and Hedges extra-long menthol, her eyes locked on the Caribbean cruise and remote-control TV she could have won.

"Maw Maw, that's your stuff!" I said, ignoring the beep and babble of the police scanner. "I don't know why you don't go be on that show."

"Well, that Chuck Woolery is one fine lookin' man—I wouldn't mind meetin' him."

The flirty way she said it cracked me up, and I giggled until she was laughing too.

"Shuts the hell up—shlomeblody's shot!" my grandfather barked.

"Come on, hon. I bet your supper's ready," Maw Maw said to me.

At the kitchen table, I sat three feet from my Paw Paw's recliner. Maw Maw and I were both waiting for him to stumble off to his bedroom. Maw Maw's bed was the cigarette-scarred couch against the back wall of the living room and mine was the little, plaid loveseat next to it. We'd lay with our heads where the two sofas met and talk late into the night. I loved it there, mostly because of Maw Maw. My grandmother had my favorite laugh. It was Beethoven beautiful, smoky, and sugar-baby sweet as it sailed around the room. She had the kind of laugh that rich women envied. It came from someplace deep inside her, someplace that my grandfather's fist could not find.

My grandmother set a steaming bowl of beef stew in front of me. She loved collecting all the character glasses from McDonald's, and she kept the Hamburglar on the top shelf reserved for me. She filled my special glass to the top with milk as I watched a square of butter melt down my favorite cornbread in the world, perfectly crispy and shaped like little corn cobs.

The black rotary phone on the wall behind the table rang. I knew it was my mama as soon as Maw Maw started talking.

"Who's on the phone?" Paw Paw shouted.

"It's Becky."

She was across town with my little brother Cory at my father's parents' house. She hated the house she grew up in and never liked to stay for long. Daddy had dropped me off earlier that morning and said he was headed to buy Christmas presents.

Paw Paw kept hollering something I couldn't understand, until I heard Maw Maw translate, "Your daddy wants you to stop at Warehouse Groceries and pick up a couple cases of beer on' count of tomorrow being Christmas."

My grandmother pulled the curly phone cord straight, stretching it as far as it would go and kept talking as she walked over to the sink to rinse the dishes. "That's the police scanner makin' all that racket. Somebody shot their self out on I-59, and your daddy wants to know who it was before he goes to bed."

A soul-jolting scream came through the phone.

Maw Maw let go of the receiver, which flew across the kitchen like a slingshot, cracking my Hamburglar glass into two pieces, sending freezing cold milk down my shirt and splashing scalding hot beef stew into my lap. It slammed hard against the pine knot wood paneling, then dangled like a hysterical puppet as another piercing scream ripped from it. Maw Maw and I grabbed for the receiver, clenching it with four hands. The fear in my grandmother's eyes scared me, so I let go.

"Becky, are you hurt?"

"Oh my God! Oh my God! I didn't believe him." Mama's screams morphed into sobs. She sounded like a wounded animal howling.

"Becky, are you okay? What's happenin'?" As the panic rose in Maw Maw's voice, a flash of somebody stabbing my mother popped into my mind.

"It's Danny... It's D-D-Danny," my mama managed to say between sobs.

"What the hell's going on?" Paw Paw yelled, trying to get up from his recliner but falling right back into so hard it rocked like it might flip.

"What's Danny?" Maw Maw asked, as confused as I was. "Is Danny trying to hurt you?"

"No—it's Danny that's shot! He...shot...his...self."

Wild World

I WAS ROCKED BY THE BLOW of a drunk man's fist before I made it out of the womb. My mama was seven months pregnant when Paw Paw hauled off and hit her in the stomach as hard as he could. My grandfather was dog-drunk, and my Mama had "talked back" when she took up for her brother Jeff in an argument.

A few weeks later, my father busted down the Chesapeake Bay Bridge toll gate because he didn't have a quarter. He made the state troopers chase my mother and him the full 17.6 miles across the bridge before he finally pulled over and jumped out of their green Karmann Ghia yelling, "My wife's having a baby! Where's the closest hospital?"

Mama, who in those days looked like Sally Field in the movie *Smokey and the Bandit*, said she could have won an Academy Award for her performance in the emergency room that day. "They were telling me, 'You're losing the baby,' and I was wailing like I was having contractions, but I knew I wasn't losing the baby, 'cause you weren't due for a month." She kept it up until the state troopers were satisfied. As soon as they left, she jumped off the metal examining table and slapped the shit out of my daddy.

My parents had known each other for ten days when my twenty-year-old father talked my teenage mother into meeting him at the stop sign on Oak Street at midnight and running away to Charleston, South Carolina, to get married. They drove all night and waited on the steps of the Eternal Father of the Sea Navy chapel until it opened. My father had just enlisted in the

Navy and was scheduled to leave for Guantanamo Bay in five days.

If John Belushi and Jack Nicholson shared a brother, he would have been my daddy. He was heavyset and his dark wavy hair was wild like it had an electric current running through it. He usually had a look in his eye like he knew something no one else did — like he had a winning lottery ticket in his back pocket and hadn't told anybody yet.

I was conceived on their wedding night in the middle of a thunderstorm in the front seat of that Karmann Ghia in the parking lot of the Charleston International Airport. Mama said, "It was lightning and thundering something awful, and your daddy kept playing that Cat Steven's song 'Wild World' on the eight-track over and over and over."

They spent their four-day honeymoon in a tiny Airstream trailer. The second day in that silver capsule, Mama said, "That's when I realized something was wrong with your daddy—when he went batshit ballistic over how I sliced bananas in circles instead of longways to make him a peanut butter and banana sandwich."

Dad headed out to Guantanamo and spent most of his time there in the brig, but he loved it because he got to play softball every day and the food was better than in the enlisted men's cafeteria. When Mama told Daddy she was pregnant with me, he went AWOL from the Navy. He snuck onto a banana boat from Cuba to Miami and hitchhiked home to Gadsden, where he surprised my mom walking through the backyard.

Daddy could talk Mama into anything. He persuaded her to call his commanding officer and tell him that she was six months pregnant and having suicidal thoughts, and that something bad might happen if she couldn't be with my father. They didn't release my dad, but they did transfer him to Pensacola, Florida, where they could be together, and Mama could go to the Navy psychiatrist.

A few days before I was born, my father took my mother on a date to the demolition derby. He said he was going to get a Coke at the concession stand. Next thing she knew, Mama saw their green Karmann Ghia on the racetrack with a big white number eight painted on the passenger side door. She watched as my father crunched their only car like a cracker in soup. She was nine months pregnant and had to climb through the driver's side window to get in to drive home.

The day when she went into labor, Daddy had to run all over the trailer park banging on doors, trying to flag down passing cars on the highway. She caught a ride to the hospital with a six-teen-year-old boy who had just gotten his driver's license that day. "I scared his little ass to death," Mama told me. She screamed, kicked, and bucked like a bronco in that boy's front seat all the way to the naval base hospital.

"For some reason I wore a wig to the hospital and was scream-ing' for Dr. Feist, the Navy psychiatrist, the whole time." Mama had just turned twenty that week and was all alone when I was born. She said, "Baby, it was you and me against the world."

Merry Christmas

NOTHING FELT REAL.

"Whhhhhhhyyyyyyyy?" Mama screamed so loud it brought me back to my grandmother's kitchen. Everything blurred into the swoosh-swoosh-swoosh of my heartbeat in my ears. I could taste the adrenaline in the back of my throat like my mouth was full of quarters. I stood in the blinking blue lights of the Christmas tree, my shirt soaking wet and milk dripping down my neck. I was drenched in shock.

What we did not know in that Twilight Zone moment, was that mom had received a phone call thirty minutes earlier from Dad's friend Buddy:

"Becky, I got a weird call from Danny—he's talking all crazy."

"What's he doing now?"

"He kept saying he was gonna pull over on the side of I-59 and shoot himself."

"Buddy, you know better than to believe him."

"Yeah, but something in his voice scared me."

"Did he say where he was?"

"At a gas station pay phone somewhere off I-59."

"Do you know how many times he's pulled that shit on me?"

She didn't bother telling Buddy that three months earlier, on their last visit to Gadsden, Dad drove her up to the top of Lookout Mountain, parked their Impala, and said, "If you're leaving again, then I'm leaving too." Then he got out of the car and walked around and opened the trunk. A few seconds later, she heard a gunshot ring through the Alabama sky. When she looked in the side mirror, he was gone. She sat terrified in the front seat for fifteen minutes before she worked up the courage to walk to the back of the car. When she did, she saw my father lying spread eagle on the red dirt road with his eyes closed. She fell to her knees beside him weeping.

Then he jumped up, grabbed her, and laughed.

"Becky, I can't believe you're dumb enough to think I'd kill myself over you."

Mom's hysterical sobs brought me back into the room. Paw Paw turned the volume on the scanner to full blast.

"Git Aimee in bed, she don't need to be hearing all this," he said.

I moved to the loveseat where I usually slept.

"Naw...git in Uncle Kelly's room."

"I ain't suppose to go in there."

"Did you hear me?" he said, his voice and eyes turning mean.

I could be outside and up a tree before he could get out of that chair. I wasn't moving until I heard what they were saying about my daddy. My grandparents crouched around the radio like God Almighty was about to reveal the meaning of life. Mama's brother Jeff was a police officer and he was at the scene now, talking back and forth with a woman, but all they said were numbers: "Eleven, forty-five, ten-four..." then beeps and bursts of static and more numbers. None of it made any sense, but I knew something horrible was happening.

I think my daddy is dead.

"Oh shit, Mary, turn up the TV!" Paw Paw demanded. "And I told you to git Aimee out of here."

"Come on, hon," Maw Maw said. "You can open your Christmas present from Uncle Kelly."

Mama was the oldest of five siblings and Kelly at sixteen was the youngest. He was her brother, but felt more like mine since he always took me places and bought me presents. Kelly's bedroom door was taboo—it stayed locked.

Maw Maw's hands were trembling so bad she couldn't get the bobby pin into the doorknob.

"I can do it," I said, and unlocked the door.

"Mary, get in here! Mary!" Paw Paw shouted.

"Hon, find that string to turn on the light."

I slung my gift from Uncle Kelly onto the bed.

That house was tiny, two bedrooms and one bath. Sneaking down the little square hall and into the kitchen, I could see my grandparents in front of the TV.

"Mary, turn it up."

"Clemmie, it's loud as it'll go."

My grandmother was on her knees, twisting the red pliers that were attached to where the volume knob had once been.

I crept into the kitchen and slid down the paneling, feeling each knot along the way through my thin t-shirt gown. Leaning my head to the side, I could see the TV screen through the skinny legs of their Formica table. A man in a gray blazer said, "Gadsden native, Danny Mayo, shot himself tonight—full story after the break."

Panic ran through me like a stampede of wild bulls, starting in my stomach and sticking in my throat. The commercials were roaring by in slow motion: "I'm a pepper, you're a pepper, wouldn't you like to be a pepper too?"

I want my daddy.

The reporter came on again: "Our sources tell us that a jet airliner has spotted Santa Claus and his reindeer somewhere over Atlanta with Rudolph leading the pack. His sled is overflowing with toys, so all you little girls and boys need to go to bed and get to sleep."

And then, breaking news: "Interstate 59 was closed for more than two hours this evening after twenty-nine-year-old Gadsden native, Danny Mayo, pulled over on the side of the interstate and shot himself. He was rushed to Holy Name Hospital."

The phone's loud ring from the wall above jarred me so badly I almost peed myself. I ran into Uncle Kelly's room and put my ear against the hollow door. I heard my grandmother talking.

"Is he alive? Shot himself in the chest? Is the bullet in his heart? What do you want me to tell Aimee?" my grandmother said.

I yanked the shoestring and the bare lightbulb in the center of the bedroom came on. It was brighter than every other light in the house combined. I could feel a hundred eyes on me. Standing in the center of the bedroom was like being shipwrecked in a sea of naked bodies. Eight-by-ten glossy centerfolds, pouty-lipped *Playboy* playmates, triangles of every shade of pubic hair, legs spread, booties in the air, boobs everywhere. I couldn't stop my eyes from exploring each one. Those posters Uncle Kelly plastered all over his walls hid a secret I wouldn't learn until years later.

My grandmother came in to tell me goodnight and I asked her, "Why is everybody sayin' Daddy shot his self? That can't be right... nobody would shoot their own self."

"Oh baby, you saw the news." Maw Maw took off her big topaz tinted glasses and wiped her eyes.

"Well, I think somebody else shot him," I said.

Someone was always after Daddy for gambling debts. Bookies called nonstop and men pounded on the door in the middle of the night. That was the main reason we were always moving. It hadn't been long since two men with guns spotted Daddy walking into a pawn shop in Gadsden and chased him until Daddy picked up a cinderblock and threw it through the front window of Alabama City Bank as he ran inside shouting, "Two guys with guns were coming in to rob the bank!" He knew nobody would be stupid enough to carry a pistol into a bank with the alarms blasting.

"Can you take me to Birmingham, Maw Maw? I need to go see him. Please."

"Just try to go to sleep, hon."

When she closed the door, I sat down on Uncle Kelly's bed. My mind raced like a blind pony. What if he's dead? Who shot him? I felt guilty wondering if Santa Claus would still come.

Uncle Kelly's burgundy sheets smelled like the Brut cologne he always wore. His room looked like it belonged in a different house, with antique Turkish rugs and his dresser and nightstand that he painted to look like white and gray marble. I unwrapped my present, a cornflower blue Holly Hobby diary that read 'Days to Remember' on the front cover. I turned to the first page and wrote in a wild scrawl across the top, "Daddy shot his sef." with a black marker that bled through the first five pages. The words looked alive and wounded like they might jump off the page and bite me. Along the bottom of the same page, in red ink, I practiced my cursive and added, "Merry Christmas...Merry Christmas...Merry Christmas."

Angels and Stars

IN MY FIRST MEMORY I'M TWO YEARS OLD, standing in a woman's living room that smells like dirty diapers and garbage. I don't know if she had a sign on her door that said 'White Trash Daycare,' but she kept a lot of the kids in our trailer park. The phone kept ringing and I felt a sense of alarm in the air. Snotty nosed children were crying and parents came to pick up their kids, scooping them up like a kangaroo in the pouch. But no one came to get me, so the faceless woman threw me on her hip and put me in her car. I thought I was going with her, but she stopped in front of our trailer, got me out of the back seat, and sat me on the rotting front steps of our mobile home. She held a cigarette between her teeth as she buttoned up my red coat.

"Sit on these steps and do not move. Your mama or daddy will be home soon."

The memory is mostly a feeling, the jolt of fear when I realized she was leaving me outside—alone in the dark. She got back in her car and I watched her tail lights until the night put them out. Cars buzzed down the interstate a hundred yards from me. Dogs and monsters growled in the pitch-black piney shadows. I was terrified. I sat there for hours, shivering and talking to the stars.

Dad came back to our trailer about 11:00 pm and found me crying and shaking in the cold. I had been out there for hours. We drove to Western Sizzlin', where mom worked, and picked her up. Later that night, mom busted in the door to the 'White Trash Daycare' when the woman refused to open it. I fell asleep in the front seat listening to her screaming at the woman.

Later that same year, I ate rat poison and almost died. My mom's sister, Sandy, dumped a box of d-CON into a bowl of Fruit Loops and stuck it under the kitchen counter at my grandparent's house. I found the cereal before the mice and mama found me with my eyes rolled into the back of my head, jerking and foaming at the mouth, having a seizure on the living room floor. They laced me up in what I thought was a backward coat. It was a straitjacket. And then blurs of white lab coats hovered over me shoving what I thought was a garden hose down my throat trying to kill me. The doctors told my mama, "Do not let her go to sleep. She could slip into a coma if she falls asleep." So she sat with me rubbing my forehead with a cool rag—the cure-all for everything in the South. Any time I tried to close my eyes, she would wipe my face again. Then she saw me grinning and laughing, and I kept asking, "How'd you do that?"

"Aimee, who are you talking to, baby?"

"That pretty woman with wings on her back," I pointed. Mom shook me until the woman was gone. I can't remember my guardian angel other than a burst of bliss, but I'm sure she's needed an eternal supply of Xanax to put up with me.

Front Row Seat to Crazy

I KNEW SOMETHING WAS WRONG with my father around the time I knew my foot was my foot. You could feel the energy surge when he walked into a room. He was bipolar, but back then everybody just called him crazy. When he was down, he stayed in bed in the dark and cussed me out when I tried to talk to him. But when he was manic, he was a superhero and life was a "Trip the Light Fantastic" adventure.

Mama worked long hours. She always had a job somewhere. Various nursing homes emptying bedpans, lifting patients. She was like a blur of white on her way out the door. Somebody had to pay the bills. Daddy never kept a job for more than a couple of months. For a while, he was a janitor at a high school and he rode on the back of a garbage truck. He told Mama he worked third shift at Johnson's Button Factory until she called one night and they told her, "We've never heard of a Danny Mayo."

Daddy gambled for a living and I usually went with him. I was his little dime-store queen, riding shotgun, standing in the front seat of our beat-up station wagon with my arm around his neck. We'd roll the windows down so I could feel the wind in my hair, and we'd sing, "Sha-la-la-la-la" along with Van Morrison's "Brown-Eyed Girl" or my first favorite, "Silly Love Songs."

We would leave for the laundromat and end up three states away at a horse track or a midnight auction. I loved the excitement of those auctions, everybody hollerin 'and the auctioneer talking fast: "Hobbit-hibbity-tibby-dibbidy...SOLD!" I'd leave with a mystery box of toys that Daddy bought for one dollar. Hoping for a Lite-Brite or Easy-Bake Oven, I usually ended up with orphaned game pieces, army men, and marbles. If I ever got a Barbie, she usually looked like a crackhead—half-naked with matted chopped-off hair, magic marker tattoos, and missing a limb.

I spent countless nights eating Astro Pops and Slim Jims in the smoky backroom of Sal's Gas Station where Daddy bet on ball games and paid his bookie. When he saw me racing all the neighborhood kids in front of Mama Opal's house, he marched up the front yard and said, "Come on, baby doll, we're going to the pawn shop."

He bought a stopwatch and a silver whistle. The next day, he was yelling at a bunch of us kids on the skinny blacktop. His eyes lit up every time I busted through that toilet paper finish line. He entered me in track meets and I set the state record for the fifty-yard dash and the hundred-yard dash by the time I was six years old.On Friday nights, when we were living in Gadsden, we'd pull up at a football game just as it was letting out. Daddy wandered through the crowd, looking for a glory days athlete with a chip on his shoulder and a son a couple of years older than I was. He'd walk up and ask, "How old's your boy?"

"Twelve."

"My daughter's eight. I bet she can outrun him."

It wasn't long until a crowd gathered. Under the stadium lights, I took off my shoes and ran barefoot, my feet like fire in the cold grass. I won with Daddy cheering me on. We'd drive away with the dashboard covered in wadded up twenty-dollar bills.

***

WHEN I WAS THREE YEARS OLD, I woke up early one morning and there was a bald man in bed with Mama and me. He hovered over her, inches from her face, watching her sleep.I tapped him on his bare shoulder and said, "Hi, I'm Aimee, what's your name?"

He busted out laughing and woke up my mama. She started screaming and swinging at him and he laughed harder. The commotion caused one of the wooden slats under the bed to collapse, and we all slid onto the floor. My paternal grandparents, whom I called by their first names, Opal and Harold, and sometimes Mama Opal and Daddy Harold, came running to the door of my dad's childhood bedroom, where we lived half the time.

"Dammit! You're gonna give somebody a damn heart attack," Harold said.

My grandfather had on a white ribbed undershirt, boxers, and socks with straps. There was a piece of toilet paper hanging off his chin with a blood spot on it, and his hair, which he usually wore in a comb-over, was sticking up like a brownish-gray wave, like something you'd see out ofDr. Seuss' Whoville.

When Harold was yelling at the man, I saw by the man's belly and baggy, white Fruit of the Loom underwear, that it was my daddy. He had gotten up in the middle of the night and shaved his head bald as a cue ball for the thirty-second thrill of scaring my mama.That was my daddy. If he was in the house, somebody was screaming. He hid behind every door in every dark room ready to jump out. I was just happy he was too fat to fit under the bed.

Opal was right behind Harold in her purple velour housecoat. She had green sponge rollers in her hair and Ponds Cold Cream caked on her face. "Danny, I don't know what's wrong with you," she said and shook her head.

"Shut up, Mother. It was funny. Why have you gotta ruin everything?"

Opal always stared at my daddy with a bemused curiosity, as if a spaceship had landed on their street and rolled an egg down her driveway and my father popped out. She spent half of her time trying to figure out what was wrong with her son and the other half having Dwight Baptist Church pray for him.

"You look like a damn serial killer," Harold said and huffed off to the bedroom.

By the time I was five, if Daddy bolted out of the bushes waving a butcher knife and wearing a bloody clown mask, I wouldn't even blink. "Danny, you've messed up her adrenal glands," Mama yelled at him.

"Becky, shut up. You work at a nursing home. You're not a doctor."

"Well, you're not supposed to scare a kid like that Danny. You're going to give her PTSD."

Silent Night

CHRISTMAS DAY I COULD FEEL the panic punching up my throat as I walked into the hospital. My chest got tight and my stomach cramped. I hated hospitals. This one reeked like a dirty birdcage, cheap disinfectant, urine, and people sick as sores. When the elevator doors opened to the intensive care unit, I saw Daddy Harold pacing in circles at the end of the long corridor, smacking his dentures like he did when he was nervous. I barreled into him and buried my face in his shirt for a big hug. He always smelled the same, Old Spice and Salem's. For the first time in my life, he didn't look happy to see me. Usually, he would be digging around in his front pocket and pull out fruity Certs or Freedent chewing gum and give me the whole pack. But this time all he had was cigarettes, his shirt was buttoned up wrong and his eyes darted, never meeting mine.

The waiting room was steeped in nicotine and tears. Birmingham was the biggest city in the area and had the only major hospital for the surrounding counties, so all the tragedies showed up here. The fear and bone raw desperation was palpable. Everyone's attention was fixed on the double doors, waiting for the doctors to come out and tell fortunes. Empty Kleenex boxes, sad little stained chairs, and the TV was playing the sitcom, *Three's Company*, with a laugh track that sounded sinister. Everyone had the same shock slapped expression, the same hysterical eyes. In the corner was the saddest Christmas tree I had ever seen, bare of ornaments and lopsided. It looked like it had the mange. It was decorated with a single strand of weakly blinking white lights that looked like they were screaming.

Mama Opal came around the corner, her blonde hair flat as a pile of hay, splotchy red patches all over her face. Her blue eyes were so swollen I could see the veins on her eyelids and her black mascara tears ran down her face and neck. She wore a lacy white Victorian blouse with dirty, dusty-pink sweatpants and burgundy penny loafers with no socks. I had lived with her half my life and had never seen her like this. She wouldn't go to the mailbox without curling her hair. She was always glamorous, a mixture of Marilyn Monroe and Lucille Ball. When she spoke, she sounded like a southern Edith Bunker, her voice bouncing all over the room. But now it sounded broken as she pulled me to her and said, "Baby, we need to pray." Opal prayed for me and everyone in our family at 5:30 every morning and I always loved to know someone was looking out for us.

Watching everyone in my family wander around zombie-like lost, I felt invisible and alone. I tried to act silly and make jokes to lighten the tension and break back into that place where kids go when a situation gets too heavy. I walked the dim halls with doors lined up like little Dominoes to death while families and friends waited to see which way they would fall. I couldn't help peeking inside. I heard machines beeping, TVs roaring, people howling out for help and moaning in pain and coughing their souls out. Instrumental Christmas music echoed from the nurse's station down the corridors.

The main desk was decorated with plastic holly, artificial mistletoe and a dancing Santa. I found my mother standing by some vending machines. I wrapped my arms around her. The doctors had told her that they couldn't find the bullet in my dad and things didn't look good.

"Aimee, your daddy wants to see you, but I don't want you going in there," she said.

"It's Christmas and I'm giving him his present," I insisted as I ran back to the waiting room and grabbed my painting. Pushing the heavy brown door open, I entered Daddy's room. Mama Opal stood by the window staring at the foot of the hospital bed. I heard her whimper, "Heavenly Father," and waited for the amen. She looked at me and burst into tears covering her face and ran out of the room. I was not prepared for what I saw when I came around the corner. Tubes and wires were everywhere like spaghetti noodles connecting my father to machines. His face was so swollen it looked waterlogged. His lips were chapped and peeling.

A tube snaked into one of his nostrils and his neck was stained yellow-orange.

I backed up against the wall. I didn't want to get too close to him. He slurred and turned his head toward me. I held the painting of blue horses out in front of me and took a step closer to the bed. "Here's your Christmas present," I said as I propped the canvas on his bedside table. A machine clacked and it startled me so bad I almost screamed.

"Come over here so I can see your face," he tried to talk, but I couldn't understand half of what he was saying. He sounded like he had a stuffed animal in his mouth—all his words were smooshed and smeared. He kept fading in and out of consciousness. Panic shot through me when I saw bright red blood soaking through his hospital gown, seeping through the over-bleached sheets. I watched the stain spread in slow motion like a crimson butterfly.

He patted the bed and wanted me to get up there with him. I kept telling myself this is my daddy, this is my daddy, but I was afraid he might go crazy again and hurt me too. But this is who I snuggled with on the couch to watch Columbo and Saturday Night Live. This is who pulled my first tooth. I focused on his hands, which mirrored my own. I knew his hands. I carefully climbed up next to him. He tried to look at me, but his eyes kept rolling back into his head.

"I love you, baby doll. No matter what, I'll always love you. Can you remember that?"

That evening on the drive back from Birmingham, I prayed almost the entire sixty-mile drive that Daddy would make it. When we got back inside the Gadsden city limits, my grandmother said, "You just took a wrong turn."

And Paw Paw said, "No, I want to show Aimee something. She needs one damn memory from Christmas that isn't a tragedy." He kept going and we pulled up in front of a house that was lit up like a Lite-Brite. I stared in wonder, and then I heard Paw Paw singing. His voice was baritone and beautiful as he softly slurred the words to "Silent Night."

Sweet Home Alabama

AS A CHILD, I WAS A DARK-HAIRED DANDELION and Daddy was the wind carrying us chaotically from state to state, trailer park to trailer park. There was always someone after my dad for gambling debts. Alabama was where we always ran back to no matter where we'd been. We flew in and out of my grandparents' homes like flies through a hole in a screen door. We lived with them as much as we lived anywhere. All I ever wanted was to stay in Alabama.

Alabama. Al-a-bam-a, just the word sang as pretty as a song on my lips and it was the song of my childhood, the sound of my voice and the place that shaped me more than any other. Alabama was where I heard my first stories, said my first prayers, and learned to dream under more stars than sky.Along the foothills of the Appalachian Mountains, a daisy-chain of tiny towns that link together within minutes of each other: Gadsden, Glencoe, and Hokes Bluff, made up the charm bracelet of my childhood. Even though my parents never owned a house in Etowah County, it was home.

Uprooted every couple of months, I was astronomically lost in the classroom. I felt like the dumbest person in the world. There were gigantic gaps in my education. I never knew what the teacher was talking about—it was like all the other kids spoke a foreign language I had never heard. I didn't know my right from my left, what a noun was, or that the United States was in North America. I didn't know how to tell time or tie my shoes, and I felt dyslexic when it came to punctuation.

When the teacher would call on me to ask me something, like what's ten times three, I would just look at her like she asked me to rebuild the engine in her car. Just when I would be about to grasp what a fraction was, I would come home to find the car packed and we were loaded up and leaving again.Everything was always changing. My school, my teacher, my address, my desk, everything I loved was either lost or left behind. Everything was different at each elementary school: where you write your name on the paper, how to write the date, how to get in line for the water fountain when you could go to the bathroom. We never stayed anywhere long enough for me to make friends. I was so lonely.

The one thing that gave me comfort in the chaos was the sky. No matter where we moved, I found her waiting in every back-yard and it made me feel like something big was watching over me, even when my parents weren't. The sky, she was kind of like my imaginary friend and I told her everything. I loved to imagine that during the day, she was wearing her softest, white cotton t-shirt and favorite faded blue jeans. And at night, she was all decked out in a little black dress with all her diamond bling. When I stared up into something so unimaginably infinite, it made me feel like everything was going to be okay.

As an adult, I tried to put together the puzzle of missing piec-es of my childhood. When I asked my mom and Opal as an adult, "Where all did we live when I was growing up?" The answers they gave me were, "Nowhere and everywhere."

Opal said, "Hon, y'all didn't really live anywhere. Y'all didn't even live together half the time."

And mom said, "You know how crazy your daddy was, we lived everywhere."

I know we lived in Nashville, Dallas, Chattanooga, but Ala-bama was the only place that felt like home. With every shooting star, birthday candle, penny heads up in a parking lot, I made the same wish: to stop moving and stay in Alabama. That Christmas Eve, when daddy shot himself, my wish finally came true.

That January, we moved in with Opal and Harold and we never returned to the basement apartment where we had been living in Chattanooga. My markers and artwork were orphaned in my little wooden desk. My Hot Wheels were left under an oak tree to rust in the rain. Uncle Kelly drove up there to get our clothes, but they had all been gobbled up by mildew.

I missed a month of third grade in the chaos that followed Christmas Eve. I alternated between my grandparents' homes. These women were wonderlands to me. Most of the time, Mama didn't know where we were spending the night, so she had no idea where to enroll me in school. That's when my great-grandmother Ginny, whom I called Mimi, stepped in.

"Well, God Almighty, none of y'all got any damn sense. She can't just not go to school. I'll enroll her somewhere close to my house and take her and pick her up every day."

Mimi was about the size of a ten-year-old and cussed a blue streak. She was my daddy's grandmother and the only one I had ever seen put him in his place. She'd stand on her front porch and cuss my daddy up one end and out the other.

"I don't know why you always gotta be leavin' town and movin' around like some kind of crazy son of a bitch. You just need to get a house and stay the hell here."Daddy loved to egg her on.

Mimi had hair the color of the moon and eyes like ancient mirrors. Every day she wore plastic pearls and polyester, and the circles of rouge that she never rubbed in looked like pink lollipops on her powdered cheeks. She was my seventy-seven-year-old sidekick, my best friend, and my favorite person in the world.

My great-grandfather T had died two years earlier and we both missed him. His name was Timothy Thomas Trudy Caper Daniel Mayo because his parents had let his five sisters name him. He got sick and tired of everybody always calling him something different and he dropped all the names and went by just the letter T. His tombstone read: "T Mayo, 1900-1977." According to Mama Opal, T was where the crazy gene came from. He wrote so many letters threatening Herbert Hoover and calling him a "blockheaded son of a bitch" that the Secret Service showed up on his front porch.

Mimi's little house in Alabama City was a two-bedroom bungalow with glass door knobs that I thought were diamonds. It felt like a genie's bottle. We lived there in our own private universe, walking hand in hand to the dime store with me skipping at her side. Everything about her smelled like candy and cigarettes. For her birthday and Christmas every year, she got the same two gifts; a carton of Salem menthols and a box of chocolate-covered cherries. Her refrigerator, which she called the icebox, always had the same contents: KitKat candy bars, ice-cold bottles of Coca-Cola, and a Pepperidge Farm coconut cake for me. Sweets were almost all she ate and her freezer looked like a winter wonderland with a tub of Neapolitan ice cream, a box of frozen shrimp, and two metal ice cube trays. It took both of us twisting, turning, pushing and pulling to break the ice free.

When I spent the night with Mimi, which was usually two or three times a week, we'd lay in her rickety double bed, sharing a heating pad and talking until one of us fell asleep. She'd tell me stories about her parents coming to America on a big boat from Italy or how she cussed out T on their wedding night because he wouldn't walk her to the outhouse. Mimi usually fell asleep first and I worried into the night that I'd wake up and find her dead because she was so old.

The last week of January, I started school at Floyd Elementary. Sixty eyeballs stared at me as I stood next to the teacher in front of the classroom. Miss King introduced me, "Class, this is Aimee Mayo."

"She's white like mayo," a voice called out and the whole room turned into a giggle box.

I sat behind a girl named Joyce, who became my first best friend. All day, I stared at her hair. It was in about thirty little ponytails. "I love your hair clasps," was the first thing I said to her. She turned around and smiled and then I realized we had something in common; the two of us had the biggest front teeth in third grade. At the end of the day, she dropped a little plastic blue barrette with birds on it on my desk.

At Floyd Elementary, I also met my first crush, a little boy named Emmanuel. Well, I called him E Annual because I couldn't say his name right. Every day on the playground, the other white girl in my class, who I called Scary Carrie, threatened to beat me up when school let out. When we'd return to the classroom, I'd spend the rest of the day watching the clock. When the bell rang, I'd bolt into my great grandmother's car. One day Mimi asked, "Why do you always come busting out those damn doors like your ass is on fire?" I told her about Scary Carrie.

"Where is she?"

I pointed.

Mimi got out of her car and marched up the grassy hill to confront my enemy. She poked her finger in Carrie's face and held the other hand on her hip. When she got back in the car, Mimi said, "She ain't gonna bother you no more."

"What'd you say?"

"I told her she better not be mean to you again, or I'll burn her little ass with my cigarette."

Graceland

THE BULLET DIDN'T KILL MY FATHER, it lodged in his shoulder blade and stayed there. As traumatic as that Christmas was, it was nothing compared to the shock of a lifetime that I got twenty years later when Dad died too young and I had an audience of over a hundred people to witness my heart breaking. I visited him in the VA hospital and he showed me his scar. I didn't want to see it and neither did Opal, but he showed it to us anyway. It went all the way across his chest, puffy and pink with a long deep cut in the center and it looked like it had spiders crawling on it.

After one peek, I closed my eyes and Opal got up and left the room. Harold got mad and started yelling, "Dammit Danny, I don't know what you're so proud of. Nobody wants to see that damn scar."

When Daddy was released from the VA hospital at the end of January, he was a different person. He was twenty-nine years old and determined to make his dreams come true. We moved in with Opal and Harold and I loved it there. I spent most of my time in the labyrinth of woods next to their house. There were magical days as I caught fuzzy, orange-dotted caterpillars, made mud pies, and dug up arrowheads in that Kudzu kingdom where vines turned everything into Gothic cathedrals, dragons, and hot air balloons. It looked like the secret museum of Edward Scissor-hands.

Every Sunday and Wednesday night, we went to Dwight Baptist Church. That's where Opal taught Sunday school. We were saturated in scripture. It seeped into everything. We learned Jesus Loves Me before we could sing our ABCs and we could recite John 3:16 before we knew our phone numbers. My cousins and I baptized each other in the bathtub. Cory and I ran around in Opal's front yard and slammed each other in the heads screaming, "Salvation!"

When my cousin Vanessa, daddy's sister Beth's daughter, saw a group of grown-ups in a circle in the front yard, we thought it was the Rapture and when we found a dead squirrel in the grill of our grandmother's car, we stood watching for Jesus to fly out of its heart.I was taught to fear the Lord and never question him. Curiosity was not encouraged. I got a slap on the hand from my vacation bible school teacher for asking, "If God wrote this bible, why's it got some king's name on the front of it?"

We were sitting in Opal's dining room eating country fried steak when she mentioned that a friend from her church said that he would hire Daddy on at the steel plant.

"Mother, I'm done wasting my life at jobs I hate."

"Danny, you got two kids to support and you need insurance. You ain't gonna get another job that's as good as that one."

Opal's helium voice grated on my dad's nerves. He always seemed like he was mad at her, but I was never really sure why.

"I'm gonna do something with music or movies or both," Dad said.

"Oh, good heavens," Opal said under her breath and got up to clear the table. A hopeless look flashed across Mama's face like she knew she was going to have to work even harder to support our family. We had lived in Nashville twice already and Daddy had written songs with people he met there. He had meetings with music publishers trying to make something happen, but it hadn't. Everybody at the table that night thought he was delusional. They'd never have believed he was on his way from being a gambling janitor to a multi-millionaire.

***

ONE AFTERNOON IN EARLY FEBRUARY, Dad came in, "Get dressed up, we're going to celebrate. I got some big news." Mom put on her brown floral skirt and a lacy, ivory blouse and I wore my sundress with the strawberries on it. We drove to the Moon River Café in Rainbow City. The only restaurants I had ever been to before were Hardee's and Runt's Chili Joint, so I was stunned by the white tablecloth and the view of the Coosa River.

Mom took one look at the menu and said, "Danny, this is too expensive."

He grinned, "Order anything you want."

I ordered popcorn shrimp and Dad devoured a seafood platter. Mama had red snapper while Cory sat in her lap and ate Jell-O and crackers. "I love eatin' these little animals," I announced. Daddy laughed so hard he said he hurt his chest where his stitches were still healing. Cory wouldn't be still. He was obsessed with the ducks on the deck of the restaurant. Daddy promised we could go feed them after dinner.

"What's going on? What are you so worked up about?" Mama finally asked.

"Guess who I booked to play the Convention Center?"

"Who?"

"Jerry Lee Lewis," Daddy said. He took a bite of a crab leg dripping with butter and it fell down his Hawaiian print shirt.

"What are you talking about Danny?"

Mama and I loved Jerry Lee Lewis. We sang Chantilly Lace all the time. Before she could ask more questions, Dad said, "Becky, watch this." He pulled what looked like a bottle cap out of his pocket and dumped something onto his plate. He stood up and yelled, "Waiter, I need a waiter over here!"

Everyone in the restaurant stared as men in navy blue jackets scurried out to our table. "Look at this," Dad said, sounding angry as he pointed to his plate. "What the hell does that look like to you?" There was a smear of ketchup, a half-eaten hush puppy and something that looked like a scab. "Do you see what this is? It's a fucking fried roach."

"Oh my God," the waiter said and jerked the plate off the table. "Just a minute, Sir."

He ran off as Daddy whispered to me, "I fried that roach in the skillet before we left." People at other tables were now dissecting their dinners.

The manager arrived at our table with a giant piece of chocolate cake in a box. "Please accept this and we will take care of your meal."

"Well, make sure there aren't any damn roaches in the cake," Daddy said as we got up to leave. Mama slung Cory on her hip and we marched out of there.

"What about the ducks?" I asked.

"Let's get the hell out of here before your dad gets us arrested," Mom said and made a beeline for the car.

No one believed Dad when he said he was going to promote concerts. But somehow, he talked Jerry Lee Lewis into doing a show at the Convention Center in Gadsden. My mom was pretty sure he was the most famous person who ever played there. The night of the performance, the place was packed. Daddy was already there when Mama, Cory, Opal, Harold and I arrived.

"Come on, I want to introduce you to Jerry Lee," Daddy said. He was talking to everybody we passed on the way to the dressing room and his voice was as animated as a twelve-year-old that had just won a baseball tournament. Daddy announced, "Hey Jerry, this is my family." Mama Opal walked into the room first.

Jerry Lee sat in a swivel chair in front of a mirror with lights around it. He spun around and said, "You've got to be the most beautiful woman I ever laid eyes on."

When he met my mama, he said the same exact thing. When it was my turn, Jerry Lee looked at Daddy and said, "How do you have a daughter this cute?" He patted his lap for me to sit down, but I stood next to his chair.

"Baby, what's your favorite song?" he asked me.

"'We Are the Champions' by Queen," I said, and everybody laughed.

"He meant one of his songs," Mama said.

"'Chantilly Lace,' we sing it all the time."

"She's a doll, Danny, and she talks just like a little Loretta Lynn."

"Well she's eight, so don't get any ideas about marrying her," Daddy said and embarrassed everybody in the room.

Thirty minutes later, we were standing on the side of the stage and I was spellbound as I watched Jerry Lee Lewis walk out. "Baby doll, he's gonna come get you to help sing a song in a minute," Daddy said.

I started to run away, but my dad grabbed my arm and pulled me back to him. "I'm just kiddin'," he hugged me.

Jerry Lee finished "Great Balls of Fire" and started walking straight toward me. My heart went off like an alarm clock, my tongue buzzed. He reached for my hand. I looked up at him, "This isn't safe. He's dangerous," I thought. His eyes were zinging like lightning bolts. His blonde curly hair was wild as a tiger. Tiny rivers of sweat had eroded the powder caked on his face.

I let him grab my hand as I followed him onto the stage. The crowd roared. When he sat down at the piano and started pounding on the keys, it was like he was trying to murder them. The wooden floor of the stage vibrated through my patent leather sandals. I was frightened and felt like I might be falling in love. That exact moment lit my spark for loving a music man.

He looked over at me and asked, "Aimee, do you want to help The Killer sing a song?" I nodded. He stood up playing with one hand while putting the microphone in my face with the other. I heard myself singing "Chantilly Lace." I was so dizzy with wonder watching Jerry Lee sitting next to me that I forgot about the crowd of over one thousand people watching us. When the song ended, they gave us a standing ovation.

***

THAT VALENTINES DAY, Daddy came in with Christmas presents. He had lost the money Mama gave him for Santa gambling before he shot himself that Christmas Eve, so he wanted to make up for it. Mine was my favorite gift I had ever received, a little blue typewriter that really worked. I sat at Opal's kitchen table, eating cherries from the jar and composing stories, while Cory rode his tricycle in circles around the living room.

Dad continued promoting concerts in Etowah County. Shows like Paul Revere and the Raiders, and J.D. Sumner and the Stamps. He started making trips to Nashville and Jim Glazer recorded a tribute song that Daddy had written about Elvis Presley. It was called "Sippin' Tupelo Honey." It wasn't a hit song, but it made its way around the South and sold about ten thousand copies.

One night that spring, Daddy got a phone call that changed our lives. It was Vernon Presley, Elvis Presley's dad. He had heard and loved Dad's song. They struck up a friendship right away and about a month later, Daddy talked Vernon into selling him two of Elvis' five cars. Then he talked Daddy Harold into taking a second mortgage out on their home to borrow money to buy them. It was crazy and nobody knew why he was doing it but our family drove to Graceland in Memphis, Tennessee, to pick up the cars. We pulled up in front of the black iron gate decorated with musical notes and I marveled at the sprawling green lawn. "Daddy, is this where the President lives?"

"No, baby doll, this is where the King lives, the 'King of Rock 'n' Roll.'"

Elvis had been dead for two years. The massive white columns on the front of the mansion looked one thousand feet high as we stepped onto that porch. Walking around the gigantic house, I was astounded by everything I saw. The walls were covered in fabric that matched the upholstery on all the sofas and chandeliers hung everywhere. There was a room full of televisions and another room filled with trophies and Grammy awards and framed gold and platinum records hanging on the walls.

Mama kept interrupting the tour to chase Cory through the house. He was a toddler and had been hyper since birth. He started walking at eight months and kept our mother running. While we were admiring the giant peacock patterned stained glass windows, I heard her yell, "Holy shit! Cory, don't move!"

My brother was standing on the arm of a white sofa. He had a huge grin on his face as he tried to hug a silver lamp twice his size. Mama got him down and said, "Come on, Aimee, let's go out by the pool before Cory breaks something." She put her hand on my shoulder and as we walked out the back door, I spotted the most incredible swing set I had ever seen. It was red with two swings, a slide and a teeter-totter and a carriage seat swing that could hold four people. I didn't get to play on it but I did get my picture taken in front of the guitar-shaped swimming pool.

"This is why we're here," Dad said as he pointed at two cars in the driveway. One was a custom made, cream-colored Cadillac station wagon. The other was a gray and burgundy Suburban. There was really nothing special about that truck other than the tinted windows. I rode back to Gadsden with Daddy in the Cadillac. I felt like a princess. Mama, Cory, and my grandparents followed in the other cars.

"Baby, there's not another Cadillac station wagon anywhere in the world," Daddy said. "This is the only one they ever made." There was a little gold plate on the dashboard about the size of a credit card engraved with 'Elvis Aaron Presley,' and underneath, 'Lisa Marie Presley.' I imagined it said 'Daniel Harold Mayo, Aimee Beth Mayo.'

After we got home, I rode with Daddy to a body shop in Gadsden. He told the guys in the garage, "Give this truck some fuckin' razzle-dazzle. It needs to look like it belonged to Elvis

Presley." They painted gold lightning bolts down both sides and the letters 'TCB' for Elvis' motto, "Taking care of business." A photo of Dad, Mom, Cory and I made the front page of the *Gadsden Times*. We were standing in front of the tricked out Suburban. Dad wore a black leather vest that was too tight and a white shirt. Mom had on a yellow dress and held Cory. I smiled a gap-toothed smile with my brown hair in braids and I wore metallic red shorts with a matching shirt. I held the Gibson guitar that Dad told everyone had belonged to Elvis. It was the first and the last photograph of the four of us together.

Polaroids

THAT MARCH, MOM AND DAD RENTED a brick ranch house on Turrentine Street in one of the more upscale neighborhoods in Gadsden. It was the nicest home we had ever lived in. The day we moved in, the smell of the brand new carpet was so intoxicating that Cory and I rolled and rolled around on the floor. I got my first bedroom suite and something I had dreamed of my whole eight years of life; a canopy bed with Holly Hobbie sheets. Mama sewed yellow and white gingham curtains to match the frilly canopy. My little blue typewriter held a place of honor on top of my cream-colored nightstand.

Daddy started working out agreements with car dealerships, charging them $2,500 to display Elvis's station wagon and truck for a weekend. The dealership would run a big advertisement in the newspaper. "See Elvis Presley's automobiles, guitars, and memorabilia. This weekend only at Bill Philip Chevrolet. If you buy a new Chevy, you can take a ride in the King of Rock 'n' Roll's custom-made Cadillac station wagon."

Daddy put Elvis's guitar on display and set up chairs around a giant movie screen, theater-style, and played a VHS of *Blue Hawaii*. He had souvenirs made up to sell to the people who came to see the cars: copies of Elvis's birth certificate, marriage certificate, driver's license, and Elvis wall tapestries, t-shirts, keychains, and pretty much everything you could put his face on. The showrooms were always packed. Elvis had been dead for two years, but half the people who came thought he was alive and hiding out somewhere. They would stare in awe through the dirty windshield covered in fingerprints as if Elvis's ashes were in the ashtray.

Daddy liked to take me with him because he made twice as much money when I came along, especially in the northern states like Ohio and New York, where my deep Alabama accent was almost as big an attraction as the cars. Customers would crowd around me, demanding, "Say white," or "Say school." My family's dialect wasn't the high-falutin' Southern drawl that might pronounce Georgia like 'Jawijuh'; we didn't talk like we were raised in Gone with the Wind, we sounded more like the poor South, more like Sling Blade. I sat behind a wobbly brown folding table selling the souvenirs, a little black metal money box in my lap, and VHS of Blue Hawaii playing on the TV behind me.

The smaller the town, the bigger the crowds. Thousands of people came out and there were plenty of freak shows. About ten percent of the men wore gigantic gold belts and white jumpsuits bedazzled with rhinestones. "Hey, uh, baby...can you let me see that calendar right there?" they'd say, trying to talk like Elvis.

Anyone that bought a car could go for a ride in the Cadillac station wagon. Every town was the same; people always stole the buttons off the leather back seats. We kept a box of beige buttons in the glove compartment and replaced them after every show. Different people joined us out on the road. A guy named Rick with a handlebar mustache, he drove the camper and Daddy and I rode in the station wagon.

We stayed at Holiday Inns and Howard Johnsons and it was heaven. My father made friends wherever he went and sometimes they came back to the motel with us. He'd give me a sock full of quarters from the money box and lock me out of our room. I wandered around playing Ms. Pac Man or sat by the pool, eating Astro Pops and Cheetos until he came looking for me.

One Sunday, Daddy left me at the house of a man who owned one of the dealerships. He had a son a couple of years younger than me and we were sitting Indian style on the boy's bedroom floor playing Chinese checkers when his Dad came in. Something about the man had scared me all day. Now he was sweaty and had his shirt off when he sat down next to me. He told his son, "Jacob, go get your friend some Kool-Aid."

Then he moved closer. His knee hit the octagon board sending marbles flying in all directions. He slid his hand under my shorts and rubbed his stubby fingers against the outside of my underwear right between my legs. At first, I thought he was looking for a runaway marble and thought that he thought it must have gone in my shorts. Then he asked, "What kind of panties do you like to wear?"

"Get away from me!" I said and kicked him as hard as I could. Then I jumped up and raced through the house and out the door. There was a trail through the woods to the car lot. I took off running downhill. It was dark and I tripped. The man was chasing me and I ran as fast as I could because I knew if he got me alone, something terrible would happen. My throat felt like a Brillo pad and my heart was pounding by the time I got back to the dealership. There were a couple of men inside when I ran in out of breath and asked, "Has anybody seen Danny Mayo?"

"No hon, we were just getting ready to go home for the night," one of the men said. Then the creepy guy came in out of breath and told them, "I can watch her. Y'all go ahead. I've got some work to do." He headed towards his office.

I ran outside and sat down on a bench. I felt like I might throw up. The man came out and I watched him pull out a red balloon from one of the displays. He handed me the balloon and said, "Don't tell anybody what we talked about."

I was terrified that as soon as the other men left, I would be trapped with him. But I saw Daddy's friend Rick loading up the last of the Elvis souvenirs. About twenty minutes later, Daddy's Cadillac came flying into the dealership and pulled in front of us. I ran to the car letting the balloon float into the night sky. I heard the man telling Daddy, "She was good. They had fun playing."

There was a plump woman with tight jeans on in the front seat, so I jumped in the back. As we pulled out of the parking lot, she turned around and said, "Hi, I'm Sheryl. Your Dad tells me you're going into the fourth grade." I ignored her and screamed, "I hate you, Daddy. Don't you ever leave me like that again!" He didn't listen and continued to put me in dangerous situations and almost got me arrested, molested, and blown to smithereens. He kept it up until my luck ran out when I was sixteen.

Back in Gadsden, life was as good as it had ever been until Mom unpacked Daddy's blue suitcase. I was sitting in the living room with Cory playing blocks, the little wooden kind with the letters and numbers on them, when I heard her scream. That was followed by a loud crash and a thud. As I ran to see what was going on, Mama hurled an antique lamp as hard as she could shattering it against the wall. She charged into the bathroom where Daddy was taking a shower and lunged at him diving through the shower curtain.

She slapped him across the face over and over, shouting, "I hate you!" They fell into the bathtub, jerking the shower curtain down and sending all the little silver clips scattering across the tile floor like tinkling bells. I heard something rip and then they rolled out into the hall.

"Becky, what the fuck is wrong with you?" my dad yelled. He grabbed her wrist, but it was too slippery from the shower. They slid around wrestling over what looked like some postcards that my mama clutched in her hand. She was laughing and sounded mad at the same time. She clawed at my dad's face. Water from the showerhead was shooting everywhere.

She tore away from him. "You want to see what's wrong with me, you fat, fucking bastard?" She showed him what was in her hands; polaroid pictures, not postcards. She was crying so hard she could barely talk. "I hate you, you fat son of a bitch!" Most of the time when they fought, Daddy called her fat, which never made sense to me because he was the one that was eighty pounds overweight.

They fell back onto the floor about five feet from where I sat holding Cory. Daddy pinned Mama under him again, "Becky, calm the fuck down!"

"You shut the fuck up, Danny. I'm showing everybody those pictures. Everybody's gonna see your fat ass fucking that whore. Do you want me to show your kids what you've been doing out on the road?"

"Becky, you're scaring them."

"I'm scaring the kids? All you fucking ever do is scare the kids."

Daddy saw Cory and me watching him. He got up and ran back into the bathroom and grabbed a towel, then he went over to Mama trying to rip the pictures away from her again. I don't know where she hid the photographs, but she began throwing clothes into a yellow plastic laundry basket. She slung my little brother onto her hip and looked at me and said, "Go get in the car."

We stayed at Maw Maw and Paw Paw's after the fight. I was used to my parents breaking up and making up. When I was five, they got divorced for almost a year and I never even knew it. Daddy did not acknowledge the breakup and just kept acting like they were married until they were again. When Mama drove us back to the house on Turrentine Street a week later, I thought my daddy would be there and we were going home.

But the house was empty. There were indentions in the carpet where my canopy bed had been. There were candy wrappers, hair bands, and my diary sitting on the floor. My clothes, my Welcome Back, Kotter tennis shoes that velcroed on the top and my little blue typewriter sat on the closet floor. "Hey Mama, where's all my furniture? Where's all my stuff?"

"It's gone. Your Daddy lost it gambling. He lost my sewing machine too," she said and packed up the last of the dishes. "Baby, go load up everything in your room."

Chapter Two

———

ALL BY MYSELF

Another One Bites the Dust

MOM LEFT DAD FOR THE LAST time in May of 1979. It all happened so fast. It felt like an invisible giant ripped open the sky and reached down and snatched up my little world like a dime-store snow globe. Then the giant shook it so violently that all the people and pieces came loose, and smashed it on the ground, the glitter water and magic turned to tears and broken glass.

Daddy disappeared after the fight over the polaroids and nobody knew where he was. We moved in with Maw Maw and Paw Paw. Mama got a job as a physical therapy assistant and she started working long hours at the hospital trying to save up money to get us a place to live and put Cory in daycare. During the week, she was always gone. On Sundays she took me to my favorite park to ride the rocket slide and catch tadpoles in the creek.

We had been living with Maw Maw and Paw Paw for about three weeks when a man knocked on the door. I ran into the little square hall off the kitchen and watched Mama introduce him to Maw Maw. "This is Mike. We're gonna go get some dinner."

He stood in the center of the room making small talk. He was so put together—the exact opposite of my dad. He wore pleated khakis, a belt and had on a green and white checkered, short-sleeved, button-down shirt. And it was tucked in perfectly. He was short and stocky, bolted down like a fire hydrant. His dark hair and beard reminded me of a lumberjack.

The second time Mike came over, I was sitting on the arm of my granddad's La-Z-Boy. He walked across the living room and said, "Hi, Aimee. I've heard a lot about you." I leaned back as far as I could, sending the signal loud and clear: "Do not come near me!"

Mom made a quick reintroduction to my grandparents, "You remember Mike. He's taking us out on the river on his boat." I hated watching Mama flirt and hang all over this stranger in my grandparent's living room. The peppy tone of her voice made me want to puke. My grandmother smiled, nodded yes, and looked over to see my reaction.

That's when I realized my parents might not get back together this time. My grandfather said, "It's supposed to rain," and went back to the ballgame.

"Okay, let's go," Mom said, taking Cory's hand and leading him to the door. "I'm staying here," I said. "Maw and me are watching a movie."

"No, Aimee, I bought you a new swimsuit and you're comin'," Mom snapped.

"I don't want to. I don't feel good."

My mother took me by the arm and led me to the back bathroom. "You're embarrassing me. Let's go." We walked outside and Mom started gushing over Mike's car. "Look Aimee, it's just like the one in *Smokey and the Bandit*." The car was a black Trans Am with T-tops and a gold eagle on the hood. Mike pulled his seat up so I could squeeze behind to get in. In the back seat was a four-year-old little girl with blonde pigtails and a giant smile on her face. "This is Leah, Mike's daughter," Mama said.

Cory was bouncing around and stood on the back seat in his sandals. Mike told him to sit down. When he didn't do it, Mike jerked him hard by the arm onto the seat. Mama didn't see it, but it set off sirens in my head that Mike was only pretending to be nice.

Cory and Leah were like twins, two little white blonde toe heads, and I was squeezed between them with my dark tangled hair. I thought we must look like a backward Oreo cookie. We flew out of my grandparent's driveway in a cloud of dust. My hair slapped me in the face and my cheeks stung from the wind, which tasted like tires and tar.

Casey Kasem came on the radio introducing a song that would forever be linked in my memory to that day. With the thump of the baseline, Freddy Mercury sang, "...and another one down, another one down, another one bites the dust."

By the time Mike got his boat into the water, we heard thunder and blackish gray clouds coming in. The sun was still shining bright, but rain was starting to sprinkle. The sky seemed as emotional as I was. Within minutes it was pouring, so we went back to the pier and docked the boat, then we ran through the storm to Mike's apartment. When we walked in, it smelled like my mama's Ciara perfume. Cory, Leah, and I were soaking wet in our swimsuits and it was cold as a refrigerator. Mama wrapped towels around us. She rambled around in the kitchen making a pot of coffee. It was like she lived there already. She and Mike disappeared down the hall and into the back bedroom to change into dry clothes. When they walked back into the living room, Mike wrapped his arms around Mama and I wanted to slap him.

"Okay, we've got something exciting to tell y'all," Mom said, as she sat down on the arm of the couch. "We got married this weekend!"

While Cory and I stayed with Maw Maw and Paw Paw, my mother and Mike had gone to Rome, Georgia to say "I do" because there was a ninety-day waiting period in Alabama before you could get hitched again after a divorce. It had been only six weeks since the fight on Turrentine Street.

I felt like I swallowed my heart. Cory was sitting beside me on the couch chewing on Mike's remote control and Leah sat there smiling and shivering. Both were oblivious to the emotional grenade that my mama had dropped on the three of us. My head felt like a beehive bashed in with a baseball bat. A thousand questions swarmed, but the only words that came out of my mouth were, "What about Daddy?"

A giant gulp formed in my throat, and I knew that I was about to explode into tears. I jumped off the couch and ran down the hall until I found the bathroom. I locked the door. Sitting on the toilet seat, I fell apart. I had never felt so alone, so helpless, there in my wet swimsuit, river water and rain still dripping from my hair. The bathroom smelled like Irish Spring soap, and something about that made me cry harder.

"Baby, unlock this door," Mom said, jiggling the handle.

"I can't believe you got married and didn't even tell me!" I yelled.

"Come on, let me in. I wanna talk to you," she said. "You know all your Daddy and me did was fight. I love Mike, and…"

"You can love him all you want, but I hate him and I hate you. I wanna live with Daddy!" I screamed.

"Well, good luck finding him," she shot back.

If Only I Could Hold You Again

THE FIRST TIME I SAW DAD after the divorce, he came to get me at Maw Maw and Paw Paw's house. I hadn't seen or talked to him in three months. When I climbed in the front seat of the Chevy two-tone truck, he was driving. He said, "Baby doll, we're gonna go to a movie and then we'll spend the night up at Opal and Harold's." Movies were our thing. Dad took me to see my first movie, *One Flew Over the Cuckoo's Nest*, when I was four years old. He loved to tell the story about how after the movie I looked up at him and said, "That Indian really liked that guy."

The drive was quiet on the way to Agricola Movie Theater. I didn't know if Dad had talked to Mom or if he even knew she had married Mike.

"Did you know Mama got married?"

"Aimee, I don't care what your Mom is doing. I don't want to talk about her," he snapped at me.

"Cory learned to swim," I said, trying to change the subject. Cory did everything early— he learned to walk at nine months. He had just turned three that August and started swimming a couple of months before his third birthday.

"Anyway, I went to high school with Mike and your mama's gonna be so bored it won't last a year," Dad said.

The movie we went to see that night changed my life. It was the *Buddy Holly Story*. Dad and I sat in the dark theater, both of our legs shaking ninety to nothing to the same silent beat. It was the first time I had ever seen someone write a song. I guess I was aware that Dad wrote songs, but I had never seen him do it. He didn't play an instrument. Usually, he'd tap the inside windowpane and sing while we were driving down the road.Growing up, I was his little dime-store queen, riding shotgun, standing in the front seat of our beat-up station wagon with my arm around his neck. We'd roll the windows down so I could feel the wind in my hair, and he'd sing the song he had written especially for me:

> *Aimee my*
> *Daddy's little pumpkin pie*
> *I don't know why*
> *I love you like I do.*

There was a scene in the movie where Buddy Holly sat on the side of the stage with his band working on lyrics and melody.Before that, I had never thought about where the songs on the radio came from, or that for every "Maggie May" or "My Sharona," someone sat down and came up with the melody, music, and words. I was captivated.

As we walked out and across the parking lot, my mind spun through "Piña Colada," "Cat's in the Cradle," and "Kung Fu Fighting." I thought about my first favorite, "Silly Love Songs" by Wings. And the first cassette I ever bought with my own money was KC and the Sunshine Band.

On the drive up the mountain that night to Opal and Harold's, I told Dad, "I'm gonna to be a songwriter."

"What makes you think you could be a songwriter, baby doll?" Dad asked.

"Because I got a title." He looked at me with a bemused smile, "Oh yeah, what is it?"

"If Only I Could Hold You Again, I'd Never Let You Go," I announced. I think I was talking about him when I said it. He came back at me and sang, "If only I could hold you again, I'd never let you go. I'd always let you know that you had a friend if only I could hold you again." We traded lines all the way to my grandparents' house.

When we sat down for supper at Opal and Harold's, Daddy said, "I sold the Elvis cars to a museum in Memphis."

It felt like he had pawned my heart. I loved those cars; we made more memories in that Cadillac than Elvis ever did. Those cars were the last piece of my old life, the souvenir of what we were. Opal was still upset about Harold giving Daddy the loan to buy the Elvis cars even though he paid it back.

Daddy told us he would be living in Nashville part-time and planned to open a video cassette rental store in Gadsden with the money he made from selling the cars.

"How are you gonna start a business if you're not even here?" Opal asked.

"What kind of store?" Harold asked.

"People come in and rent beta or VHS tapes of movies."

"How do you watch the movies?" Harold asked.

"You watch them on a VCR machine. I'll rent those, too. Dad, I want you to run the store."

"Nobody gives a flip about taking movies home," Opal said.

"It's gonna make a lot of money and it will give Harold something to do," Dad told my grandmother.

Opal started collecting the plates for the dishwasher and mumbled under her breath, "He's gonna lose all his cotton pickin' money on some kind of store nobody's ever heard of."

A Few Acres

THAT SEPTEMBER I STARTED FOURTH GRADE at Hokes Bluff Elementary. It was the first time I stayed at the same school all year, but my life was about to change more than it ever had.

As black as my last school had been, this one was all white. Scary white. It was the most racist school around. Men stood on the roof with rifles when a black family tried to enroll their son. When I asked Mama about this, she said, "It makes me sick how they act, but I don't really have a choice right now, Aimee."

Uncle Kelly went to Hokes Bluff High School so he could drop me off every morning and pick me up every afternoon while Mama was at work. Most teenage boys would be embarrassed to have a nine-year-old tagging along, but Uncle Kelly took me everywhere. He was the best looking guy at Hokes Bluff. He had

curly, sandy blonde hair and muscles from lifting weights. Every
day on the way home from school he bought me Pop Rocks and
a Coca-Cola.

Dad called every few weeks and promised to pick me up. I
waited outside on Maw Maw and Paw Paw's rusty, green glider
for hours until they made me come inside because I was getting
eaten up by mosquitoes. When Dad did finally show up, three
weeks later, it had been months since I had seen him. Paw Paw
went outside to talk to him and told me to stay in the house. I
heard him through the screen window.

"Danny, I've had enough of you calling this house and telling
her you're coming to get her. Every time she waits for you. Every
time she believes you. I don't know why."

Mom and Mike rented a two-bedroom apartment in Gadsden
and moved in. Thankfully, Mom didn't have a way to get me to
school and get herself to work on time, so during the week I spent
most of the time at Maw Maw and Paw Paw's. I knew every nook
and cranny of that house and I loved being there. At night I waited in the living room watching the back wall for the headlights of
Uncle Kelly's truck. If he was in a good mood, or had been drinking, we would dance in the living room to "Call Me" by Blondie
and "YMCA" by the Village People. He would spin me around
in circles and dip me dramatically until I was dizzy.

Maw Maw and I stayed up late, passing the little movie channel guide back and forth deciding on what movies to watch. In
the bathroom she kept a stack of Frederick's of Hollywood catalogs sitting next to the toilet. They were dog eared and waterlogged. Sometimes we played a game we called My Page, Your
Page. We sat side by side and flip through those catalogs laughing
at all the weird police woman lingerie and all the naughty nurse
costumes. Anything on the right page was mine and anything on
the left page was hers. I loved everything that glittered and she
loved the high heels. Sometimes it made me sad when I looked at
her white canvas, dollar store tennis shoes, but she seemed happy
just looking at the catalogs. My grandmother found joy in simple
things like sitting on the swing with the sun in her face.

Mike sold his boat, Trans Am, and his motorcycle to buy a
few acres of land in Glencoe a few miles from Maw Maw and Paw
Paw's place. Mike spent every Sunday for the next eight months

in the punishing Alabama sunshine making his and my Mama's dream come true. He worked from daylight to dark, running the plumbing and electrical, and hanging sheetrock. This was Mama's first house of her own. She sewed curtains, and picked paint colors and wallpaper for each room.

We moved into the new house that March. Cory and I each had our own bedrooms and Leah had a bedroom too, but she only came over on the weekends. Not long after we settled, Mike's brother David bought the lot next door and began construction. His daughter, Cathy, was a year younger than me, and he had a son Cory's age, so every day we played in the woods on the side of our house, building forts and exploring for treasures.

Mike was off in the summer and watched Cory and me while Mom was at work Monday through Friday from 8:00 am to 4:00 pm. Cory was like a jackrabbit on crack, everywhere all the time. It was easy to see that he got on Mike's nerves and he had a quick fuse. It wasn't long until everything he said to Cory was in a mean tone.

Cory told everybody everywhere we went, "I've got two daddies." The problem was, neither one of them wanted the job. I'm not sure he even knew which one was his real dad. The first time we sat down at the table for dinner in our new house, I asked, "Can Daddy come?" and I begged Mom to get back with my father every time we were alone.

I tried my best not to talk to Mike for the first few months we lived there. He was a stranger and watching him and Mom made me sick. Mom turned into someone new married to Mike. She had a different last name. I flinched every time she wrote it on a check. I gagged every time she said it. I wanted her to be a Mayo like Cory and me. They were blissful newlyweds and we were prisoners of our mom's heart.

45 RPM

WE HAD BEEN IN THE NEW HOUSE for about a month when Dad called and said he was coming over because he had a surprise for me. I fantasized about him and Mike getting into a fight, but I also felt guilty, like I was betraying Daddy for living in the same house with some other man. I expected Dad to hate Mike, but he sat down at the kitchen table like nothing had even happened. "Hey, Becky, go fix me something to drink," Dad yelled out to Mom. She was in the laundry room.

Daddy and Mike went to high school together and were in the same grade until Daddy quit his sophomore year. "How's it going', Mike?" Dad asked. He didn't sound mad at all.

"It's going good. How you been, Danny?" Mike acted completely different in front of my Dad. He was patient with Cory and he spoke in a more positive and peppy tone. He laughed more, but in a fake, nervous way.

"Let's go," I tried to pull Daddy by the hand.

"Hang on, I want to tell your Mom about the new store I'm opening on Broad Street. It's called Bear Video and I'm gonna rent movies. It's gonna change everything. You'll be able to rent a movie and take it home and watch it." Every time Dad described the concept of the store, it confused people because no one knew what beta max or VHS tapes were. No one in our town had a VCR or knew what he was talking about.

"Okay, baby doll, I've got something extra special for you," Daddy said, and handed me a shoebox. He brought Cory a Hot Wheels track, Spiderman Underoos, and cowboy boots.

I ran to my room and plopped down on the floor. Dad followed me and yelled at my Mom, "Hey Becky, get in here. I want you to see this." I opened the shoebox and it was full of 45 rpm vinyl records still in their sleeves. Each one had the same song, "Lottie, Lottie, Low," performed by Danny Mayo and the Black Girls.

I flipped to the B side and saw the title "If Only I Could Hold You Again," and under it read, "Written by Aimee Mayo and Danny Mayo," in white letters on the black label. That moment locked the dream of becoming a songwriter into my heart. I knew for sure that was what I wanted to do when I grew up. I kept reading it over and over, and I couldn't believe my name was on a REAL record.

Daddy hired some studio musicians, recorded a demo of our song in Nashville, and he sang it with a full band. I loved his voice. He sounded like a mixture of Van Morrison and Randy

Newman, except that he couldn't control his voice the same way. I listened to those records until they were all worn out. I played the song for everyone who came in our house. That day, Mom came into the bedroom to listen and she loved the song. It was years later before I realized that a lot of the lyrics were written for my mom. There was one part in the bridge that said, "You and I could have made it, but my lies got in the way. I know you won't believe it, but still I gotta say, 'Baby I love you. Baby I need you.'"

I was ready to go the freaking hell go. Mama followed us outside and I climbed up into the truck. "Come on, Becky, ride with us downtown. I want to show you the store. It's gonna make a fortune," he said as he started the engine. "Danny, I can't just leave with you, what about Mike?"

Dad leaned out the window and said, "You're gonna wish you never divorced me." He slammed the truck into reverse and pulled out of the driveway.

Glencoe Middle School

GLENCOE MIDDLE SCHOOL WAS MY tenth "new" school. On my first day I was the only kid in the fifth grade not wearing shorts. August in Alabama is so humid that you're swimming in sweat the second you step outside, but I had on candy-striped, thick denim overalls to cover the black and blue checkerboard bruises up and down my legs.

I don't remember what that first beating was for. Mama was at work, and Cory and I were playing in the yard when Mike told me to come inside and go to my bedroom. I heard him stomp down the hall, and then he came in with a belt. "Bend over," he demanded.

The sheer force of the first lash hit me so hard I peed my pants. I tried to run away, but Mike grabbed my wrist and hit me over and over and over. The more I tried to escape, the madder he got. I tried to block him with my free hand, dancing like a spastic around the room, dodging that brown leather belt. He hit me so many times that I stopped counting.

"Be still," he kept screaming, but I couldn't. I thrashed and bucked and tried to crawl under my bed to get away from him. He hit me about thirty times before he stopped.

"And don't go crying to your mama about this either," he said, and walked out.

When he left the room, I crawled over to my door and shut it, crying so hard that I couldn't breathe. I went into the bathroom across the hall and climbed up on the counter to inspect the damage in the mirror. I had a horseshoe-shaped blood clot where the buckle hit my lower back, a pink slash inside my right thigh that had a bloody line on it, and more on my neck and wrist. I was covered in red welts. I got into the bathtub, the water stinging every place Mike had lashed me.

I cried until my face was red and wet with tears and my lips were numb. I was in shock that this could happen, that a grown-up could do that to a kid. I wanted to call Daddy and tell him, but I hadn't seen him in weeks and didn't know where he was. I stayed locked in the bathroom and waited for my mama to get home from work.

I heard her talking in the kitchen and smelled Hamburger Helper cooking. "Mama!" I yelled and ran to the front of the house to tell her what happened.

She was sitting in Mike's lap on the couch, laughing and watching *The Andy Griffith Show*. Cory was on the living room floor playing with his Hot Wheels.

"What is it, baby?" Mama asked. Mike stared straight at the TV.

I heard myself say, "I don't feel good. I'm going to bed."

I don't know why I didn't tell her. Maybe because I was afraid of it happening again, or maybe because I thought nothing would happen at all. My mom was so haunted by her own childhood that she could not see the horror in mine. If the walls could talk in the house where my Mama grew up, they would just cry.

Night after night she watched Paw Paw beat my angel grandmother with a bottle of whiskey in one hand and her dignity in the other. He smeared her face in spaghetti sauce on the cracked linoleum floor as he blacked her eyes and bruised every inch of her body.

When Mama was thirteen, she found her mother on the bathroom floor in a puddle of blood. She had been five months pregnant and my grandfather beat a baby out of her. All they kept was the secret.

Every night as the sun slid down the Alabama sky, my grandfather's words blurred into slurs and everybody got ready for the whiskey nightmare show to begin. Mama, who was the oldest of five, hurried to hide her brothers and sisters. She always put Kelly, her baby brother, in the broom closet in the small, square hall. She gave him a flashlight to play with so he wouldn't cry. He sat alone in the spider-webbed darkness. She helped Sandy squeeze behind the old cabinet TV. Then Mom gave pillows to Jeff and Debbie and they all got in bed and covered their heads to drown out the sound of their mother being beaten. When the sobs faded into a whimper, the children lay still, afraid to move, praying their daddy would die during the night and their mother would still be alive come morning.

Fuck that McMuffin

I KEPT WAITING FOR DADDY to come save me. To somehow know what was going on and swoop in like a bipolar Superman and take me out of there, but he didn't even call on my birthday.Seventy percent of the time, when he promised to come to get us, Cory waited on the front porch with his Hulk Hogan backpack until Mama made him come in and go to bed. I had learned that "yes" really meant "maybe" with Dad.

One night he came to pick me up to go to a movie on a school night and said we'd spend the night up at Opal's. Then he'd take me to school the next day. I still saw Opal and Harold every Thursday night when they'd come by and take me to Hardee's, my favorite restaurant.

Dad got up late the next morning and we didn't leave the house until 10:00 am. We went through the McDonald's drive-through and he ordered two Egg McMuffins.

"I want a chicken biscuit!" I kept telling him, but he ignored me.

"You can take the egg off."

"It gets stuck in the cheese."

The drive-thru girl gave us the food and Dad tossed me my breakfast.

A couple of minutes later, he took a turn going the wrong way.

"Where are you taking me?" I asked him.

"To school."

He was headed toward Hokes Bluff Elementary, where I had gone the year before.

"I go to Glencoe Middle School. I don't know where you're going."

For some reason he thought I was lying and kept driving me there anyway.

"I don't know what you're doing. I'm not going in there."

"Aimee, eat that damn McMuffin!" He snapped at me.

I rolled down the the window and said, "Fuck that McMuffin!" and slung it out on Meighan Blvd.

He got mad, then asked, "Do you really go to Glencoe?"

"Why would I lie about where I go to school?" I said and got out and slammed the door.

He didn't even know where I went to school or what grade I was in.

I felt like an orphan whose parents were living.

Black and Blue

I TURNED TEN THAT SEPTEMBER. A few weeks later, report cards arrived and so did my next beating. When Mike saw that I received a D in math, he said, "Go to your room."

Fear took over. I didn't want to obey, but I didn't know what else to do. The sounds of the clink of him taking off his belt and coming down the hall made me heave with fear. He came in after me with the belt again and told me to bend over. His face was blood red and the look in his eyes was like a rabid animal.

I had changed schools so many times over the years and it always took me a while to catch up. My parents had never even asked to see my report card and now all of a sudden this stranger was obsessed with it. The beatings continued after every report card and any other chance he got.

A couple of months later, I had another D in math. I made a plan on the school bus. I ran to my bedroom as soon as I got home. I threw all the clothes out of my drawers and then I pushed my dresser up against the door to block it. Mike always knew the day that report cards came and he kept knocking asking to see mine, but I ignored him. Mama got home from the hospital a couple of hours after Cory and I got out of school. She said, "Aimee, baby, what's going on? Why don't you open your door?" but I refused.

"He's not whipping me again," I said, leaning up against the dresser.

"She's so dramatic. All I asked is to see her grades," Mike stomped down the hall. When it was time for supper, he came back to the door. "I promise I'm not going to whip you if you have a bad grade," he said sarcastically, as if he had been talked into it by my mama.

A few days later, I was outside playing with Leah and my step-cousin, Cathi, and they both started crying when Mike came up and yanked me by the arm. He dragged me across the front yard and into the living room.

"Look at this floor."

Cory had trailed grass and dirt across the carpet when he came in to use the bathroom. "I vacuumed, I swear." The fear in my voice made me sick. "This happened after…"

Mike started hitting me before I could finish. Mike had made a paddle in the woodworking shop and he had cut holes in it so that it would sting a little more. The beatings always happened in private. When I cried or screamed or begged, it seemed his fury fed on that. The rage he went into when he beat us was fueled by our fear. I never knew how many times he was going to hit me, and that was the worst part.

The time he hurt me most, Mike didn't touch me at all. Cory and I were playing outside and I was trying to break in my new softball glove. Cory was almost four and had been playing with Mike's yard shears. He tried to cut an extension cord. I heard Cory screaming and ran around the side of the house. I saw Mike jerk Cory up by the wrist and lift him off of the ground like a rag doll. "Are you just trying to get electrocuted?" Mike yelled in his face.

"I'm sorry, I'm sorry," Cory cried. I heard the same panic rising in his voice that always overtook mine.

Mike grabbed the thick, orange extension cord, made it into a lasso and started swinging. Every time he hit Cory, I felt it. I knew by the way Cory was crying that Mike was really hurting him. I stood there buzzing with hatred. I wanted to run and attack my stepfather to make him stop, but I was too scared to move. When it was finally over, Cory fell limp and I raced over to him. He was hyperventilating, trying to apologize to Mike.

"I won't do it again. Yes, sir. I'm so sorry." He was sobbing and mumbling and not making sense. He went to that hysterical place that I went when Mike was hitting me, but he got stuck there.

It was a Saturday, so Mama was home. I ran in the house, "Cory's hurt. Come quick!"

"Oh my God!" she ran at Mike. "What did you do?"

"Becky, I thought he was gonna get electrocuted. It scared me. I didn't mean to hurt him."

"Who could do this to a four-year-old? Something is bad wrong with you."

When Mike looked at Cory standing there by the steps of the side porch, he seemed as shocked as Mama about what he had done. He knelt down and told Cory, "I'm sorry, are you okay?" There was panic in his voice. "Cory, I didn't mean to hurt you like that."

"It's okay. It's okay," Cory tried to get the words out, but he still hadn't caught his breath. Cory forgave him on the spot.

"Do not come in this house. Get away from us," Mama's voice broke into sobs. She grabbed Cory's hand and walked him inside and I followed them. She tried to clean the bloody cuts all over him and he begged her not to touch them. A couple of the gashes on his legs and one on his arm were so deep they looked like we might have to go to the hospital. That night I heard them fighting. Mama screamed at Mike, "I could have your ass put in jail. I could ruin your life."

"Becky, somebody's got to discipline these kids and Danny sure as hell ain't gonna do it."

"I can't be with someone who could do that to my child. We're moving out," Mom said. I was the first one packed.

Mama made minimum wage and didn't know how she was

going to support us. Daddy was making good money at the video stores, so he paid the deposit and the first two months' rent at Pine Ridge Apartments. Opal and Harold got involved. Opal had seen my bruises when I got out of the bathtub at her house a few weeks earlier. They wanted to have Mike arrested and my dad threatened him, "Lay another hand on one of my kids and I'll kill you."

Daddy took Mom and Cory and me out to eat at Ruby Tuesdays and shopping at the Gadsden Mall. He bought me a satin, champagne-colored satin comforter and Mama a lamp for her bedside table. He kept coming over and took us out to eat every night for the next couple of weeks. My parents were being nice to each other, laughing about old times.

"Becky, remember that night when I woke you up banging on the front door?"

"Yeah, you were naked on the porch saying you'd been robbed."

"And you got up and cooked me chicken wings at 4:00 am?"

"Yeah, and then I found your clothes in the azalea bush when I went to the mailbox that morning."

I was so happy listening to them. I thought they might be getting back together, but Daddy disappeared again, and Mike started dropping by. I heard him crying to Mama, "Becky, I just went into a rage. I don't even remember doing it."

Two weeks later, Mom told me we were moving back in with Mike. "Everybody deserves a second chance."

I felt like a piece of nothing—empty. I couldn't even cry. Mike promised that he would never hit Cory or me again. He kept that promise to me, but I had a new kind of punishment coming my way that would make me beg for a beating.

Bear Video

THAT DECEMBER, I heard my name ring out on the intercom at school. When I got to the office, the principal, Miss Farley, said, "Your stepmom's here to check you out. Sign the sheet."

"I don't have a stepmom." I said confused.

"Well, then who's that lady out there?" She nodded toward a woman I'd never seen in my life. She was standing in front of the trophy case in the hallway. She looked like she had wandered in from the movie, *Flashdance*—a thick mane of wild, strawberry blonde hair, shiny, teal tights with burgundy leg warmers, and some sort of plum leotard with a tiny belt fastened around her waist. I had never seen leg warmers in real life; they hadn't made it to the Gadsden Mall yet.

"I think she's here to get somebody else," I said.

"Well let's find out what's going on," the school secretary suggested, and I followed her out of the office.

"Hi, Aimee! I recognize you from your pictures," Susan said in a thick Cajun accent.

I imagined her spinning around a pole, doing a fancy kick, and breaking into the chorus of "What a Feeling."

"Aimee, I'm Susan, your new stepmom." She lunged and wrapped her arms around me in a big hug. I could feel her heartbeat in my face.

"Oh," was all I said back to her.

At first I thought it was another one of Dad's stupid jokes. I kept waiting for him to pop around the corner.

"Your dad wanted me to come to check you out of school. He's waiting at the new house we rented."

I followed her out the double doors to the car, our feet crunching on the gravel of the school parking lot. My hands were sweating and I didn't know what to say. I had already forgotten her name.

As we walked up to a silver convertible Mercedes, I said, "Wow. I love your car." I studied the dotted caramel leather and the cool wood dashboard.

She looked at me as if I were strange and said, "This is your dad's car."

My heart sank. Daddy hadn't told me he was married. I had never seen this car, and we were about to drive to a house that I didn't know he lived in—a rented Tudor in downtown Gadsden.

We drove to the elementary school and picked up Cory. When we arrived at Dad's new house and walked in, there were piles and piles of colorful hand-stitched quilts everywhere; butterflies, tulips, and every pattern you could imagine. Some of the stacks were taller than I was.

"Hey, baby doll," Daddy said, walking into the living room with a plate of fried chicken. "What did you think when Susan showed up to get you at school?" he laughed.

I wanted to ask him why he didn't tell me he was married, but all I said was, "Where'd you get all these quilts?"

"Come check this out," he said, and I followed him into the den. There were posters and stuffed animals, necklaces and bracelets, and all kinds of figurines of some weird, gray, long-necked creature. "What is this thing? What are you doing with all this stuff?" I asked.

"It looks like Steven Spielberg's fucking basement in here," Dad said.

Then I picked up the crazy looking stuffed animal, it's finger lit up and said, "ET phone home."

"It's a new movie, *ET*, and it's gonna be huge. I'm selling this stuff at the new video stores and I'm taking the quilts to sell at the flea market." Dad announced the grand opening of Bear Video a couple of weeks before Christmas. It was the first video store in northeast Alabama. The flagship store was on Broad Street in downtown Gadsden. There was a giant ten-foot tall taxidermy grizzly bear in the front window. Other kids stared at it from the street, but I got to examine it up close. Every new movie came with a poster and the walls were covered in them: *Tootsie*, *Risky Business*, *Trading Places*. Soon Daddy opened Bear Pavilion ten minutes away in Rainbow City, and Bear Junction ten minutes away in Glencoe.

On the weekends the line snaked out the door and down the block. Business was booming. Daddy put an XXX room in the back of each store, probably just to upset Opal. I wasn't allowed in there, but I snuck in any chance I got to study the boxes: *Deep Throat, Black and White, Babysitters Need to Be Punished.* Mama Opal complained about those movies nonstop. She taught Sunday school at Dwight Baptist Church and this was an embarrassment to the whole family.

Susan was wonderful. She loved photography and took pictures of Cory and me leaning us up against trees and posed by a wood fence. She taught me how to use her Minolta camera, and whenever we spent the night with her and Dad, she always cooked pot roast for Cory and me and helped us with our homework. That Christmas, Mom gave me a ventriloquist doll that I had picked out from the JC Penny catalog. Dad gave me a bunch of *ET* shit. I had been asking for white speed skates with pink wheels and black Gloria Vanderbilt corduroy pants with the white swan on the pocket.

Dad worked a lot getting the video store set up. He taught Harold how to run Bear Video, and my Aunt Debbie, my mom's younger sister, ran Bear Junction, the video store in Glencoe. Dad stayed close to all Mom's brothers and sisters. Every time I saw him, I begged Daddy to let me move in with him and Susan, but he always said no. She even offered to drive me to school, but he refused, saying that he didn't have time to watch me. Then he turned around and let his friend Sonny's fifteen-year-old son, Sean, move in when he got kicked out of the house for shoplifting.

Sean had been in and out of juvenile detention centers since he was twelve and was always aggressive towards Cory and me. Sean had shoulder-length dirty blonde hair and a permanent sunburn.

One night, Daddy, Cory, and Susan were out at the grocery store and no one was in the house but Sean and me. He got mad when I didn't want to go to his room and he chased me, pinning me down on the beige shag carpet in the living room. "I'm gonna rape you," he said. I clawed him in the face to get him off me, which only made him mad. I ran into the bathroom and locked the door.

Then he tried to pop the lock, so I climbed out the window and waited in the neighbor's driveway until everyone got home. Susan was afraid of him too. Daddy finally made Sean leave when he found out he kept a gun in the house.

Ten months after Dad and Susan were married, he called her one day and said he didn't love her anymore and wasn't coming back. Dad let the lease go on the rental house and ran off, leaving her with no car, no money, stranded in Gadsden. She was devastated and no one knew what to do. Opal and I tried to console her. She cried for days, "How could he do that? How could he be so cruel? Why did he just marry me if he didn't love me? He called out of the blue and said, 'I don't love you'. He didn't even tell me what I did wrong, why he left."

"You didn't do anything wrong. He did, he's an idiot," I said. I was furious with Dad. Uncle Kelly and Mike had to move Susan and all those quilts back to Shreveport.

Chapter Three

—

BOHEMIAN RHAPSODY

Egg Magician

BACK AT HOME, MIKE mastered the art of making me miserable. I felt like I was in some kind of weird psychological experiment. I got grounded for anything and everything he could come up with: leaving lights on, running too much bathwater, eating too many potato chips, not shutting the broken door all the way, letting the cat in. Grounded at my house meant I couldn't go anywhere for six weeks at a time. I couldn't talk on the phone; I couldn't do anything. My bedroom became a jail cell and I was in solitary confinement.

I stayed grounded for most of sixth grade, and then again in seventh grade I was trapped in my bedroom for eight months for failing typing class. Since I had taught myself how to type in my own freestyle way on my little, blue typewriter, I could never catch on to not looking at my hands. It would have been easier to just start walking everywhere backwards.

During those years confined to the house, I was under permanent surveillance. And if Mike wasn't watching me and waiting for me to do something wrong, his brother, David, who lived next door was. He was a part-time helicopter pilot for the Air National Guard, and he wore Army fatigues year-round and patrolled the yard like it was Vietnam. I couldn't walk to the mailbox without him barking at me, "Where are you going? What are you doing?"

Everything I did irritated both of them. It didn't help that Daddy was making a lot of money from the video stores, but refused to pay Mom one cent of child support. Every few months a dented cardboard box would show up in the mail with clothes Dad picked out for us. Usually I loved what he got me: leopard print cowboy boots, neon parachute pants, a blue and red Jordache sweat suit, which was my favorite outfit. Harold gave Mama money when she asked for it, but I could tell Mike was resentful that he had to provide for and take care of two kids who weren't his when his own daughter didn't even live with him. He paid child support like clockwork, but I think he felt guilty he wasn't doing enough for Leah.

Every night after school my job was to wash the dinner dishes, pots, and pans. Mike inspected every single one microscopically to make sure that there wasn't a speck of food caught in a crevice on the bottom of a plate or a faint lipstick smudge on a glass. If he found one spot anywhere, I had to start all over and wash each dish again.

My bedroom felt like a hamster cage, and I was caught in a spinning wheel, with diaries and mixtapes my only escapes. Time crawled like a geriatric snail. Mike put a giant antique grandfather clock at the end of the hall right by my bedroom so I could hear the tick-tock, tick-tock of the seconds of my childhood that he was stealing. Then every hour on the hour I heard the outburst from a demented bird screaming, "Cuckoo! Cuckoo!"

On Saturdays and Sundays, Mike always insisted that Mama make eggs. Once he learned that I hated them. I did not want to get out of bed those mornings because I was nauseated by the smell. When I sat down at the table, I gagged when I saw that slimy slop that tasted like snot.

I always requested scrambled because they were easier to get rid of. Sometimes I spit the eggs into my iced tea and kept my hand sealed around the base of the glass. I snuck them onto my brother's plate, slung them into the plant behind my chair, stuck them into my pockets, panties, and socks, or into a wadded-up napkin in my lap. Mike refused to get up from the table until he made sure my plate was clean. Sometimes I got my revenge and held him hostage. If an Auburn game was on TV, I wouldn't touch my eggs so that he'd be trapped watching me instead of the team he loved.

The only thing I hated more than eggs were English peas. When Mom made them for lunch one Saturday, Mike would not take his eyes off me, so I couldn't use my tricks to get rid of them. I wanted to go outside and play kickball with some neighbor kids, so gulping down the peas seemed like the easiest way to eat them. But what I didn't expect was that they would come right back up. I threw up all over my plate, which made Mike furious.

"You're gonna eat that!" he yelled.

"I'm not eating puke!"

"If you don't eat the mess you made, I'm gonna serve you green peas for supper every night this week!"

So, I ate it. I didn't gag. I looked straight into Mike's eyes, took a giant spoonful, and swallowed that pea sludge, chasing it down with Coca-Cola, then I ran outside to play kickball.

We were fire and gasoline, and our epic power struggle continued until five years later when I burned down our house.

Tone Deaf

DURING THE SCHOOL YEAR, Cory and I went months without hearing from Daddy. He would just appear like an early moon or rainbow. The summer I was eleven, he picked Cory and I up in a dark green Rolls Royce with a bumper sticker on the back that read, 'My Other Car's a Rolls Royce.' It was the first time we stayed in his one-bedroom condo on Nashville's Music Row. It was located right across the street from the famous RCA Studio B, where Dolly Parton recorded, "I Will Always Love You" and "Jolene," and where Elvis sang, "Are You Lonesome Tonight?" We went on a guided tour and walked through the hallowed rooms where so many hit songs were made. In the control room and vocal booth I felt the weight of all the magical music moments that happened there.

On our first night in Nashville, after we finished dinner at The Cooker, Daddy said, "Let's go downtown and look for hookers." "Like prostitutes?" I asked. "Yeah, they're everywhere."

We drove up and down Broadway in his Rolls. "They love this fucking car. Watch this," he said as he pulled over to the curb. "Okay, you two crouch down in the back seat and when one of them comes over here, Cory, jump up and scare 'em." I was confused. "Hurry up, duck down in the back seat."

"What are we doing?"

"Just do what I said." A lady with teased blonde hair leaned inside the window, showcasing her cleavage. She reached her huge hand with burgundy fingernails through the window and touched Dad's thigh. "How much, baby?" she asked. Cory popped up like a jack-in-the-box and scared the shit out of her. She slapped my Daddy across the face and then we drove away.

"Here's another thing you won't see back home." Daddy pulled up next to a man with a sign that read, 'Hungry,' and gave him our leftovers. The man blew us a kiss. I had never seen anyone homeless and I couldn't stop thinking about it for the rest of the trip.

Daddy never had a driver's license and usually he had outstanding warrants in at least three states, so he had to get creative when we got pulled over. Frequent license plate changes and high-speed police chases were just a part of being with him. Cory and I were always dragged into helping him. If I was in the car with him and he got pulled over, he commanded, "Act retarded," which meant picking my nose and yelling out every few seconds. It worked. The cops were always quick to forgive a stressed-out dad, but they wanted the hell away from me too.

When Cory was about twelve, we got pulled over on Hillsboro Road, one of the busiest roads in Green Hills. Daddy told us, "I've got a warrant out for not appearing in court. If he asks for my license, I'm going to jail." He handed Cory a plastic cup from Captain D's and said, "Cory, I need you to hold this cup like your life depends on it. When I give you the signal, jump out of the car and take off running back to the apartment and don't talk to anybody."

"I don't want to," Cory argued.

"I'll give you twenty bucks. Get ready." Daddy got out of the car and went to talk to the officer. We saw him wave his hand behind his back for Cory to bolt. Seconds later, Dad started shouting at the cop, "Oh my God, where's my son? My son! My autistic son! He just ran away. This is your fault. I'll have your badge," he kept yelling. "If he loses that cup, all hell's gonna break loose."

The police officer called in back up and they drove all over the neighborhood looking for my little brother.

Twenty minutes later, my dad suggested, "Well, maybe we should check my apartment. He may have run back there, it's about a mile away." We found Cory sitting by himself on the Royal Arms Apartment steps, rocking back and forth, clutching that blue, plastic cup like his life depended on it.

I heard one of the officers tell him, "I'm a policeman. I'm your friend."

Dad was still in full theatrics as he screamed at the cop that pulled us over, "You'd better be glad he didn't get lost." The cop was so rattled, he forgot why he had stopped my dad. By the end of that trip, I had learned how to call the bail bonds guy and bail Daddy out of jail.

***

FOR TEN DAYS I BEGGED DADDY to take us to Barbara Mandrell Studios. It was at the edge of Music Row next to a country music museum, and out front it read, "Make your own record." Finally, the day before we were leaving to go home, he said he would take me if I would stand in line. Over fifty people were waiting to get inside into the air conditioning. Every person's recording was played on the speakers outside and in the lobby. When someone was a really great singer, everyone applauded.

I waited in line while Dad and Cory walked across the street to Arnold's Country Kitchen to eat lunch. When they made it back, it was our turn. There were three huge binders filled with hundreds of songs. I chose "The Rose" by Bette Midler because I loved the poetic lyrics. The attendant led me into a small vocal booth and helped me adjust the headphones and microphone adjusted.

When the music started, I felt the blood rushing through my

arms. The words were on the TV screen, but I missed my cue. The engineer stopped the track and said, "I'll point at you when it's time to come in."

I nodded and watched him through the glass window of the vocal booth. The music started again and I heard my voice singing. I closed my eyes and poured everything I had into it. My voice broke with emotion in the last two words of the song because I started to cry.

As I finished, Cory and Dad busted into the vocal booth and the attendant plugged in another set of headphones so they could sing together. They had chosen the song, "Jungle Love" by Morris Day and the Time. Dad started by doing an "Oh-ooh-aah-aah" kind of psychotic chimpanzee call. Cory was almost six years old and fearless. He jerked the microphone up to his mouth and sang the lyrics in a low, husky voice. He wore a red and white striped tank top, blue terry cloth shorts, and danced like Michael Jackson. Dad did all the answer background vocals: "Oe e O e O..."

Afterward, we waited in the lobby with dozens of red-faced, sweaty strangers until it was our turn to listen to me sing. I thought I might puke when I heard the intro to my song. Then my voice was playing over the loudspeakers. I had never heard my voice recorded like that.

At the end of the chorus I missed a note and lost my place. When I sang the last words of the song, my voice broke with emotion. When the song ended, I waited for Daddy's response.

"Baby doll, you're tone-deaf."

"What does that mean?"

"It means you don't need to sing in front of anybody, ever."

That's when I noticed that the people around us had heard him, and they gave me sad looks as if to say, "Sorry you can't sing."

I waited at the window for the lady to give me my cassette and stared down at the floor so I wouldn't cry.

On the drive back to Alabama, Dad played his and Cory's recording of "Jungle Love" over and over. Then I finally got to play mine and I put my cassette into the stereo, but after two lines Dad popped it out and said, "It's so out of tune, I can't listen to it." Part of me wanted to rip the ribbon out and throw it out the window, but another, a deeper part of me wanted to keep it for-ever.

"I don't think I'm tone-deaf," I argued with him.

"You are, trust me," he said. That's the whole point. People who are tone-deaf don't know they're tone-deaf."

"I don't believe you! Mrs. Griffin gives me a solo in every musical!"

"There must be some bad singers at your school," he laughed.

Dad swerved into the Shoney's for dinner. After we finished our meal at the all-you-can-eat buffet, he paid Cory a dollar to sing "Swinging" by John Anderson for everybody in the restau-rant. People at some of the other tables tipped Cory and he left with a pocketful of change. As we walked out, Daddy told me, "He's the entertainer."

All by Myself

THROUGHOUT MIDDLE SCHOOL I hated Fridays. Every-one seemed so happy. The lunchroom ladies hummed as we went through the line, even the strict teachers laughed on Fridays. By the time the bell rang at 3:00 pm, the whole school was buzzing with anticipation, thick as honey in the halls. There were cheer-leaders throwing pompoms in the air, rehearsing routines. Jocks were going over football plays. There were groups of eighth-grade girls, my friends, huddled at the lockers laughing and planning everything from spend the night parties to skating rink celebra-tions. Talking about which boys they were going to meet at the mall.

"What are you wearing to Mindy's party? What time are we going to the concert?" Their words felt like wind-up chattering teeth chasing me through the school. I had to fight with every-thing inside myself not to burst into tears. I could not make eye contact with anyone on my walk to the classroom or during the hour-long study hall while I waited for the school bus to make its first round, and then come back to pick up the leftovers.

I was the last stop. Every school bus trip began the same

way—loud and wild—until Mr. Hodge and I rode alone. He had more moles than teeth, and the ones he had jutted out at the bottom like a llama. I stared at the back of his bald head until I heard the hiss of the brakes. Then I raced down our dirt road.

Music and words were my sanctuary. I disappeared into songs as I sat on my bedroom floor every weekend, recording Casey Kasem and the Top 40 Countdown. I wrote out all my favorite lyrics. I cried whenever Lionel Richie's love ballads played. I sang "Time After Time" by Cyndi Lauper into the heating vent so I could hear my voice echo like a microphone.

My bedroom was my world, and writing—lists, dreams, lyrics, plans, and poetry—kept me from going insane. Writing gave me a sense of control in a life where I had none and holding a pen in my hand calmed me down. I wrote for hours every night, compulsively filling spiral notebooks and diaries with my tiniest handwriting to make them last longer, but I still filled one a week.

Spending so much time alone, I felt myself getting weird, but I did not know what was wrong with me. It would be years before I learned what Obsessive Compulsive Disorder was. In the 1980s, OCD was kind of like HBO, it hadn't made it deep into Alabama yet.

I became obsessed with poetry. Emily Dickinson and Elizabeth Barret Browning were my secret friends. They had been dead for decades, but we girls spent our weekends together. They were both trapped in their homes by their tyrannical fathers and wrote endlessly, just like me. I was in awe of the love story between Elizabeth Barrett and Robert Browning. Her overbearing father kept her at home, and Robert began sending her letters straight from his heart. She had been sickly and spent most of her time at her desk, writing. Then, like some kind of Shakespeare Superman, Robert came to her rescue. They eloped and spent their honeymoon in Paris. I would cry, reading the words they had written to each other: "How do I love thee? I love you with the breath, smiles, tears, of all my life; and, if God choose, I shall but love thee better after death." Robert loved Elizabeth with a passion I had never known existed. She died in his arms, and he said, "She died smilingly, happily, and with a face like a girl's." Reading the poetry they wrote to each other, I realized that I had never heard people talk to each other like that. I knew that I wanted to be with someone who loved me like that. They were soulmates.

I began to write poems and songs to my future soulmate. Every day after school I sat on my bedroom floor drawing my dream house, which was always the same—it had a turret and sunken living room, tennis court and swimming pool, a stream running beside the house with a little bridge over it, and weeping willow trees in the front yard. I dreamed of a big, passionate, extraordinary love, and Robert and Elizabeth made me believe it was possible.

Affair of the Heart

THE FIRST TIME I SAW RICK SPRINGFIELD, I thought I was having a heart attack...in my panties. Standing in front of my grandparent's old cabinet TV, a warm, flushing feeling flooded through me and melted into a soft pulsating rhythm between my legs. It was like a heartbeat I never knew I had. And this throbbing ache kept perfect beat with the opening guitar riff of "Jessie's Girl," the song playing in the video on *Night Tracks*.

As I gazed into Rick's hypnotic hazel eyes, the TV screen disappeared, and the whole world made sense. I cannot adequately express the force of raw love jolting through my eleven-year-old veins. But, for the first time, I knew why I was on Earth: to marry this man. He would be the poetic justice to my sad and shitty life.

Spending so much time in solitude in my room, I survived in my imagination, and it now swirled around one fantasy—Richard Lewis Springthorpe, III. It seemed like I dreamed him into being like he was born on the pages of my diary. I bought all his cassettes, and his music made me feel less alone during the loneliest years of my life. Sprawled on my bedroom floor in an oasis of spiral-bound notebooks, I wrote out the lyrics to all of his songs and felt such a deep and profound connection to him that I knew he was my soulmate.

Rick was more than my first love; he was my after-school special, my favorite hobby, my football game on a Friday night.

While I was grounded, the only place I was allowed to go was to Food World with Mom—that was the highlight of my weekend because she always let me get a magazine. While she grocery-shopped, I sat cross-legged on the cool floor and gorged myself on every glossy 8x10 and interview of Rick I could find in *Teen Beat, Tiger Beat, Bop,* and *Seventeen.* The decision about which magazine to purchase was torture. Eventually I began to tear out every picture and article about Rick I could find, slipping the loose pages into the magazine Mom bought me and praying that they wouldn't fall out when the checkout girl rang it up. I rationalized my theft because since Rick and I were getting married, they kind of belonged to me anyway. Plus, I saw old women rip out recipes all the time, and Rick was the recipe for my future.

When I read that Rick would be playing at the Jefferson Civic Center in Birmingham, I knew two things:

1. I had to get a bra.
2. I would be at that concert, even if I had to run away from home.

Terrified that Mike would ground me for something stupid, I morphed myself into a modern-day Laura Ingalls: "Yes, Pa." I jumped to obey all of Mike's kooky commands. I ignored his negative commentary on every move I made. I bit my tongue when I had a smartass reply to make. I vacuumed with passion and scrubbed the hell out of the dishes. And, for the first time, I made all A's and one B on my report card.

Mama took me to Sears to buy the concert tickets the day they went on sale. I stared at them, running my fingers across the raised black print: "Rick Springfield—Success Hasn't Spoiled Me Yet Tour." Then Mama and I went on a quest for my first bra in the intimates section of the store.

"Here it is!" I held up a sexy leopard and lace bra.

"No."

"I'm the one wearing it, not you."

"It's a push-up bra, and you ain't got nothing to push up."

"Oh yeah, it needs to be blue anyway."

"Why blue?"

"It just does." I did not want to tell her blue was Rick's favorite color or that the sole reason I needed a bra was so I could throw it to him on stage.

The day of the concert I was in a state of excitement border-ing insanity. During the hour-long drive to Birmingham, we lis-tened to all my Rick cassettes while I sang every word.

"Thank you, Mama!" I hugged her as we walked through the doors to the Civic Center.

When we found our seats, they were almost at the top of the balcony level. Roger Staubach couldn't throw a bra and hit Rick from where I was. I burst into tears.

"Why are you crying?"

"These seats might as well be in outer space."

"We bought 'em the day they went on sale."

"At 5:30 at night."

"Aimee, I have to work."

To make everything a million times worse, I saw Staci and a group of girls from my school on the floor level. Watching them thirty rows from the stage felt like I was being stabbed. I had to get down there.

"Mama, I see Staci and Charla. I gotta go down there. Please?"

"If you stay where I can see you."

The lights went out and some band I had never heard of start-ed playing. My fluorescent yellow parachute pants Daddy sent me from Key West glowed in the dark. So did the words on my t-shirt, 'Aimee 'n' Rick,' which I'd made with neon pink puffy paint.

"How could you not see me?" I started laughing and kissed Mom on the cheek. Racing down the stairs, I realized a security lady was checking everyone's ticket with a flashlight before they could go down on the floor level. I spent the whole first act wav-ing and shouting, trying to get Staci's attention. Finally, at inter-mission, she saw me.

"If you let me borrow your ticket stub to get down there, I'll give you ten bucks."

"Okay...but bring it right back." She held it up, and I grabbed it.

"Thank you!" I hugged Staci, giving her the ten dollar bill.

The opening act was over, and I began fighting my way to the front row. Most of the girls in the first twenty rows were a foot taller than I was. The closer I got to the stage, the more violent the girls became. I put my head down, plowing through them like

Sonic the Hedgehog, making my way through angry elbows, kicking legs, and overstuffed purses stumbling toward the stage, shoving and squeezing, until at last I had one hand on the steel gate that held back the frenzy of girls. With all of my power I pulled myself to it, clenching with both hands. I latched my arms and locked my legs around the gate. My heart was pounding, and my hair was soaking wet from a beer that got dumped down the back of my shirt. I was covered in other people's sweat and couldn't get the taste of hairspray out of my mouth.

The lights went out, triggering a roar that felt both primal and scary. Everyone thrust forward, crushing my chest against the steel bars, and nearly knocking the breath out of me, but it would have taken a chainsaw to remove my fingers from that gate.

Suddenly, Rick was right in front of me, standing on a giant amplifier, wearing a white tank top, white pants, and red bandanas tied around one of his ankles. Looking straight into my young eyes, he sang, "I get excited, just thinking what you might be like. I get excited, there's Heaven in your eyes tonight."

Then everything went black like somebody had unplugged my world. I came to with smelling salts in my face and two security guards hovering above me, waving their arms like fans.

"What happened? I shouted over the music.

"You fainted!"

Laying on the floor on the side of the stage, the stairs to Rick were three feet away. I thought about making a run for it. A security man helped me to my feet and asked for my ticket stub.

"I must have dropped it."

"Go get some water and cool off. Don't go back down front."

"Okay."

Rick started singing "Love is Alright Tonight."

I walked toward the seats, then ran back into the crowd and fought my way to the front again. Resting my arms on the gate, I caught my breath. It was time to throw my bra to Rick. Since I had only worn a bra twice in my life, I was having problems getting it unlatched with my arms pinned by the crowd. I almost strangled myself trying to take it off without removing my shirt. The girl next to me had to help tug the tangled straps loose from my neck. When Rick was right in front of me, I threw my bra at him as hard as I could. It grazed the top of his black combat boot and went straight into the pit between the gate and the stage. He didn't even see it.

By the end of the show, I had screamed until I could barely talk. After the encore, the lights came on and I stared at the stage, crying. Then I remembered my bra. Peering over the gate into the valley of bras and panties and rose petals, I poked a security man and whispered, "Can you hand me that baby blue bra?"

Mama bought me a tour book with the best pictures of Rick I had ever seen. On the drive back to Glencoe, lying across the backseat of Mama's brown Chevy Chevette, I gazed up at the night sky and swore to myself and the stars, "I'm gonna meet Rick Springfield...the next time he's in Alabama...I don't care what I have to do."

During the twelve months that followed, all I could talk about, think about, and dream about was Rick. I wouldn't shut up about him. I made a huge button that announced, "I Love Rick's Bod" and wore it to school every day. I signed everyone's annual, Aimee Springfield, and my schoolwork too. When Mrs. Farrow, the principal, saw "Rick Springfield is fine as hell" written in blue Sharpie in a stall in the girls' bathroom, I got a paddling, and no one even asked if I did it.

A year later, Rick came to Alabama! For months I waited to get tickets to his "Living in Oz" tour. I picked out my outfit in advance—cheetah print, denim jeans that zipped at the ankles, an off-the-shoulder, white top, and my first pair of heels—hot pink pumps. I was ready for my next encounter with my future husband.

When the day finally arrived, it was like the cathedral of my soul was throwing a revival. I felt like Aretha Franklin was singing "Hallelujah" in my chest. My friend, Brook, went to the concert with Mama and me. Brook knew all about my plans to find a way backstage. We listened to "Affair of the Heart" and "Human Touch" over and over on the fifty-mile drive to Birmingham. When we got to the Civic Center, we found our seats up in the balcony and I told Mama, "Brook and me are gonna go look at t-shirts."

I had to find a way to get to Rick. My heart ached, knowing we were in the same building. Brook and I found an area that went behind the stage. The back of the arena was blocked off by a black partition wall with accordion doors and a "Do Not Enter "sign.

"We gotta squeeze through this opening and see what's behind here."

"We're gonna get in trouble, Aimee," Brook said. "I'm not going."

"Tell Mama I'll be back after I meet Rick and not to be mad at me."

Knowing it was now or never, I wriggled through. The space was so narrow that my head got stuck. Once I was in, I immediately realized I could only move forward. There was no turning back, not that I would have. All the lights went out, and the whole building was shaking. Corey Hart, the opening act, began to sing some song I had never heard, and I tried to figure out where to go. At the bottom of the stairs I saw an octagon of light, an opening to somewhere.

A blinding spotlight began scouring the area behind the stage. Not wanting the light to find me, I dropped to the floor and slithered, face-first, down about seventy five stairs. At the bottom, I found some sort of lower level. The only problem was there was a ten-foot drop. When I saw a black equipment crate about the size of a refrigerator with 'SPRINGFIELD' stenciled on it in white letters, I jumped.

I hit the crate, twisted my ankle, and broke the heel off one of my new pink pumps. I sat down to examine my throbbing foot. A big guy with long, black braids and an Iron Maiden t-shirt came at me out of nowhere. "Hey, are you supposed to be down here?" I jumped down from the crate and took off half running, half limping and hid under a tour bus. This wasn't backstage. I was in some stupid garage. The big guy and another shorter guy, squatted down to my level. "Come on out. There's nowhere to run."

I could not run if I wanted to. My ankle felt broken. As I rolled out, I realized my white shirt had gum, dirt, and every kind of shit in Birmingham all over the front of it. I had popped the button off my skin-tight cheetah print pants when I slid on my stomach down the stairs, and they were wide open.

"You're outta here," the big guy said.

Corey Hart was singing "I Wear My Sunglasses at Night" while I was led out the back door of the arena. As the big black metal door slowly shut, I heard the short guy say, "These girls are out of control."

I tried the doorknob, but it was locked. I could see the men walking away through the little square window. Not only was I going to get grounded forever, but I was going to miss the whole concert. Sitting there with my knees pulled into my chest against the brick wall, I could feel the drums vibrating through my body. The crowd erupted into applause, and I exploded into tears when I heard Rick singing "Jessie's Girl."

Sobbing and singing along, I rested my head on my knees. Why am I so stupid? I cried harder. All year I've waited for this night and I ruined it. Then I heard footsteps beside me.

"Sweetie, are you okay?" A stranger's voice pulled me out of my self-hatred, and I followed a pair of black converse tennis shoes up to a cute, skinny guy in a Ramones t-shirt with a big camera slung over his shoulder. Mom had let me wear make-up to the show, and I had caked it on like Tammy Faye Bakker. My face must have looked like a dirty rainbow, and my neck was sticky from tears.

"I'm from Glencoe, and that's an hour from here. I don't know where my Mama is. I'm gonna be in so much trouble. I missed the whole concert and those guys won't let me back in."

"I'll get you back to your mom."

He started banging on the door so hard I could tell he was pissed. The short guy who kicked me out opened it, and the photographer went off on him, "Who in the hell stuck a little kid outside on the street in downtown Birmingham? Are you fucking kidding me?"

The guy shrugged.

"You better be glad she didn't wander off or get hurt."

Reaching for my hand, the photographer pulled me up. I stood holding my pink pumps in front of my unzipped pants.

"How old are you?"

"Twelve."

The big guy walked up. "We were gonna let her back in. These girls are nuts, man."

"Tell her how to get back to the main floor."

"Take those stairs up to the third floor and look for someone in a yellow jacket. They can take you back to your seat."

"Yes sir," I said to the big guy, trying to make peace. I hugged the photographer, thanking him.

"Hurry, or you're gonna get stuck in the crowd letting out."

Hobbling up the stairs, I heard something that stopped me. It was the unmistakable voice that my heart had memorized by watching the movie *Hard to Hold* over two hundred times until I broke the VHS tape from repeatedly pausing it on the scene with Rick's naked butt.

As I spun around, the world shifted into slow motion. An intense tingling exploded through my arms and legs, my pulse pounded in my ears, and my eyes locked on Rick Springfield. I dropped my shoes and ran at him like a panther in heat. He was shirtless and dripping sweat, his head down as he dried his jet-black hair with a towel. His perfect chest glistened. I pounced, and he didn't know what hit him. I grabbed his arm in a bear hug. It was so slick that I slid down it. Then, in the passion of the moment, I licked his delicious sweat off my arm.

I wanted to kiss him, but I couldn't reach his face, so I stared straight into his hazel eyes and said, "We're getting married! I know it in my soul. You might think I'm just a kid, but I swear to you—we are getting married."

Rick looked down at my wide-open cheetah pants, and the hair and gum stuck to my shirt, and started laughing. Everyone around him joined in. The big guy was bent over, holding his stomach. He was cracking up so hard. I didn't care. I was breathless with wonder because my dream did exist. He was real, and he was right in front of me. I had felt butterflies in my stomach before, but this was more like pterodactyls flying around.

"I am serious!" I stomped my hurt foot and heard myself start to get mad as they all laughed harder. Somebody threw Rick a t-shirt, and he put it on and hopped inside a blue van, still smiling.

Delirious with adrenaline, I took off to find my mother. My heart was on fire with love. I could still taste Rick's salty sweat on my lips. I finally found her standing with a police officer in the almost empty venue.

"Mom! I've got so much…"

Clap! I heard the slap across my cheek more than I felt it. My whole body was zinging numb.

"Where the hell have you been?"

"With my husband!" I screamed at her.

She glared at me with a mix of fury and embarrassment and dug her fingernails into my arm, almost jerking it out of the socket. "Look at your pants! Why are you barefoot?"

"Feel my shirt!" I shrieked.

"Why are you all wet?"

"It's Rick's sweat!"

Mom's anger slowly turned to relief, and I told her and Brook everything on our way to the car. "I'm not gonna tell Mike about this, but don't ever ask me to take you to another concert."

"Don't be mad at me on the best night of my whole life."

As we drove home, I began planning my future with Rick. On the day I get out of high school, using all of my graduation money, I'll buy a one-way ticket to L.A., then rent a white V.W. Rabbit and find a star map to Rick's house. Since he probably has a mansion with a big gate like Graceland, I can park on the street and wait for him to pull out of the driveway. By then I'll almost be eighteen and he will be thirty-nine. Every day of my senior year I will do the Jane Fonda workout religiously, and I'll wear a white sundress and have a wavy perm and perfect tan. When his black Mercedes comes driving down the street, I'll pull out in front of him and cause a fender bender. When he gets out to see if I am okay, I'll be like, "Oh my gosh! Rick! Remember that little girl from Alabama? That was me. I'm all grown up now and ready to rock your world!"

***

THE DAY MY HEART EXPLODED LIKE a Chinese rocket, I was standing in line at Food World. Out of the corner of my eye,

I saw Rick in a little, yellow square on the cover of the *National Enquirer* with the headline: "Rick Springfield Secretly Married for Months." My whole being felt the lightning bolt of shock, buzzing through my teeth, down my spine, and into my core.

Tears welled and I almost threw up. My brain felt like a tater tot thrown into hot grease...frying...malfunction...sensory overload. Oh my God! I heard the words without saying them. Grabbing the magazine, I slung it on the checkout belt.

"Baby, you already got your..." her voice trailed off into the air when she read the cover. Mom still had on her white hospital uniform, and the drive home was silent. We pulled into the driveway, and I ran straight to my room.

"This can't be true!" I collapsed on my bed. I did not want to read the words. Staring in disbelief at a picture of Rick and some blonde bitch with their arms wrapped around each other like a dumbass pretzel. Oh. My. God! The next page showcased a photo of them wearing some kind of fucked-up karate suits and another one of them eating wedding cake. Motherfucker, I told you we were getting married. You bastard fuck-stick piece of shit-fucking-loser-lying-jerk-face asshole!

In yellow letters on a black background was the word that could not be real. Pregnant. I read it ten times trying to scramble the letters, trying to believe I could be seeing wrong. Wild with grief, I started ripping down all of his 8x10s, crumpling the pictures and tearing through his lying face. There were scars where the tape had stuck for years. I threw all of them in a metal trash can and took it to the porch and started a blazing bonfire. I grabbed a gallon of milk and poured it all over the ashes of my dreams.

Hysterical, I ran back to my room. I felt the death of my own heart. It was now an empty black casket inside my chest. I began jerking out the pages of the tour books that held ten-thousand wasted kisses.

"What are you yelling about in here?" Mike came stomping through my door.

"Fucking get out of my fucking room!" I screamed so loud I thought a tonsil was gonna fly out.

"You're grounded!"

"Ground me forever, motherfucker! My fucking life is over!" With both my hands balled in tight fists, I fell down to the floor in a fetal position, sobbing. Mike stared at me, almost said something, then went to find my mother.

I felt cheated on, lied to, betrayed, and most of all, like my life was over. If only I could have told my twelve-year-old self that in twenty years Rick Springfield is going to come to your house (on Valentine's Day!) and you're going to write a song together. You are going to have his cellphone number and email address. You will keep his Starbucks cup with "Rick "written in black Sharpie until it molds over. Even if I could have relayed the message, it wouldn't have made any sense in 1984.

Fat Farms

EVERY SUMMER BEGINNING IN SEVENTH GRADE when Dad came to get us, he was in a different car, at a drastically different weight, and with a different woman. Daddy pulled into the driveway, two weeks late, in a car that looked like it came out of a cartoon. It was a white Volkswagen Thing with a big brown bear face painted on the hood.

"Aimee Paimee Pie!" Dad called out.

"Daddy!" I ran to him.

"Hey, baby doll." I couldn't believe my eyes—he was as thin as I had ever seen him and seemed taller and more handsome. He had lost at least seventy pounds and had a golden tan and a diamond stud earring, which made me furious, because he had told me I couldn't get my ears pierced until I was thirteen.

"How are you so tan?" I asked.

"I've spent a couple of months in Key West at a fat farm called 'The Rice House,'" he said.

"What's a fat farm?" I asked.

"It's where people go to lose weight. I'm taking you and Cory to a fat farm in North Carolina this summer." Dad took a cardboard box out of the VW's trunk and went around to open the passenger-side door. A Goth-looking girl got out of the car. I was crushed. Cory and I hadn't seen Daddy in a few months, and I thought it was going to be just us.

"Aimee, this is Chantel."

"Hi," I said, equally furious and fascinated.

We followed him into the house. He was dropping t-shirts behind him like a flower girl scattering rose petals. He dumped out the cardboard box on the dining room table, creating a rainbow of colored shirts.

"Gadsden won't have these for another year—they just came out!"

"What are they?" Mama asked.

"Coca-Cola's got a clothing line. It's gonna be huge!" He kept digging in the box and slinging everybody shirts. "For you, baby doll," he said, tossing me a yellow one, and then a royal blue rugby shirt, both with white collars and the iconic cursive logo across the front.

Chantel stood in the corner of the kitchen, fidgeting with her gigantic hobo purse. She had a gorgeous face and was a little on the plump side. She wore deep-purple lipstick and had a tooth that looked like a Rockette kicking—it shot out while the others stayed in line. Her jet-black hair was cut in a short, blunt bob with dramatic bangs. She wore a miniskirt and black-and-white-striped knee-high socks with Doc Marten combat boots. Everything about her intrigued me. I ran to my bedroom to change my clothes.

Daddy sat at the kitchen table with Mike. When Chantel went to the bathroom, Daddy told Mike, "You wouldn't believe these girls at the fat farms—hands down, the wildest girls I've met anywhere." He said it loud enough to make sure Mom heard him too. Dad always loved a girl with a little junk in the trunk. "Most of them aren't even that fat, but they all have low self-esteem, and they'll do anything. I mean ANYTHING!" Dad said, his eyes getting big.

Mama pulled Daddy aside. "Danny, how old is she?"

"She'll be eighteen on her next birthday."

"What's wrong with you? You're gonna go to jail."

"Becky, you'll believe anything! She's twenty-five."

Chantel was eight years younger than Dad. When she came back into the kitchen, Daddy said, "Hey, Chantel, show 'em your boobs."

"Danny, whatayou, retahdid?" Chantel asked in her thick Boston accent.

I stared at her.

"Come on, Chantel, show 'em. They won't believe it," Dad begged.

"Get outta hiyeah. I'm not showin' ya ex-wife and kids my tits." She laughed and walked out to the car.

I grabbed my suitcase and followed. Finally, I'd be free from Mike's surveillance! Chantel and I sat in the back seat and Cory sat in the front. We tried to talk, but between the wind, her strong Boston accent, and my deep Southern twang, we could barely communicate.

That night around my grandparents' dining room table, Opal stared at Chantel like she was an alien. Opal had made my favorite dinner: chicken-fried steak, mashed potatoes, and biscuits. As we ate, Daddy whispered, "Show 'em ...show 'em. They won't believe it."

"Danny, ya fuckin' nuts. I'm not doing it. Shut up about my tits already."

Mama Opal was stunned. A cuss word for her was "fiddle-sticks "and this girl just said "fuck "and "tits "at her dining room table. Daddy and Chantel kept arguing, and then Daddy said, "Chantel's got something she wants to show you."

She stood and lifted her shirt. Mama Opal said, "Oh my Lord...oh Lord!" at such a high decibel, her voice shook the room. She turned away and then looked back at Chantel's chest in disbelief. Cory was almost six, and he stared straight at those knockers. They were huge and she had big, silver rings like you might see in a cow's nose, pierced through both nipples.

I started laughing and Harold's mouth dropped open so wide that I thought his dentures might fall out. A couple of seconds later, he was laughing too. This was the 1980s in small-town Alabama—none of us had ever seen anything like this.

"Ah, ya happy now, ya fuckin' weirdo?" Chantel dropped her shirt down. "Danny said he wouldn't take me to the airport tonight if I didn't show ya's my tits."

Opal fled to the kitchen and started washing dishes.

***

IT WAS AROUND THIS TIME when Dad changed his name to Bear. No one knew why or where it came from. Some thought it was after Bear Bryant, the legendary football coach of Alabama, but I knew that wasn't right. Dad couldn't stand him. They got into a heated argument at a bar over a trick punt football play my Dad told Bear Bryant they should use in a game. Bear Bryant said it would never work. The Steelers won a game with it about ten years later.

The following morning, we dropped Chantel at the airport, and Daddy, Cory, and I drove to Durham, North Carolina, the diet capital of the world. Duke Towers was the new fat farm where Dad was staying. It was a weight-loss program for wealthy people from all over the world. Everyone there called Dad either "Bear" or "Danny Bear." Most guests stayed for a few weeks or months in hopes of shedding extra pounds via diet, hiking, and fitness programs. It was a mecca for the rich and obese. I had never seen anything like it. Daddy was one of the thinner people there. Almost everyone else was at least a hundred pounds overweight.

There were about fifty apartments at Duke Towers, and Daddy's consisted of a small kitchen, living room, and a bedroom in the back with two double beds—one for him and one for Cory and me. The brick building was two levels, and all the doors opened onto a swimming pool and garden.

During the day, Dr. Kenner, a bald man with piercing blue eyes, lectured everyone around the pool, talking about high blood pressure, heart disease, and getting off medications once and for all. My job was to watch Cory, and looking after him was like chasing a flea. Mama put him on Ritalin to calm him down so he could sit still in his seat at school. But it gave him headaches, so he didn't have to take it in the summer.

There were supermodels, comedians, trust fund kids. More characters than Shakespeare could dream up! The first famous person I met at Duke Towers was the actor Dom DeLuise. He was on a green float in the middle of the pool. "You know him, baby doll, he's in the *Cannonball Run* movies," my dad reminded me. There was a man with thinning hair and big, black glasses, smoking a cigar, and dad said, "Hey, Mario. This is my daughter, Aimee." Then he told me, "He wrote the greatest movie of all time, *The Godfather*."

I saw a guy in his early twenties who reminded me of the character from *Charlie and the Chocolate Factory*, the one who swelled up bigger and bigger like she was going to pop. His name was Davy, and he was too heavy to walk, so he got around in a wheelchair. He was about seventeen, and the first time I met him, Daddy said, "I'll give you twenty bucks if you'll go flirt with him and make him feel good. He never gets any attention from girls."

Everyone was supposed to be on a strict rice diet, but they all knew where you could get the best ice cream or pizza close to the complex. Our first night there, Daddy gathered up a group of the heaviest people and took us to an all-you-can-eat seafood buffet. My father loved to watch the owner get more and more upset as people piled up plate after plate of crab legs, lobster, and fried shrimp. Finally, the manager came to the table and told us we had to leave.

I think Daddy paid his rent at the fat farm by gambling. He made a bet with a guy named Scooter, who owned a restaurant chain of chicken restaurants, that he could walk fifty miles in one day. We went to the store and bought some wooden beads and string. "I need three hundred beads," he said, without pausing to add up how many laps around the track fifty miles would be. He always did rapid-fire math in his head, no matter how big the numbers.

I was his assistant for the walk. Daddy hung the string on the window in front of his apartment, and for each lap, he moved a bead. I brought him Gatorade, and about thirty hours after he started, when the sun was coming up, Scooter came out and gave him $5,000.

My father's favorite person to gamble with was Ira, a Jewish millionaire from New York. Ira loved Bruce Springsteen, so when Springsteen came to town, Ira said, "I'd pay five grand for tickets to that show."

Daddy shot back, "I bet you ten thousand dollars I can get you into that concert for free and you can meet Bruce."

"Danny, do you know him?" Ira asked.

"No, but I know how to meet him."

That afternoon we drove to a pawn shop and Dad purchased the biggest camera the guy had. We bought a copy of *USA Today* at the gas station and headed to Kinko's. I watched as Dad cut out the blue square *USA Today* logo. He made a copy, laminated it, punched a hole in the top, put it on a shoestring, and did it again. Now he had two laminated backstage passes.

Around midnight, Daddy and Ira came back to Duke Towers after the concert. They were both drunk. Daddy had pretended he was a reporter and he'd talked his way backstage to conduct an "interview" with The Boss.

"Danny, you're fucking crazy," Ira said. "I can't believe we just walked straight in." He laughed and handed Dad a check for ten grand.

Cory started gambling too. Ira had a giant jar full of change and told Cory, "If you can guess how much change is in the jar, and you get within ten dollars of the total, you can have it."

Cory guessed $300, then spent the rest of the day in a mountain of quarters, dimes, and nickels, counting it until he found out that he had won. Cory bought a hundred dollars' worth of Garbage Pail Kids trading cards and candy.

Dad was like a rock star at that fat farm. Most of the women didn't stay more than a couple of weeks, he went through them like paper towels. Dad loved Jewish girls with a little meat on their bones. He playfully called them JAPs. I had never heard the term, so he explained that it stood for "Jewish-American Princess." He loved to tease them by saying things like, "The only thing Rochelle knows how to make for dinner is reservations." Rochelle, like every other girl, threw her arms around my dad and giggled.

He was thirty-three and living it up, falling in love every other week. We went to the Crisco Disco every Saturday and it was a sight to see: 400-pound women dancing like Madonna, totally uninhibited. It was beautiful.

Our last night at Duke Towers, Dad came in drunk. I heard him rattling around in the kitchen, then stumbled into the bedroom. He fell into his bed and something started to stink. I couldn't figure out what it was, so I got up and turned on the light. Daddy was passed out and grinning. He had red lipstick smeared all over his face and an empty can of sardines sitting on his chest.

French Tickler

IN EIGHTH GRADE I MET this little bitch, Little Debbie. She might as well have stolen my boyfriends herself. Yes, I'm talking about Little Debbie, the delicious snack cakes that come ten to a carton for ninety-nine cents. The girl on the box looks so sweet, like a little Shirley Temple with her innocent eyes, strawberry blonde curls, and straw hat. She seems friendly, but if you look a little closer, you'll see that her soft smile is more of a smirk.

Maybe because she felt sorry for me being trapped in the house all the time, Mom started bringing home these boxes of lies: Star Crunch, Zebra Cakes, Oatmeal Cream Pies, Nutty Buddies. I packed on thirty pounds the summer before I turned thirteen.

"Unwrap a smile," the carton said, instead of stating the truth: "Unwrap a Smith and Wesson, because you're going to want to shoot your fat ass after you eat all this shit." I spent endless hours during the first months of eighth grade in front of my full-length mirror, trying to find some way to camouflage the roll of belly fat that hung over the top of my Jordache jeans like a mushroom.

Every morning I sat in front of my Clairol Three Way Makeup Mirror, trying to accentuate my jawline with a dark brown eyeliner pencil using shades and shadows to cover up my double chin, but I never did it right and usually just looked like I had a dirty neck.

The weekend I turned 13, I went to the mall with my sidekick Stephanie and we met up with the guy she liked, Phil. Behind him lurked Shelby, the tallest teenager I had ever seen. He was six-foot-four, and skinny as a broom with a mouth full of metal and gorgeous gray-green eyes. I was trying to decide if I thought he was cute or not when he said, "I'm in a band." I knew right then I wanted to be his girlfriend.

We snuck out and went cruising in circles around the parking lot in Phil's blue Camaro. My mama would have died if she knew I left the mall in a boy's car. I couldn't believe it myself. Stephanie sat in the front seat flirting with Phil. I sat in the backseat with Shelby. I was terrified he was going to try to kiss me, but I had always wondered about making out with someone with braces. Would it be like licking a barbed wire fence? Or taste like a flagpole? What if the wires cut my tongue to bloody bits?

Shelby looked over at me and smiled, but we were too awkward to know what to say to each other, when—Bang! Bang! Bang!

Out of nowhere came machine gunfire. It was sudden and loud. I thought we were being attacked. "Oh my God!" I screamed, just about the time I realized that music was blasting through a speaker behind my head. Phil had wanted to show off his new subwoofers, so he cranked up Aldo Nova's "Life is Just a Fantasy" as loud as it would go and scared me so bad, I peed my pants. I could feel the warm urine seeping through my Jordache jeans and into the tan upholstery. I was mortified.

I tapped Phil on the shoulder, "Take me to the bathroom."

He pulled into the Burger King parking lot and I jumped out of the car and ran into Burger King trying to cover my bottom with my gold hobo purse. I climbed up on the bathroom counter and stuck my crotch up against the automatic hand dryer. I was contorted like a praying mantis and kept having to hit the steel button with my knee to restart the machine. The air got hotter each time and I was afraid I was going to burn my labia off.

Stephanie burst in, "What the hell are you doing?" she asked in her ditsy yet sarcastic Valley Girl voice.

"When that dumb ass, Phil, blasted his music, I peed my pants. Look at them, they're soaking wet."

When we finally got back to the car, with a flip of his sandy blonde feathered hair, Phil said, "We were worried you guys ditched us."

"Aimee was sick," Stephanie said but couldn't stop laughing. The upholstery on my side of the back seat had a stain the shape of a turtle and it smelled like a Porta-Potty. There was no way Shelby didn't know. My chest was constricted with panic as I waited for him to say something, but he just reached for my hand. We were boyfriend and girlfriend for almost a year, but we hardly ever saw each other. I was always grounded. Half the time, I could not even talk to Shelby.

Mike took to scotch taping doors to see if I opened them and rigged the phone cord, taking it barely out of the wall to see if I used it. He was always trying to catch me talking to Shelby. Our passion played out in handwritten love letters. He would leave me one in our black mailbox at the end of our dirt road every day on his way home from school and pick one up from me. It was kind of like a prison pen-pal romance. We had to get by with stolen moments.

Whenever I spent the night with Maw Maw and Paw Paw, I'd walk to the Big B drugstore behind their house. Shelby would meet me in the parking lot where we would profess our love, catch up with each other and kiss for about fifteen or twenty minutes. Somehow we managed to spend Christmas together and Shelby showered me with presents. He gave me my first real jewelry; a pair of 14-carat gold crescent earrings, and a bottle of Lauren perfume and my favorite pillows that spelled out our names in puffy yellow letters. He sewed them in his Home Ec class.

That night we lay under the stars on the new trampoline my family had gotten that day and ate spaghetti sucking the noodles out of each other's mouths and laughing. Everything was perfect until I lit one of the Roman candle fireworks our Dad had given Cory for Christmas. Instead of shooting into the sky in a burst of sparks and magic, it shrieked and exploded into the black fabric of the trampoline. Cory ran in the house yelling, "Aimee just tore a giant hole in the trampoline."

Mike came out and started screaming in my face, "I swear to God I don't know what's wrong with you. You ruin everything."

"It was an accident."

"Yeah, it always is."

Mom joined him and told me to go to my room. "Now."

"Can I tell Shelby bye?"

"No, he's going home." She turned to Shelby, who was standing with his hands in his pockets by the side steps to the house. "You need to call your mother to come pick you up."

"You're not going to be seeing Aimee for a while," Mike said and followed me in the house.

Shelby sat on the front porch swing shivering in his black Members Only jacket while he waited for his mom to pick him up. I could hear the swing squeaking through my bedroom window. I fell asleep crying on those puffy, yellow pillows that night, and almost every night for the next three months.

Finally, the fateful day arrived. Shelby called me when I was at Opal and Harold's and said, "I can't do this anymore."

"Please don't break up with me," I was hysterical.

"Who wants to date a girl that can't go anywhere. I don't even feel like I have a girlfriend. I can't even talk to you." That's when I knew I had to do something to save our love.

"Listen Shelby, I'll find a way to see you this weekend and I'm ready to do it."

"Do what?"

"It."

"What?"

"Have sex," I whispered.

"How?"

"I don't know how but I'll figure it out." I was desperate. After we hung up, I worked on my plan. I had to figure out somewhere that Mom and Mike would let me go. I thought about it for hours and then I saw the light: church. How could they not let me go to church?

The next night at supper I burst into tears, "I've been so depressed. I don't know what to do. I need help. They're having a revival this week at North Baptist. Please let me go."

In Alabama we learn young that you never, never, never go to church in a tent. Ringling Brothers ain't got nothing on a revival in backwoods, deep Alabama. People are shaking and shouting and laying hands, leaping into the air like bullfrogs, prophets in overalls with shaggy beards and snake bites, people falling to the ground and hollering, filled with the Holy Spirit. I picked the one church that I knew Mama and Mike hated. We had visited once and a guy in front of us started having what looked like a seizure, speaking in tongues. We got up and left before the service was over.

It worked. That Sunday night, Mom drove me to North Baptist. I walked in the front door and straight out the back. Shelby was waiting in the parking lot acting all Rico Suave as he leaned against the driver's side of his mom's white Mercedes. He looked different than I remembered him. His legs were so skinny he reminded me of that Planter's Peanut character. His eyes lit up when he saw me. He tried to hug me, but I dove into the car, "Let's get the hell out of here before somebody catches us."

I stayed ducked down in the front seat for most of the three-mile drive to Shelby's Victorian house. It looked like it belonged in Key West or Charleston. Before I met him, I had always wondered who lived there. It was a mansion compared to most of the aluminum siding bungalows in Hokes Bluff. We walked up the steps to the wrap-around porch. As I watched Shelby turn the key in the lock, something clicked in my heart, and I said to myself, "When you walk out of this door, you will no longer be a virgin."

Standing in the foyer on the checkerboard tile with giant palm trees, I could smell Shelby's mom. She always wore so much Poison perfume. It was like tear gas.

"Shelby, I think your mom's here."

"She's in Florida with her boyfriend, Eric."

In the kitchen, a black wrought iron cage hung in the back corner of the room.

"Hey, Friday," I said as I watched the African gray parrot climb down toward me using his black curved beak. I reached through to pet him.

"Get your hand back! He'll bite you—he's nuts."

As I stared into Friday's light yellow eyes, it was as if he could see into my soul. He seemed to know exactly what was about to happen. It was as if he was trying to tell me, "Don't do it. Don't do it." I was about to start crying when with freakishly perfect precision, the bird started ringing like a telephone.

"Hey, what's up?" he answered in Shelby's mom's voice.

"How does he do that?"

"I don't know. Let's go." Shelby took my hand and I followed him upstairs. We walked into his bedroom, the odor of Poison perfume dissolving into Polo cologne and piña colada incense. It was almost dark except for the flocked neon Led Zeppelin and Pink Floyd posters glowing in the blacklight. On Shelby's dresser was a little brass heart-shaped frame with a picture of us taken when we were standing in the Big B parking lot freezing. My nose was red, and I was wearing my granddad's naval officer's hat and an airbrushed sweatshirt that announced, "I'm a Goonie!"

Shelby fell back across the bed and patted the Star Wars bedspread. "Come here."

It was thrilling and terrifying being alone with him. We started kissing as warmth rushed through my stomach. My whole body tingled and burned with a strange new sensation. His kisses tasted like the cinnamon gum he was chewing.

"Do you know how long I've waited for this?" he asked as he kicked off his shoes. He slid his t-shirt over his head and I saw his chest for the first time. There was a small, apple-sized patch of hair in the middle that trailed down to his green boxers.

I unzipped my pleated gaucho pants and stepped out of them.

He unbuttoned my blouse and unhooked my bra clumsily. Goosebumps pricked up on my skin. I was self-conscious of my fat roll from all the Little Debbies. I was embarrassed standing there with my breasts exposed, so I scooted under the covers. I couldn't believe I was in Shelby's bed, naked except for my socks. I was so achingly vulnerable; there was no way I was taking those socks off.

We had never done anything more than kiss and now here I was about to do it. I pulled the sheets over my breasts, confused about what should happen next; we'd skipped second and third bases. Shelby climbed in bed on top of me. His body was burning hot. Wrapping my arms around him was like holding a roll of paper towels. He kept licking my ear and it was freaking me out. Why was he trying to give me a wet willie?

When he finally stopped, I looked into his eyes, his long lashes slowly blinking as he said, "Aimee, I love you."

I took a deep breath and got ready.

"Shelby! Shelby!" Damn...it was his mother!

"Oh my God—get off me!"

"What's wrong, baby?"

"Your mom!"

"That's just Friday."

"It's not!"

He stood up wearing nothing but his boxers, marched out of the room. "Shut the fuck up, Friday!" he yelled from the top of the stairs. The bird, hearing its name, went batshit—squawking and talking, and ringing and singing, going off like a slot machine.

In the chaos, I realized how scared I was. I didn't want to do this; in fact, I might never want to. As usual, I had gotten myself into a mammoth mess of my own making and didn't know how to get out of it. I'd been consumed by the fear of how lonely my life would be without Shelby.

He came back in and shut the door. He put a cassette in the boombox on his dresser. Led Zeppelin blasted "Kashmir "through the little speakers. The heavy bass intro to the song sounded like my virginity crawling away. I was screaming inside, but I tried to act calm. Shelby trembled and twitched and wouldn't leave my damn ears alone. He kept kissing the lobe and blowing hot air, and then it felt like he was trying to give me a hickey. His penis shot straight up like the flag on a mailbox. Boing!

I had never seen a guy's thing—not up close. I didn't count our neighbor Mr. Joe who used to sit on his front porch in jersey workout shorts with his junk hanging out of the leg opening. That looked more like a pinkish purple blob.

My legs shook uncontrollably as I watched Shelby try to put a rubber on. "Hang on just a second." Every time he would almost get it on, it rolled up and he'd start all over. "I'm gonna wear two," he said.

"Yeah, I'll die if I get pregnant."

"Oh shit! That rubber came off."

It was total confusion. Everything about us was awkward and out of sync. He tried to insert his penis in me, but the condom kept rolling up. He put on the second one and I couldn't stop trembling. Then both rubbers rolled up. I suppose I could have helped, but there was no way I was touching him down there.

Shelby's eager, glittering eyes looked into mine, searching intensely. He wrapped his lanky legs around me, and his hip bones scraped against mine. My heart was beating so fast that I thought it might jump out of my body. A warm feeling sparked down my thighs, followed by a fluttering sensation in my stomach, like some part of my insides was melting.

"I've got a surprise for you!" He reached over and jerked his nightstand drawer open. While he was digging around, Robert Plant finished the last chords of "Stairway to Heaven." Shelby finally pulled out a purple metallic packet. "Girls are supposed to really dig these."

The shiny wrapper read: French Tickler. I watched as Shelby tore the foil open with his teeth, then picked the corner out of his braces. When he figured it out, he had on two rubbers, plus the tickle thing, and his boner looked like some sort of weird dog chew toy.

I stared down at it as he kept trying to ram it in, but the rubbers kept rolling up on each other.

"Is it in?"

"I don't know."

"Is it in now?

He thrust and thrust between my legs, but he couldn't penetrate.

"What about now?"

"I don't think…" and then it felt like I'd been stabbed with a knife.

I pushed him off me, but then he rubbed up against me, touched my boobs, and moaned in pleasure. We laid there in silence until Shelby said, "It will be better next time. I got the wrong kind of rubbers."

The digital clock on his nightstand read 7:57 pm.

"Holy shit, we've gotta go!"

On the drive back to the church, something was different. Something was going on in my stomach. We were flying down Rabbit Town Road and I felt a twitching, like a magic bean jumping in my belly.

"Oh my God…the baby kicked!"

"What are you talking about?"

"I think I'm pregnant."

Shelby swerved, almost hitting a fence where a bunch of cows were standing by the side of the road.

"Don't say that."

A tsunami of guilt hit. "I know I'm pregnant. I feel different."

Shame was radiating through me. People were walking out of church when we pulled into the parking lot in back. Shelby tried to kiss me, but I jumped out of the car, burst through the back door of the church, and ran straight into Brother David, the preacher. I was sure he could smell the sex all over me. I felt like the biggest whore on earth. I wanted to go throw myself on the altar and repent.

I hated myself. I didn't like Shelby much anymore, either.

I know I'm pregnant. God is going to punish me for this. I snuck out of church to lose my virginity, making me the biggest sinner that's ever lived.

The heartbeat in my stomach grew stronger. There was definitely a baby in there. I asked my friends Stephanie and Laurie. "Can you get pregnant if it goes in one time?"

"Yes, you can get pregnant if you even touch sperm."

There was nowhere to find the answers to my questions. In Alabama, discussing sex meant acknowledging it, or worse, condoning it. We had seen one grainy video projected on our homeroom wall at the beginning of eighth grade, but there wasn't a lot of information. A guy beside a chain-link fence looked at the camera and said, "I got gonorrhea, and you can get it too." The camera panned to a girl sitting on the curb, crying. They showed people walking in a city built from the bones of a T-Rex with an over-dubbed TV voice warning, "The chances of seeing a dinosaur in today's world are very slim. But the chances of contracting another prehistoric monster are very real. That monster is a venereal disease." As teenage girls, we did the best we could with what information we could get.

After three weeks of agony and praying, I made an appointment at Save a Life, where you go to take a pregnancy test. Stephanie and her aunt gave me a ride. It was still two days before I was supposed to start my period, but I couldn't wait. While we sat in the lobby, looking around at the sad, empty faces of all the other girls, a nurse came and led me into a small room. I climbed up onto the examining table.

"Can I ask you a question?" I looked up at her, biting my lip.

"That's what I'm here for."

"Well, can you get pregnant if your boyfriend wears two condoms and a French tickler and you're not sure his...thing went inside you? His..." I had to close my eyes to say the word, "...penis."

She told me to wait a minute.

When she came back, she had a clipboard. That couldn't be good.

"Let me ask you a few questions," she began. "How long have you been sexually active?"

"One time."

"Did you use prophylactics?"

Tears welled up in my eyes. I didn't understand what she was talking about. It sounded like science words.

"You know, protection—condoms, jellies, foams, diaphragm."

"Yeah. We used three, including the French tickler."

She looked at me as if I were some kind of slut. "Pee in this cup and put it in the window when you're done. I'll be back in about fifteen minutes."

I filled the little cup to almost overflowing to make sure she had enough for the test, left it where I'd been instructed, and hurried back into the examination room.

The nurse came in a few minutes later. "Okay. I'm not quite sure what you and your boyfriend have been doing, but the good news is you're not pregnant."

Jumping off the table, I hugged her. "Thank you!"

She handed me a pamphlet. "Take this and read it."

"I will," I said. "Thank you again!" and I ran to the waiting room to find Stephanie and her aunt.

That night, I broke up with Shelby in the Piggly Wiggly parking lot. The whole experience scared me into celibacy for the next few years.

Chapter Four

———

FIRE AND RAIN

High School and Hormones

CORY AND I SPENT THE SUMMER after eighth grade with Dad at the fat farm, The Rice House in Key West. I loved it. It was a nonstop party. I made grape leaves with Egyptian twins, went to see Cyndi Lauper in concert, and made so many friends. I loved the freedom. I could do whatever I wanted except wear make-up. Dad freaked out if I wore lipstick or eyeliner and he would always embarrass me saying, "Go get that shit off your face!"

That summer, Cyndi Lauper was on tour and Daddy took me to her concert and I fought my way to the front row. I found a place to sit on the metal, X-shaped poles that supported the sound system and I held myself there with my arms on the stage. I wanted to be Cyndi Lauper and I couldn't believe I was so close to her.

When she started singing "She Bop," she bounced all over the stage, jumping up and down and her barefoot stomped on my pinky finger. I let go and people were pushing so hard that the next thing I knew I was under the stage and couldn't get out. I spent the rest of the concert listening to the thump of Cyndi Lauper's feet above me.

We went on a road trip with Opal and Dad. They took us to the Hershey Park in Pennsylvania, and we toured an Amish farm. We went to the Norman Rockwell Museum in Massachusetts and my favorite, to New York to see the musical, *Annie*. It was one of the most fun summers of my life, which made it even harder to go back to bedroom prison.

The great thing about a September birthday was that it came before report cards did. I was allowed to have a big party when I turned fourteen and invite boys over. Teenagers were parked all the way down our dirt road. My gift from Mom and Mike was a microphone and amplifier. We all hung out on the front porch and danced to Prince's "1999" and Ready for the World's "Oh Sheila." That's the night that I met Billy Joe Rickles. He had dark brown hair cut in a mullet, was skinny, and was the lead singer of a local rock band. I was in love. All the girls were in love with him. He drove a checkerboard van and on the back double doors it read, "Don't laugh, your daughter may be in here."

The next weekend, Billy Joe took me to the Glencoe Homecoming Dance. The smell of the gym floor and his leather jacket, I melted away in his arms as we slow danced to Bryan Adams' "Heaven." When I liked a boy, I latched on like a barnacle. Then, as always, October came and I got grounded again. Being grounded in ninth grade was torture. High school and hormones added to the hopelessness I had felt for so long. One Friday night, my friend Stephanie called me from a party to tell me that Billy Joe was making out with his ex-girlfriend, Shayla, in the bathroom.

"Put him on the phone right now," I said.

"Aimee, they're in there with the door locked and I'm about to leave to go home."

I heard Mike headed to the kitchen to try to catch me on the phone. That was it. I could not spend one more night wondering what my friends were doing. I couldn't survive one more Monday at school hearing all the details about the boy I loved and who he was kissing. I snapped. "I've got a headache," I said and slipped past Mom and Mike who were on the couch watching The Greatest American Hero on TV.

I tiptoed up the stairs and opened the mirrored cabinet in Mama's bathroom. It was like a mini Walgreens. I grabbed a bunch of prescription bottles and tucked them into the elastic band of my sweatpants. As I walked back downstairs, the bottles shook like miniature maracas. I went straight to the bathroom connected to my bedroom and locked the door.

I dumped the baby blue, pink, and yellow pills into the lid of my hot rollers. They looked like a candy necklace. Gazing out the little poster-sized window, I looked up at the moon and said, "God, I don't want to die. Please just get me out of this house." I swallowed a handful of pills and washed them down with a swig of strawberry flavored Slim Fast.

About twenty minutes later, my mind went haywire: What if I took too many? What if I end up paralyzed or brain-dead? What if this doesn't kill me? What if it does? Please, God, don't let me die. Oh my God, I could die. I can't believe I did this. Why did I do this?

Then I thought, what if nothing happened at all and Mama saw that I had taken all her medicine? She'd go batshit and I'd be grounded forever. I ran to the phone in the kitchen. I didn't care if Mike caught me. I had to tell someone what I had done and I was afraid to tell Mom. I called my friend Stephanie and she could tell by my voice something was wrong. My speech was slurred. I told her I loved her and what I had done.

I hung up and went back to my room. That's when I remembered to write my suicide note just in case. I dipped my quill calligraphy pen with a feather on the end into my India ink from art class and dove straight into Sylvia Plath mode. At the top of the page, I wrote a poem called Birthday of Eternity using the most dramatic looping and swooping handwriting I could produce:

Dear World,

How can you really die if you're not allowed to live?

Sprawling out across my bed, I wrote and watched my teardrops hit the paper and smear the ink. This suicide letter will be famous. It will be a poem the whole world knows. My Cyndi Lauper posters began to morph and swirl. My legs were hot and cold at the same time and felt like goldfish were swimming through them. I was shaking so hard that I thought I might have a seizure.

Stephanie called Mama and Mama called 9-1-1. I don't remember the ambulance ride to the hospital except for paramedics slapping my face and shaking my shoulders, trying to keep me awake.

In the emergency room, a heavyset nurse shoved a Big Gulp

sized glass of chalky, black liquid in my face and barked, "Drink this and drink all of it." It tasted like a milkshake made of ashes. Everyone kept asking, "What did you take? You have to remember what you took." Mama brought the pill bottles. She cried and told the nurse, "I bought a new bottle of Excedrin PM today. If she had taken those, it would have killed her."

Psych Ward

I WOKE UP THE NEXT MORNING in the psych ward. I thought my dad was the craziest person in Gadsden, Alabama, until I spent a week on the fifth floor at the Baptist hospital. I was the only teenager there and it felt like I had been shot out of a cannon into a Quentin Tarantino movie. Anything could happen at any moment and it did. There was a man who did nothing but write down numbers, a lady who whispered to the curtains, and two guys who thought they were Jesus, so that was a problem. People were kept calm by a flea market of powerful psychotropic medications that left them drooling in wheelchairs staring into space. The most difficult patients were always doped up so that they would cause less trouble. And there were people that the world had forgotten with swollen eyes, chapped lips, and broken hearts.

Being locked behind steel doors in a place that looked like the inside of an armored truck was a million times better than being trapped in my room. The psych ward was a nonstop feast of pudding, popsicles, Jell-O, grape juice, Coca-Cola with crushed ice, and my favorite, the zig zaggy straws that bend at the top. I had my own TV with a remote control that turned on the lights and thirty channels. I could lower and raise my bed, and use the phone any time I wanted before 10:00 pm. I could go to sleep at whatever time I wanted.

The hospital psychiatrist made me take the crazy test and I busted out laughing when I read the questions: *Do you secretly want to hurt animals? Do you hate your whole family?*

On my second night, a commotion outside my room woke me up. The nurses were yelling, "Mr. Jacobs, get back to your room!"

There was a naked man who looked like he was in his eighties. He reminded me of Gollum from Lord of the Rings—humpbacked, with sagging, silvery skin, and gray-white pubic hair sticking out every which way. He was horrifying and hilarious at the same time.

The community room smelled like cigarettes, dirty hair, and gardenias. There was a lady in there who never spoke until she looked at me one morning and said, "Let's get the fuck out of here." A man who sat by the window would never shut up. On my fourth day in there, I asked him who he was talking to.

"God," he whispered.

My favorite thing about the psych ward was that everyone played BINGO and they were serious as a fucking heart attack about it. When someone yelled, "BINGO!" they might get bitch slapped by a bowl of banana pudding or stabbed in the hand with a plastic fork.

When my time was up in the looney bin, I didn't want to go home. I begged Mom to let me move in with Maw Maw and Paw Paw. She finally gave in. I finished my ninth grade year living in Uncle Kelly's old bedroom. After he graduated, he rented a duplex in downtown Gadsden closer to where he worked at the decorator store. Uncle Kelly could paint anything and everything that customers commissioned: family portraits, sailboats, cows, flowers. The store sold his paintings and took a percentage.

Paw Paw still got drunk every night. I knew all the stories of how he beat her black and blue when my mama was growing up. After he had triple bypass surgery in his late fifties and Maw Maw nursed him back to health, he switched from hard liquor to beer and mellowed out in his old age. I did not witness the horrific abuse my mother, aunts, and uncles endured every day of their childhood. I should have hated my grandfather for all the pain he caused, but it's hard to hate someone who loves you.

During the week Maw Maw made me cheese toast every morning and my friend, Trey, who was a junior at Glencoe High School, brought me home from school. I could go out with my friends one night a week and talk on the phone whenever I wanted. I felt like a typical teenager for the first time. On Saturdays, Maw Maw and I would get up early and go to yard sales and find treasures like a glittery cigarette case and vintage clothes.

Tokyo Road

I MOVED BACK IN WITH MOM AND MIKE in the tenth grade. I don't know if my suicide attempt scared him or if he got sick of the nonstop power struggle, but Mike didn't go out of his way to be mean to me anymore. There was still tension every time we were in a room together, but we tolerated each other. He took a second job, and every afternoon he came in with a brown paper bag from McDonald's and went straight upstairs. The only way I knew he was in the house was from the sound of the TV coming from his bedroom.

Mom worked all day at the Baptist hospital, then drove an hour to the University of Alabama in Birmingham where she was studying to be a physical therapist. She got home around 10:00 pm and studied until she fell asleep. Cory was nine years old, and every day after school he came in and made a bowl of SpaghettiOs and played outside until dark. Nobody seemed to care what we did. Somehow our house went from Fort Knox to a free for all.

We had to make up things to do in Gadsden. On the weekends, kids from all the local high schools drove in circles around Sonic. The cops gave you a ticket if you passed by them more than three times, so we had to find other ways to entertain ourselves. Sometimes we got in a truck and went mud riding and ended up head to-toe covered in mud. Occasionally we parked on Tokyo Road, a dead-end dirt road out in the woods where everyone sat on tailgates under the stars and drank beer and hung out.

For a while, on Friday nights, we met and got into groups of ten and went on scavenger hunts. I was always in charge of making the lists, and every weekend they got crazier:

1. Telephone receiver from a payphone
2. Live duck
3. Plastic spoon (from a stranger—you have to knock on the door and ask to borrow it)
4. Window cling sign from Taco Bell, McDonald's, or Wendy's

5. Bag of fertilizer from Kmart
6. Six-pack of beer
7. Flag from someone's mailbox.

Whoever made it back to Tokyo Road with everything on the list first, won. It was so fun watching boys wrestle ducks and try to catch them. But sometimes it was a dangerous game. I almost knocked my front teeth out trying to pull a black payphone receiver off of the thick, silver cord in front of Piggly Wiggly by sticking it between the handles on a grocery buggy and yanking it until it came off and hit me in the mouth, busting my lip and leaving a bruise like a Groucho Marx mustache for almost a month.

My three best friends, Laurie, Stephanie, and Brooke, used to visit this crazy alcoholic woman in her seventies. She had red hair and white roots and her name was Ruth. On weekends, we knocked on her front door and sat in her living room while she told us a bunch of insane shit, like how she had a tattoo of a cat on her pussy and killed her ex-husband. After about ten minutes of talking, we gave her money and walked around the corner to the MAPCO. She bought us beer and we always let her keep the change to buy herself some cigarettes.

We went to Noccalula Falls, my favorite place in Gadsden, and climbed underneath the hundred-foot waterfall. We wandered through hidden caverns. No one had a boat or jet ski, so we all put our cigarettes in a cellophane bag and piled onto an air mattress and floated all day down the Coca-Cola colored Coosa River, letting it take us wherever it wanted to. We usually ended up miles from Gadsden, and when it got close to dark, we wandered up the riverbank to find the closest payphone and call for a ride home.

Burning Down the House

IN ELEVENTH GRADE I DID SOMETHING in a split second that changed my life forever. It was an unusually windy day in May—the Friday of Mother's Day weekend—the kind of day when doors slam shut and papers fly away like doves. The kind of day when you can feel something in the air wants to pick a fight.

I sat in study hall watching dogwood petals and little, pink mimosa blossoms floating like confetti through the crank-operated windows of our classroom. Spring in Alabama looks like the trees are all dressed up and going to the prom: Valentino gowns, sherbet-colored ruffles, frills, and Chantilly lace.

My favorite teacher and the school counselor, Miss Boozer, had a date. She had been excited about it all week. I overheard her say, "Oh no, I forgot my gold sandals. I'm gonna have to wear Reeboks with my dress."

"I've got gold sandals," I said, almost jumping out of my seat. She stared down at my flowered Doc Marten boots and asked, "Here at school?"

"No, at my house about a mile away."

"What size?"

"Seven."

She looked back at the clock above the chalkboard and then asked me,

"Can you be back here before the bell rings?"

"I can if somebody drives me. I don't have a car."

"Can someone run Aimee to her house?" she asked the class. Almost every hand went up and I looked straight at Jeffrey. "Okay, Jeffrey, can you take her?" she asked.

"Yeah okay, I wanted a cigarette anyway," he mumbled, trying to be cool.

I had a crush on Jeffrey all through middle school and he had escorted me in the Glencoe Homecoming Court for the past three years, but right after the football games were over, he acted like I was a leper. He had pushed me up against the trampoline in my friend Laurie's back yard and kissed me once and he had tried to get me to stick my hand down his pants in my grandmother's dining room, saying that there was a carrot in there. But I wouldn't do it. But even so, my heart was fluttering as I followed him to his car.

I knew every detail of Jeffrey's silver Monte Carlo even though I had never been inside it. I knew the airbrushed tag on the front, "Cothran #1," the fuzzy black and white dice hanging from his rear-view mirror and the wooden beads on his seat covers. I had always imagined what they would feel like rolling up and down my back. When I slid into the front seat beside him, the car smelled like cigarettes, Prell shampoo, and piña coladas. It smelled like Jeffery.

We flew down the road with the windows open, my hair flying in my face and mouth every time I tried to talk. "Get me a cigarette," he said, "they're under the seat." I grabbed the silver Zippo lighter in the broken ash tray and lit a Marlboro Light for each of us. His dashboard drumming wasn't thumping nearly as loud as my heart. He popped in a Beastie Boys cassette.

Every time he took a turn, I scooted a little closer to him on the bench seat until our legs were almost touching. When we pulled into the driveway, he parked the car and felt a burst of excitement as I waited for him to grab me and passionately kiss me, biting my bottom lip like he had the previous summer by the trampoline. "What the fuck are you doing?" he snapped. "Go get the shoes."

"You're an idiot," I said as I got out. I ran to the side door, flicking my cigarette before I went inside. Mike's bloodhound nose could detect even a molecule of smoke. I grabbed the brand new metallic sandals from my closet and dashed back to the car. Jeffrey and I didn't speak on the drive back. After school, my friend Brook and I were sitting in the parking lot and we saw Miss Boozer. She was wearing my gold sandals and fell into the ditch trying to climb into her boyfriend's dirty Jeep. Back at Brook's house we were lying across her bed talking when her mom burst into the bedroom. "Get in the car. We gotta go," she said.

"Go where?"

"We gotta get Aimee home."

"Why? What's wrong?" I asked.

"Something's going on at your house."

"What do you mean?"

"It's on fire."

"There's no way. I was there thirty minutes ago!"

Brook's mom was usually a nervous wreck with a panicked look in her eye like a possum about to be crushed by a truck. Now her hands were shaking so badly that she could hardly hold the steering wheel of her Honda Civic.

As we got close to my house, I smelled the thick smoke in the air. When we turned the corner of Allen Drive, I saw two police cars with their sirens wailing and four fire trucks lined up down our dirt road.

"Let me out!" I screamed. "I gotta get out!" I jumped out of the backseat before the car came to a stop.

"You gotta move that van!" a cop was screaming at a white news van with a tiny satellite dish on top.

I ran as fast as I could down our dirt road. The smell of smoke burned my eyes and stung my throat. My mind could not process what I saw; our house in flames fifty feet high. It looked like an orange demonic monster was devouring our lives.

The fire had already taken the living room and kitchen, and the roof was ablaze. I watched firefighters screaming at each other and dragging gigantic hoses through the ditch and across the front yard. Another fire truck showed up as flames began shooting off the roof, threatening the acre of pine trees on the left side of our house. Neighbors huddled in my step-cousin's yard, on the dirt road, and in our driveway. They stood with their hands over their mouths.

Mike's brother, David, who lived next door, told the firefighter, "I smelled smoke and came out," he said. "And damn, I couldn't believe it—the whole side of the house was on fire."

A couple of older women who lived down the street were trying to comfort my mother, but she was inconsolable. The more the fire crackled, the crazier she became. Suddenly she collapsed, sobbing uncontrollably, lying on her back in the grass.

"No, no, no—oh God, please, please no!" she screamed.

"Becky, don't start that shit!" Mike shouted.

"Everything we have is gone!"

A woman with big red hair knelt next to my mother, trying to hold her, but she kept wailing, "My whole life is gone."

Cory sat on his skateboard in the driveway; orange flickers reflected in his blue eyes as he watched the flames crawl through his bedroom window. "What about my baseball cards?" he asked, but nobody answered.

I watched Blackie, the crazy neighborhood dog that we'd kind of adopted since he was always hanging around our house, while he ran in circles, hysterical with joy. That dog loved fire so much that Cory gave him sparklers to eat every Fourth of July. This disaster was the best day of Blackie's life.

I heard Mike ask the chief what had started the fire. "You're gonna have to wait for the marshal to make his report, but if ya ask me, I'd say it started over yonder by that there trash can," he said, reaching into the front pocket of his orange overalls. The fire chief pulled out a pouch of Red Man tobacco and stuck his fat fingers into it, pinching out a massive dip. He put it into his mouth and reached for another pinch until his cheek jutted out like a giant tumor. Mike flinched every time he spat a brownish-black wad onto the driveway.

"There was a gas can sitting behind the trash can," Mike said.

"Well, shit, there's your answer. Somebody threw a cigarette down over there, and psssshowww!" Tobacco juice sprayed as he made the explosion sound.

Everything began to slow down and distort. I felt my knees giving out as I bent over, trying to catch my breath. My brain was stuck, replaying the scene from forty-five minutes earlier when I casually flicked my cigarette before going inside for the gold sandals. Oh my God. I did this. This is all my fault. My mind was spinning like a roulette wheel: guilt, fear, horror, panic, and back around again to guilt.

The fire chief caught me as I began to fall and eased me down onto the grass. My mother crawled over and hugged me. "Oh, baby, everything we have is gone. It's all gone." We watched the flames devour the curtains she had hand-sewn for the front picture window. And the two taxidermy deer head were on fire.

Mike's green eyes were red and watery as he stood in the driveway, hands in his pockets, watching the destruction of the house he had built nail by nail. Now it was ashes in the wind, along with the burned remains of two generations of family pictures, GI Joe action figures, diplomas, baseball trophies, and everything we owned.

Nobody could ever know that I had started the fire—it didn't matter that it was an accident. If Mike found out I was responsible for burning the house to the ground, I had no idea what would happen, but it would be bad.

It took every fire truck in three counties to put out the fire.

That first night, as the blackened skeleton of our house dripped and smoked into the starry sky, my aunt took charge and drove us to Walmart. My mama walked in and stood like a zombie, eyes dead, staring straight ahead.

A clerk came up to her and asked, "Ma'am, can I help you?" Mama started to cry.

"Can I help you find something? What do you need?"

In a brittle whisper, my mama replied, "Everything."

***

IT WAS FORTY EIGHT HOURS before they let us back inside. On Mother's Day we walked through the charred door. I gagged at the smell of smoke and soot. Everything around us was black, crispy, lined with dark silver ash. We kicked through the soggy wreckage, trying to find anything we could salvage. Miraculously the steel, cow print trunk in my closet saved my diaries and poetry, and Cory's baseball cards had survived in their metal box.

Everything else looked like it was out of a surreal nightmare world; broken glass, twisted metal, the television melted into the carpet, mirrors and windows dripping like liquid, and a carton of eggs cooked by the heat in the remains of the fridge. What hadn't been consumed by the fire was destroyed by smoke or water. We began a guessing game holding up objects and trying to figure out what they had been. That puddle of beige plastic, that was the phone. The melted mess of swirling colors that looked like taffy on the floor was all my cassette tapes. As I stood in the center of my bedroom, blackened pages of poetry flew in the breeze above me. I could see the beautiful blue sky above the burned out roof. I looked up and asked, "Why did this happen?" Then I whispered, "Please God, don't let anybody ever find out I did this."

We lived in a motel for the next few weeks and then moved back into Broadmoor Apartment Complex, where Mike had lived when he and Mom first started dating. It took a while for the impact to sink in. Every time I turned to look for something small, like a toothbrush, or ponytail holder or socks, I felt the suffocating shame of what I had done swallow me again. Whenever someone mentioned something they'd lost, I wanted to confess, to let the truth flood out of me like a dirty river. Every night the secret sat on my chest like a skyscraper and the guilt ate through me like acid. But I kept my mouth shut.

Metallica Toes

I STILL DREAMED OF MEETING A BOY in a band and running away with him. I wouldn't look twice at one who couldn't play "Eruption "by Eddie Van Halen on the guitar.

When two students from each high school in Etowah County were chosen to tour the Atlanta College of Art, our art teacher, Mr. Bentley, picked my friend, Katy, and me. Mr. B. loved my abstract paintings and always hung them up where everyone in the classroom could see. On the day of the trip, he told me, "You're going to love this college, Aimee. It's far out, like you."

We were waiting to get on the school bus for the field trip when I saw Ty Phillips for the first time. It was like he walked out of a Guns N' Roses video. He was skinny with long, dark, curly hair and about a hundred rubber bracelets up his right arm. What sealed the deal was that he had on one red Converse sneaker and one black. I'd never seen a boy like him in Glencoe. I had found my rock star in a town full of rednecks.

I wore a long, lime green, vintage cape that I'd bought at an estate sale with Maw Maw and I followed Ty to the bus and flung my cape over my shoulder as I sat down behind him. I flirted with him for the whole two-hour drive to Atlanta. We walked side-by-side through the college, looking at all the paintings and sculptures, and by the end of the day, we were wandering around the Lenox Mall so in love that we bought matching John Lennon style sunglasses.

When the bus got back to Gadsden, Ty asked for a ride home. I grabbed Katy's arm and begged. "Please, we got to take him." Ty didn't live far from me, so we dropped him off at his house. He invited us to come to his room. The walls were covered in Metallica and Megadeth posters and he kept a pet python in an aquarium. Ty picked up his red Alvarez electric guitar, plugged it into the amp, and I watched as he played "Welcome to the Jungle." I'm pretty sure I ovulated for the first time.

From that day on, for the rest of high school, I spent more time in his bedroom than I did in mine. Before we left, another long-haired boy walked into Ty's room and asked, "What time's practice?" This was Ty's best friend, Jerry, and the bass player in Ty's band. It wasn't long until Ty, Jerry, and I were like the Three Musketeers. Going anywhere with them was asking for dirty looks, but I didn't care. I loved it. In Alabama back then, if a boy had long hair, he might as well have carved Satan into his forehead for the way people treated us everywhere we went.

Ty and I dated for the next few years. I spent most weekends sitting on a Marshall amp watching their rock band, Vertigo, play "Crazy Train" by Ozzy Osborne or writing poetry for them to turn into songs. Jerry's mom, Miss Annette, drove us to concerts in Nashville and Birmingham, and both times we found ways to meet the bands, and both times it ended in disaster. When we went to see Metallica at Starwood, I got into the mosh pit and messed up my feet so bad I could barely walk.

We waited outside after the concert for an hour, hoping someone could get us a backstage pass. A group of twenty-somethings came out and had red triangle all-access stickers stuck to their shirts. "Can we please have your passes?" I asked.

"Yeah, but I don't think the band's coming out."

We walked into a backstage room with long tables full of covered catering: mashed potatoes, chicken, green beans, and desserts. The opening band, Megadeth, was there and Ty asked to have his picture taken with the lead singer, Dave Mustaine. When Ty put his arm around Dave's neck, his watch got caught in Dave's blondish red hair and someone had to cut it out. A few minutes later, Metallica's lead singer, James Hetfield came out. I was sitting on the end of a folding table and he sat down on the opposite end. It collapsed into the floor and he looked at me like it was my fault.

When Jane's Addiction played in Birmingham, Miss Annette rented a motel room for us to stay the night. Back at our Budget Motel after the concert, we saw Perry Farrell, the lead singer for Jane's Addiction, on the top floor balcony across the street. We shouted to him from the parking lot of our Holiday Inn up. "You should come to our room. You should come to our room to party."

"Why would we come over there?" Perry waved his arms around, showing the penthouse rooftop where the band was hanging out.

"You should come over here because we got green tea malts," I yelled at him. We had watched a documentary on the band over and over again where Perry talked about his favorite drink. I didn't even know what a green tea malt was, but I guess he realized what big fans we were because moments later we saw about twenty people crossing the street headed straight for us. They came into our room and Perry started jumping on one of the double beds. Fifteen minutes later, there was a hole in the ceiling, a lamp was broken and the door was off the hinges. I was being escorted to the motel office by a police officer as he spoke into his walkie talkie, saying, "I've got a female Caucasian..."

"I'm not Caucasian! I'm not Caucasian," I screamed at him. Why was he calling me some race I had never heard of? He looked at me like I was crazy and ended up letting me go after Miss Annette paid the manager to have the broken door fixed.

Daddy and Oprah

DADDY CALLED TO SAY he was going to be on *The Oprah Winfrey Show* and he told us what day it came on and I waited anxiously all week. The theme of the show was weight loss. It was Oprah's most famous episode and she had a contest to see who could lose the most weight in a month's time. There was also a competition between the people of Raleigh and Durham North Carolina, the diet capital of the world. When the show started, I couldn't believe what Dad had on. He looked flat out crazy. He had on snakeskin wrestling boots that were knee high and he had his blue jeans tucked into them. He had on some kind of weird royal blue blazer and when Oprah finally made her way over to him to quiz his eating habits, she said, "Danny, how did you lose 45 pounds in one short month?"

He started screaming, "Stand up girls! Girls, stand up!" Nothing happened but he just kept on. "Girls, girls, stand up," and then a row of cute black girls finally stood up and Dad said, "I lost my weight thanks to my haram," and Oprah just stared at him, speechless.

Chapter Five

——

RUST & STARDUST

Target Bullseye

LATER ON IN HIGH SCHOOL, Dad got his first song recorded. It was called "Heartbeat" and the title track to the Oak Ridge Boys record. Throughout high school, Cory and I spent time with Dad in Nashville. The more we were there, the more I fell in love with it. Dad began having hits on the radio and getting big checks in the mail for songwriting royalties.

Money to him was like fun tickets. Dad was either broke or making it rain. Most of the time, I loved it when he was manic. I rode on the magic carpet of mental illness with him, we went to the horse races and gambling boat casinos. Dad took Cory and me to Target one night and gave both of us a red shopping cart. "Okay, here's what we're doing. You've got fifteen minutes to go get everything you need for school."

Standing in the front of the store with a Big Gulp of Dr. Pepper, Dad hit the timer and said, "On your mark ... get set... GO!"hon

Cory and I tore off in different directions, zig-zagging through the aisles slinging jeans, sweaters, hiking boots, hats, notebooks, markers, and pens into our carts. The only rules were no makeup or music cassettes for me, and no baseball cards or video games for Cory. My dad and brother were intensely competitive. That night in the parking lot of Target, everything turned dark the moment we walked out. "I'll bet you twenty bucks I can beat you back to the truck," Dad said.

"Okay, go!" Cory yelled and they took off and then fought for an hour over who won the race. They always wanted me to be the judge.

That same night we ended up at a random tennis court at midnight where they battled it out with rackets in the pouring rain with thunder roaring like cannons in the sky.

"Get in the damn truck before somebody gets electrocuted." I yelled out the window, but they wouldn't stop."

Cory won, and in the Silverado on the way back to the apartment, I sat between them. They disagreed about who won the game of tennis until it turned into a raging fight.

"Cory, I don't even know if you're my son or not," Dad screamed. "Your mom was fooling around on me when she got pregnant with you."

"Your mom was fooling around on me when she got pregnant with you." That wasn't true and that broke Cory's heart. It infuriated me. Cory took a swing across me at Dad hitting him in the jaw and I burst out crying. Dad swerved, just missing a head-on collision with a BMW. He could be so vicious to both of us. He used words like 'knives.' But that night what he said to Cory, I hated him in that moment.

Cory had Opal's blonde hair and blue eyes and everything else about him looked just like Daddy. The same two little moles in a line above his full red lips, pigeon legs and his hand and feet. They stood, walked and talked exactly alike. Dad was the one that cheated on Mom throughout their marriage.

Fuzzy Duck

THE SUMMER BEFORE ELEVENTH GRADE, Dad came to Gadsden one weekend and took me out to The Fuzzy Duck, the biggest bar in town. The Pirates of the Mississippi, a band that Daddy helped put together and named, was playing there. He had written almost every song on their record. We all joined in as they played a song that would go on to be one of their biggest hits, "Feed Jake." Dad wrote the lyrics to the song in jail. He had been up for three days straight. It was one of those songs that means something different to every listener. Some called it the first gay country love song. Some said it was about life and loss of innocence. And some people thought it was about a dog. I believe it was Dad's story of moving to Nashville, chasing his dream. I don't know where the dog named Jake came from. He never had a dog named Jake.

> *I'm standing at the crossroads in life*
> *And I don't know where to go*
> *You know you got my heart, babe*
> *But music's got my soul*
> *Let me play it one more time*
> *Tell the truth and make it right*
> *And hope they understand me*
> *Now I lay me down to sleep*
> *And pray the Lord my soul to keep*
> *If I die before I wake, feed Jake*
> *He's been a good dog*
> *My best friend right through it all*
> *If I die before I wake, feed Jake*

Daddy was like a celebrity when he came to town. It was so rare for someone to get out of Gadsden and go for their dreams. Most of the men worked at the Goodyear Tire plant. That factory kept our town going. Paw Paw lied about his age when he was fourteen and started working there, spending the next fifty years breathing in black tire fumes. Most of my dad's friends worked there too.

I was almost sixteen, so Daddy had to talk the owner into letting me into The Fuzzy Duck.

"Okay, Danny, but I'd better not see her drinking any alcohol. I could lose my license."

When we sat down, the first thing Dad did was order me a drink. "Hey, baby, I got you a Jack and Coke. That way, it'll look like you got a soft drink," he said.

By the end of the night I'd had four or five Jack and Cokes, and when the lights came on, I couldn't find Daddy anywhere. I went up and asked the bartender, "Do you know where Danny Mayo went?"

"Yeah, he paid his tab and left about an hour ago."

A guy stepped up. "My name's Doug. I know your dad from Nashville. He went home with that waitress with the red hair.

My heart sank. I couldn't really call my mom shit-faced from a bar at 2:30 in the morning. How in the world was I going to get home?

As if answering my unspoken question, Doug said, "If you need a ride, I can run you home."

I followed him out to his dirty, blue Chevelle and tried to give him directions. I was so drunk it took me a minute to realize he was going the wrong way. "You missed the turn to my house," I told him, but he kept going straight down Meighan Boulevard.

"I need to run in my motel room for a second," Doug said.

I felt like I might be sick. We pulled into the parking lot of the cheap Redwood Inn. He got out and ran into his room. I watched the door which he left cracked open and waited on him for about fifteen minutes. I had to pee, so I went inside to go to the bathroom. Even though I was blind drunk, I worried that being alone with him was a bad idea once I got inside. I reassured myself, he's a friend of my dad's and everybody knows Dad is crazy. He's not going to do anything.

When I stepped out of the bathroom, I was beyond shocked by his sudden kiss and surprising strength as he pushed me back on to the bed.

"No, no, I want to go home. Please get off me." I tried to shove him but he pinned me down with all his weight.

"I'm gonna be sick, I really am." I kneed him between the legs which only made him mad and he jerked my jeans open and pulled them down to my knees. His face was oily and covered in acne scars. His chin stubble rubbed me raw. His sour breath was hot on my neck and my whole face was wet from him trying to kiss me while I kept my mouth shut. I said, 'NO,' over and over until it didn't matter anymore. I heard him grunting and disconnected myself from what was happening. When he was done, he stood up and zipped his pants.

I got up off the bed. The room was dark and the TV was on a dead channel. I walked straight out to his car. I pointed out where he should turn and he drove me home in silence. When I took off my jeans to take a shower, I realized he had used a rubber because it was stuck to my inner thigh. I was thankful I was so wasted when it happened.

The next day I asked Daddy about his friend Doug and he said, "I don't know that guy. I've seen him hanging around Opryland Publishing. He's trying to get people to listen to his songs."

Being sixteen, I didn't think he raped me. I didn't tell anybody for years. Since it didn't happen in a dark alley and he didn't pull a knife on me or wear a ski mask, I blamed myself for being so stupid to go inside his motel room. I felt guilty like I had cheated on Ty.

We had just moved back into the house. It had been rebuilt after the fire, and I remember the smell of new paint on the walls. I felt disgusting, dirty, and alone and I couldn't get his smell off my face. My inner thighs ached. I took a scalding hot shower until the water turned cold. I thank God that I had been blackout drunk when it happened. I could force it out of my mind most of the time, except when I had to drive past the decrepit Redwood Inn. I refused to give him any more power to control me in any way. I put the shame on him. It was his to carry. Between that and the consuming guilt from burning down the house, I didn't think things could get worse. I was wrong.

Hope Chest

WHEN I TURNED SIXTEEN, I imagined that I would come home from school and find a Pulsar with T-tops—my dream car. But all I found was a burnt birthday cake sitting on the kitchen table with a note that read, "Happy Sweet Sixteen. I love you, Mom."

Dad refused to get me a car. Harold felt sorry for me and bought me a beige Monte Carlo with bullet holes in the passenger side door. Every time I used the brakes, the car shook and I only had it for about six weeks until it broke down. At the end of my junior year, Dad gave me a red, four-door Mercedes that I loved, but I only had it for a few months before he got mad and took it away. He wanted me to skip two weeks of school and my junior prom to fly to L.A. and babysit his co-writer's kids while he and the parents worked.

The summer before my senior year of high school, Mama Opal gave me an antique hope chest for my birthday. Two long drawers popped out from the hinges and it had a little, gold keyhole, but the key was lost long before the chest found me. She said the hope chest was a tradition passed down from her grandmother to her. She explained the concept; this is where you save things for your future as a wife and mother.

I got my first job at Wendy's fast food restaurant and used every paycheck to purchase something to put in that hope chest. Even when all I could afford was a strawberry-scented votive candle, it went in the chest. Whether it was an orphaned piece of patterned china from the flea market or a John Lennon magnet, each small item was a deposit into my dream life. I had over a hundred matchbooks from everywhere I had been with Dad. I would unfold my pink flamingo shower curtain, breathing in the plastic smell, my favorite smell in the world. It was like the scent of an inflatable pool float; the scent of fun. I had a watermelon printed serving tray and pitcher with eight matching glasses that I had on layaway all summer until I finally paid it off. I had an owl timer for the kitchen, and a Betty Boop towel set, a pink spatula, an orange Art Deco sunburst clock that my Uncle Kelly bought me at a yard sale, a Hello Kitty fuzzy bath mat and a black and white cow spotted tea kettle.

Opening that mahogany chest, the thick scent of cedar was so intense that it was like it was wrapping its arms around me. It was the perfume of freedom, of flying away like an eagle into a new world. When I was down, I would drag out everything in my dream box and sit on the floor and go through it. It was kind of like entering the door to Narnia. I dreamed about moving to Nashville and getting an awesome apartment and writing songs every day. This life I was looking forward to was every bit as real to me as the life I was living. In some ways, it seemed more real. Ty may have been my on-again, off-again boyfriend, but I shared my dreams with Jerry because deep down, I knew Ty would never leave Alabama. Being a dreamer in a small town is kind of like being a vampire, as soon as anybody finds out, you could get staked in the heart.

BMI Awards - Senior Year

THAT NOVEMBER, AFTER I HAD turned seventeen, Dad invited me to the BMI Awards with him. He called last minute, "Hey, baby doll, I want you to be my date for the BMI songwriting awards. I'm winning something this year for 'If I Had You.'"

The song had gone number one and it was one of the top fifty most played of 1989. Since it was last minute, I had to get a dress fast in Nashville, and the only one I could find in my size was a yellow ruffled strapless gown. The event was black-tie and everyone had on evening gowns. I had never been anywhere like the building we walked into. We followed the red carpet up the stairs and had our picture taken with Francis Preston, the lady who was President of BMI. I had seen her photographs with Paul McCartney and Paul Simon, and pretty much every badass songwriter.

Daddy looked straight out crazy. He had on a black leather vest that he bought at Goodwill and a floral, button-down shirt, acid-washed jeans, and knee-high, lace-up wrestling boots that looked like something Hulk Hogan might wear in the ring. He disappeared the moment we walked in and I had to go find our table. He was mingling and drinking way too much. When they called his name to come to the stage, they announced, "'If I Had You,' Danny Mayo," with the other songwriters. He came straight at me, "Aimee, go get my award."

"No!"

"Dammit, Aimee, can't you do one thing I ask you to?"

"I'm not going up there. You go get it." I didn't want to walk on that stage until they called MY name and it was for MY song. One of the publishers on the song came up behind Dad and put his arm around him to help him up the stairs. Dad was so drunk he almost fell just as he was about to step on stage. Then as they took the picture, he was holding his award upside down and he rubbed his hand on Jimmy Baskin's head, his publisher, and knocked his toupee off on the floor on the stage. I was mortified.

As we were leaving the awards, the president of DECCA Records walked over and said, "Hey, Danny, I want you to meet this new artist, Radney. He's the lead singer of a new band. They've had three hits this year."

Dad said, "Nice to meet you, Rodney."

And the guy said, "It's Radney."

Then Dad said, "Whatever dickhead," and walked off and left me standing there.

He told another new artist, Michael Atkins, "My daughter thinks you look like Weird Al Yankovic." I had said that because of his dark curly hair, but I never dreamed Daddy would tell him. I could tell at that moment he didn't like me and never would. Dad was too drunk to drive, so I had to find a phone and call a taxi. When they arrived to pick us up before the awards were over, we pulled out of the parking lot...and then I realized that Dad left his award.

Jerry and I

JERRY AND I VISITED NASHVILLE a couple of times during my senior year. Dad liked Jerry because he was so chill— he was easy to hang out with. He didn't bring the drama that usually came with a teenager. Jerry had a lot of health problems growing up and spent most of his childhood on steroids and medication that made him gain weight. I think Dad bonded with Jerry since they had both battled their weight growing up. Dad said, "Jerry's an old soul," and after he took us to see the movie, *Do the Right Thing*, Dad nicknamed Jerry "Radio Raheem" after one of the characters.

We went to songwriter clubs and concerts with Dad. On one of our trips we drove up and down Music Row where all the publishing houses are. We watched all the songwriters walk up and down 16th and 17th Avenues with guitars strapped to their backs. Jerry and I made a pact. We promised each other we were moving to Nashville after I graduated.

"I'll find a cool band to play bass for and you can write songs," he said.

"Yeah, and we'll make it together on rent even if we have to work three jobs. It will be so worth it," I told him.

That May I designed an orange, sequined dress and Mom made me it for me to wear to the prom.

Every day that week, Laurie, Stephanie, Brooke, and I laid out on the roof to get the darkest tan we could before the dance. I made some Aimee's Supersonic Tanning Tonic with baby oil, butter, and iodine, and all week everyone smelled something that stank, but couldn't figure it out until my mom jerked up my arm and I realized it was me that stank. We had all baked that nasty rotten smell into our skin and had to go to the prom that way.

Promise Me

I GRADUATED FROM GLENCOE HIGH school in 1989. I was seventeen and ready to start my new life, but I was stuck until I saved enough cash to get to Tennessee. Most of my friends took their graduation money and went on a senior trip to the "Redneck Riviera," also known as Panama City, Florida. But I went to Walmart and bought a microwave and a Sanyo remote control TV and a VCR for my dream apartment in Nashville. Uncle Kelly bought me an expensive coffee table from the interior design store where he worked. It had a glass top that opened so I could display all my matchbooks that I had collected from my adventures with Dad.

One day that summer, Maw Maw called and said that she had a surprise for me. When I got to her house, she was so excited.

"Okay, hon, sit down at the table and close your eyes."

"What are you doing?" I asked. I couldn't help peeking.

I watched her climb up on a chair and reach on the top shelf above the refrigerator. She pulled down a big Maxwell House coffee can about the size of a bucket of paint. When I took the lid off, it was full of quarters, dimes, and nickels. "Oh my gosh, how much money is this?" I asked her. "I don't know, but I've been saving it for a couple of years waiting on you to graduate." I jumped up and hugged her. "You can add this to the money you're saving to move to Nashville," she said, and I started to cry.

Maw Maw was the one person that believed in my dreams as much as I did. When I was down, she always made me feel better. In my town, people saw being optimistic as a weakness and being a dreamer made somebody a damn fool. But I never felt that way when I poured my heart out to my grandmother. She was always there like a silver-haired, drunken angel holding a red Dixie cup full of Budweiser in her hand. My grandmother is where everybody went to talk. She listened without judging and she could keep a secret. The grapevine didn't grow at her house.

"Hon, I want to talk to you for a minute," she said and sat down next to me while we sorted through all the quarters and dimes. "Okay, what is it?'

"I don't want you to live your life like I've lived mine," she said and started to cry. "I need you to promise me two things; that you'll go after your dreams no matter how big they are and that you'll marry somebody that's good to you. Don't make my mistakes."

That was the closest I had ever heard her come to calling her marriage to my grandfather a mistake. Even after all the bruises and beatings, she still loved him somehow. "Aimee, I want you to promise me."

"Maw Maw, there's no way I'd be with somebody that would hit me, I swear to you."

She took off her smoky gray topaz glasses and wiped a tear. "I'd beat the shit out of 'em in their sleep," I said, trying to make her smile. Generations of women in my family were born on a carousel of abuse. They came into this world with a painted pony waiting, a saved seat on the sad ride that their lives would become. My grandmother endured a voiceless and choiceless existence, caught in an endless cycle of being controlled by a man. These women didn't live—they survived. When I made her that promise, I had no idea how I would break it.

Veterinarian

THAT FALL, I WATCHED SOME OF my friends get married and some of them move off to colleges like Auburn and Alabama Universities. They shot like neon fireworks out into their new lives and I felt sewn to the ground in Gadsden. I begged Daddy to pay for me to go to college at Belmont University in Nashville, but he refused. Daddy could have paid for my whole graduating class to go to college with the money he had lost gambling. He lived in Florida now, with some new girl he met at the fat farm in Key West. I almost never saw him, but when I did, all we did was fight. When he came back to Alabama, he told me, "I've decided I'll pay for you to go to college in Tennessee if you want to go."

"Yes, I want to go. You're gonna pay for me to go to Belmont?" I jumped up and hugged him. Belmont School of Music was located at the edge of Music Row and I saw the students lugging their instruments in and out of buildings every time I was in Nashville with Daddy.

"Aimee, I'm not gonna waste my money on a music degree. You can't do anything with a music degree."

"You just said you'd pay for me to go to school in Tennessee. Do you want me to go to Vanderbilt?"

"Good Lord, Aimee, you'd never be smart enough to get into Vanderbilt. But if you want to go, I'll pay for you to go to Columbia State Community College."

"What are you talking about?" I asked.

"It's around an hour outside of Nashville and it's got one of the best veterinarian programs in the country."

"I don't want to be a veterinarian."

"But Aimee, you love animals."

"Yeah, but I don't want to fucking operate on them."

"Then forget it. Your grades probably aren't good enough to get in anyway."

"Why can't you let me go somewhere I want to go, like Belmont, to study music or the Atlanta College of Art?"

"That's stupid. If you want to draw, just draw," Daddy said. "If I'm paying for you to go to school, I'm picking where you go and that's it."

"Why can't you ever help me? I've begged you to let me stay in your apartment while you're gone in Nashville. And then you let some stupid southern rock band you don't even know stay there instead. You've got five cars and you won't let me drive one. You won't even help me to get my transmission fixed. I'm so sick of you. Just stay away from me."

Cruel Summer

I DECIDED THAT IF I WAS GOING TO MOVE TO NASH-VILLE, I had to do it by myself. I worked at Big Lots Closeout Clearance Store, and every couple of months I put in an application at the Record Bar. It was the only music shop and it was in the Gadsden Mall. That way, I could at least be around music and get discounts on cassettes and albums. But they never called.

That spring, I entered a county-wide art competition at the Gadsden Mall. The first prize was a full scholarship to Gadsden State Community College. The judges loved my piece. It was called, "A Cannibal's Stomach."

I had worked on it my whole senior year, carving thin white lines on a black piece of scratchboard. Every day in art class I added something new to the drawing, and the finished artwork had everything from a seahorse to a roller coaster, an accordion to a giraffe to a grocery buggy.

Mr. Norton, the head of the art department at Gadsden State, said it was one of the most original entries he had ever seen, and I won. It wasn't Nashville, but it was better than nothing so I enrolled. I worked part-time and kept saving money.

Ty was a year younger than me and he was still in high school. I broke up with him when I started college, but after a couple of weeks, I realized how much I loved him and wanted him back. There was no one else in that town that I could imagine dating. Everybody knew everybody, so I couldn't go out with anybody that hadn't dated one of my friends or cousins. Ty didn't answer the phone when I called him, but I thought we would get back together. We always got back together. Meanwhile, I still had Jerry, and about once a month we would park out on DeSoto Road and dream about moving to Nashville. But he was dating a new girl and they were getting serious.

I had been in school for about six months when Mom and Mike were weirdly in agreement with Dad that there was nowhere that I could get a job with an art degree. My high school art teacher, Mr. Bentley, rotated between all our district schools, so I'd have to wait around for him to die if I ever wanted a job. Mom, Dad and Mike were convinced I needed to change my major to something in the medical field where there were lots of jobs.

Everyone in my family had different plans for my future. I navigated my way through their negative commentary about who I was and who I would become. Any time I mentioned becoming a songwriter, I got the same response: "Be realistic." I wondered why being realistic was always a negative concept. I wanted to scream at them, "Do you know me at all?"

Mom had completed her training, graduated at the top of her class, and was now a physical therapist. She worked from 8:00 am – 4:00 pm at the hospital, then worked for home health patients afterwards. I decided to take their advice and change my major to occupational therapy, because at least that way I could get a job in Nashville at one of the hospitals. I hated my classes and everything my anatomy and physiology teacher said sounded like the parents from the Charlie Brown cartoons: "Whah, whah, whah."

When I interned at the hospital, I felt like an emotional lint roller. If I saw a family crying, I ended up crying with them. I was useless.

My favorite classes were English 101 and American Literature. Miss Pruitt taught both and she always chose my poetry to read aloud. She encouraged me to enter a statewide essay contest that paid $1,000 to the winner. If I won, I could use that money to move to Nashville, so I poured my heart out working on it. A few weeks later, Miss Pruitt kept me after class and said, "I've got some fantastic news. You won the contest!"

Seconds later, Miss Clark, the Dean of the English Department, knocked on the door and I overheard her talking to Miss Pruitt out in the hall. "Yes, we all agree she wrote the best paper, but we can't give this award to someone who doesn't even understand basic punctuation and grammar. Honestly, I don't know how she graduated high school."

It went from pride to shame in a millisecond. My whole life I've felt dyslexic when it came to punctuation. I don't know if it's because I wrote for so long in my diaries without commas and semicolons, but I've been insecure and embarrassed about my skills ever since. But I'd find a way to make it as a writer the one place I could without understanding punctuation; as a songwriter.

After class, I sat in my Dodge Laser in the parking lot, crying until I had to go to work. That same week, Mr. Norton found out I had dropped most of my art classes and he was furious. "Lots of students want this opportunity and you wasted it and embarrassed me in front of the whole school board by not even talking to me before you changed your major. We've rescinded your scholarship, turn in your books at the library."

Lost

IT HAD BEEN ALMOST TWO YEARS since I graduated from high school and I was as hopeless as I had ever been. I felt stuck in the wrong life. Everything was going wrong. We found out that Maw Maw had lung cancer. The doctor gave her six months to live. We watched her deteriorate right in front of our eyes. She had suffered so much in her life, so seeing her at eighty pounds with no hair or eyebrows, in so much pain, gasping for breath was unbearable and unfair.

For her funeral, my mama did her makeup and all my aunts and uncles pitched in to buy Maw Maw a green silk dress. It was the first new dress I had ever seen her wear. My grandfather fell to his knees at her casket and wailed, "Mary, I'm so sorry. I'm so sorry. I wish I could take it back. I wish I could take it all back." His words echoed cold off the floor.

Our whole family came apart without my grandmother. Mom started spending more and more time in bed and lost thirty pounds in a month. Uncle Kelly wrecked his silver 300 ZX going ninety miles an hour, and a few days later he announced to the family that he was gay.

Uncle Kelly got a job at the Goodyear Tire Plant in Union City, Tennessee and moved a couple of weeks later. I don't know if he plastered all of those centerfolds to his walls to try to turn himself straight or convince Paw Paw that he liked girls, but I do know he carried that secret growing up. Back then, in deep Alabama, boys who came out of the closet could end up in a casket.

It was so hard to go see Paw Paw without my grandmother there. The house felt like a ghost. Paw Paw sat stewing in regret in his recliner. I spent most of my time in the bathroom, smelling her Primo perfume and going through her things. Her hair was still in the brush and her stack of waterlogged Frederick's of Hollywood catalogs still sat on the floor.

All of my problems ganged up on me. I fell into a depression. I blamed myself for what happened at the cheap hotel and the guilt from burning down the house felt like a giant sitting on my chest. I had lost my scholarship, the essay contest, and my boyfriend. Now Maw Maw and Uncle Kelly were both gone, and Jerry had fallen in love with a girl from Birmingham. Ty was dating the most beautiful girl I had ever seen. She looked like my beauty idol, Brooke Shields, like she had just walked out of the movie The Blue Lagoon.

Dr. Dooney, the psychiatrist, put me on antidepressants. I took them, but they made me numb like I was floating alone in a dark ocean and I didn't care if a great white shark bit off my torso or if I sank to the bottom of the black water.

Rust and Stardust

I WAS NINETEEN THE NIGHT I ALMOST ended my life before it had even begun. After I got off work I drove to the Chevron station to see if anyone was hanging out, then I talked my friend Andy into selling me a twelve pack of Coors Light tallboys. I drove around aimlessly until I realized I didn't have anybody to drink the beer with. Everyone was gone. I rode by Ty's house, but he was probably out with his new girlfriend, Rachel. I rode by Jerry's, but he had moved to Birmingham. I wanted to talk to Uncle Kelly, but he lived five and a half hours away now.

I parked out on DeSoto Road, the dead-end dirt road in the woods where Jerry and I always went to dream. Laying with my back against the dirty windshield of my silver Dodge Laser, I grabbed my fifth Coors Light tallboy and killed it. The rusty hood of my car looked like pizza crust and the hot engine burned the back of my thighs through my jeans. I didn't care. I didn't care about anything. "How is this my life?" I asked, staring up at the stars. The moon was hiding and the night was alive around me. Crickets buzzed like a billion broken clocks and I could see the magic smear of the Milky Way arching across the darkness.

"Why would you let me believe for so long in a dream that could never come true? I want to know why," I screamed at the sky. It was October, and red and gold leaves somersaulted all around me. It looked like I was in a snow globe. The wind raced through the pine trees as hysterical as I was. It sounded like it was screaming the same question back at me, "Why?"

"What the fuck?" I screamed at the stars, God, the universe, anything that could hear me. Dogs barked in the distance as tears rolled down my face and pooled in my ears. I was sick of being trapped in that fatalistic town where factory smoke hung in the air like dream repellant.

What did I think? That after my high school graduation, abracadabra, a red carpet was going to roll out and lead me straight to the life of my dreams? That I would wander off into this watercolor sunset of some Jack Kerouac paperback where I was a hit songwriter and madly in love with my soul mate? "How can I be such a fucking idiot?" I asked the clouds moving above me. I could see absolutely no way out of Glencoe, Alabama. My dumbass $300 car wouldn't make it past the Etowah County line, much less to Tennessee.

"So this is my destiny? Stacking expired cans of cat food working at Big Lots? This is why I was born?" I yelled at the night. "Well guess what? You win. I'm done!"

***

AFTER I FINISHED THE TWELVE PACK, I drove around the corner to Ty's house and parked in his driveway. His car was still gone. I knew he was out with his gorgeous new girlfriend. I found the spare key above the door frame in his garage and went inside to wait on him to get home. Ty's mom spent weeknights in Birmingham where her job was.

Ty's bedroom still smelled like cinnamon from the box of one thousand Atomic Fireball candies that I gave him for his birthday. There were souvenirs of us everywhere. The Mardi Gras beads from our trip to New Orleans hung on his dresser around a big green bottle of Jägermeister. I picked up the 1.75 liters, 35% alcohol bottle from his dresser, twisted off the top and took a giant swig. I was so drunk from the Coors Light tallboys that I could barely focus my eyes, but I couldn't stop staring at the little cross and the little deer on the green bottle.

Something inside me wanted to see how drunk I could get. How far into the darkness I could go. The licorice-nickel taste of the liquor almost made me sick, but I was still drinking it when Ty came in a little after 1:00 am.

"Aimee, I don't want you coming over here all fucked up. You know I'm dating Rachel," he said. I was crying and tried to put my arms around his waist and moved in to kiss him, but he pushed me away.

"I love you," I said.

"You can't even stand up, so I know you can't drive. I'm calling your mom."

"Well go a fuckin' head, because she won't answer the phone," I said. I held onto the wall and led myself down the hall into the bathroom. I tried to look at my eyes in the mirror but I stumbled and fell backward into the bathtub. When I pulled myself up, I sat on the rim of the tub and found myself eye level with a razor blade someone had left lying on the counter. Something compelled me to pick it up.

My dream of having a better life was gone. And without it there was nothing.

I grabbed the razor blade and sat on the cold tile floor. I gently ran the blade against my right wrist again and again using more pressure each time until crimson blood bloomed through my skin and dripped like red rain off my arm. I was spinning. I was crying and I thought I might throw up.

Then I led the sharp blade along my left wrist. This time I went deeper and felt the rattled blue adrenaline pumping through my body. The pain made me feel closer to what I was searching for. I was talking to God the whole time, "What's wrong with me? Why am I so fucked up? I don't know what you want me to do." I answered every question with a cut. "Will you please help me?

I need you to show me what to do. I can't do this anymore." I prayed that if I died, God would forgive me. It felt like someone unplugged the world, but a part of me waited inside a black elevator that could go either way.

Somebody shook my shoulder and I tried to open my eyes. Somebody put something over my face. I looked up from the floor and saw Mama standing in the doorway in blood-soaked sweatpants. Paramedics knelt around me, "Stay with us. Open your eyes. Stay with us."

My mother fell to her knees crying. When I saw the look in her eyes, it tore me open with guilt. "Baby, why would you do this?"

"I love you, Mom. I'm so sorry," I said, trying to take the oxygen mask off. The paramedics lifted me onto a stretcher. One of them almost slipped in the pool of blood on the bathroom floor. I faded in and out of consciousness as they rolled me strapped to the stretcher through Ty's living room. *Headbangers Ball* was playing on the TV as they pushed me through the kitchen and out the door into the garage. I heard a loud scraping sound as the stretcher got stuck and I thought they were going to dump me down the stairs.

Inside the ambulance, I felt like I was in some kind of tin can dream. Everything the paramedics said echoed like I was listening from inside a conch shell. I kept my eyes closed, too humiliated to look at anyone. I faded out and came to, shivering on a cold metal table in the emergency room. I smelled the strong smell of rubbing alcohol and heard voices and saw white lab coats hovering above me in the bright light.

I saw my mama in the corner and started yelling at the nurses, "Get my mama out of here. I don't want her to see this. Mom, I'm sorry. I love you."

A doctor in a white lab coat hovered over me. His nose was almost touching mine and his breath was warm on my face and neck. "Your blood alcohol level is dangerously high and we can't give you anything to numb you. Do you understand? Nod if you understand."

"I don't care," I mumbled.

I saw the doctor pick up silver scissors, a needle, and black thread but I couldn't watch him sew me up like a dress. I thought I was ready for the pain. I felt like I deserved it. I closed my eyes as tight as I could and then came the rush of cobalt blue pain. It was so big, so powerful, there was nothing to do but go with it. Each stitch filled me with a silent hysteria. I was praying to pass out. I felt it take my threshold for pain and shatter it into stardust.

Chapter Six

———

SOMEWHERE
OVER THE RAINBOW

Waking Up

I WOKE ALONE IN A BLURRY room to the sound of beeping. Something was biting at the top of my hand and tubes tugged at me every time I moved. My head throbbed so hard that I couldn't focus my eyes. Looking down, I saw I was wearing a paper-thin, backward hospital gown. The front was open, exposing my breasts and the sticky little electrodes that connected me to monitors and blinking machines. Gauze bandages were wound up both of my wrists like sleeves to nowhere. Blood dripped from my hand onto the floor from where I'd pulled the IV loose.

"Give me my fuckin' cigarettes," I heard a man scream right outside my door.

On the bedside table, I saw my neon Converse high tops. They were covered in starfish splatters of blood. The shoelaces were gone. My mouth watered from nausea from the overwhelming smell of urine and disinfectant. When I saw the windows were covered with bars, I sprang up. Electric pain shot through my arm. It was so intense that I almost screamed. The pain was coming from a place inside me that I'd never been aware of. It felt like my veins were trying to eat their way out of my arms. I sat completely still paralyzed by fear of the pain reoccurring.

Flashes of the night before jolted through my mind; the blood on the bathroom floor, Mama standing in the doorway and the horror in her eyes. Oh my God, what have I done? Red hot shame radiated through every cell inside me. My mind rang like a cymbal clashing a million vibrations through me.

"Please God, please don't let this be real. Please. Please don't let this be real," I repeated it over and over until the words became only sounds that I couldn't stop saying, and then another flash from the night before came at me.

I had to see what I had done. I maneuvered my way through the tubes and unlatched the bag connected to my IV. I was so dizzy that I almost fell, but I made my way into the bathroom. I stood at the sink. There was no mirror on the wall and I was glad because I did not want to see my face. There was a stabbing feeling in my throat and my entire being buzzed as I unwrapped the bandage. I pulled the last piece of gauze off.

When I saw my wrist, I felt my chest heave forward and I began throwing up in the toilet. Tears ran down my face and I just kept staring at it. The scar sat up swollen and red around the edges. It looked like some kind of thick upside-down centipede with black legs.

Seeing this wounded me in a spiritual way that I knew would be a part of me forever. I was crying so hard that I couldn't see the tape to cover the scar back up. "What have I done, oh my God in Heaven, what have I done?" My mind exploded in emotions. "What is wrong with me? I could be dead right now. I could be gone." The thought of my mama having to plan my funeral went through my mind.

I will never believe that anyone who tries to take their life really wants to die. I think they are just trying to make the pain stop. The best thing I ever heard about suicide is something Phil Donahue said, that suicide is a permanent solution for a temporary problem.

I put my hand across my chest to feel my heart drumming wildly and I kept it there. I had to get down on my knees for this prayer. I cried in a way I had never cried before or since. "I am so sorry for what I have done. Thank you, God, for this beating heart. Thank you for showing me grace." Inhaling as deep a breath as I could, I exhaled, "I'm alive."

***

MY SECOND DAY IN THE PSYCH WARD, now completely sober, I was as shocked as anyone at what I had done. Mama slept in the yellow, vinyl chair beside the bed, and every time I looked at her, I saw the flash of the moment I wanted to erase the most; the agony in her eyes when she looked down at me covered in blood on the bathroom floor. I hated myself for hurting her like that. She and everyone else had one question,

"Why?" I ached for the answer too. I don't know how I could do something like that.

When I looked at my bandages, a terrifying chill shot through my bones. I tried to block it out, but it just kept coming. My mind replayed the events of the night over and over. I had been down, but I wasn't that down. If I hadn't seen that razor blade, I would have passed out on the couch. I hadn't been thinking about killing myself. I didn't leave the house with the intention of never coming back. I did not want to die. I wanted the exact opposite, to live.

The nurses took everything from the bag that my mama brought me; the hairdryer, the fingernail file. They made her pull the shoelaces from her Keds sneakers. "I'm not gonna kill myself with my mom's shoestrings," I said joking.

The nurse shot me a mean look. No one listened no matter how hard I tried to explain that I didn't know why I did what I did. The hospital staff watched every move I made like I might try to escape or do something else to hurt myself. Dr. Dooney burst into my hospital room. He was the same psychiatrist that I had seen when I was fourteen who put me on so much Lithium that I passed out cold shopping with Mom at Fashion Bug. He reminded me of Captain Kangaroo with an eye twitch.

Sitting down on the arm of the chair next to me, he flipped through some papers on a clipboard. "I think we need to get you on an antidepressant," he said.

"I'm on one."

"And who prescribed them?"

"You did." It would be years before I learned that the antidepressant I was on when I tried to kill myself had been found to cause suicidal feelings and behavior in children and teenagers.

"Okay, did you drink alcohol last night?" he asked.

"Yes."

"How much?"

"A lot."

"What did you drink?"

"Twelve Coors Light tallboys and a big bottle of Jägermeister."

"Do you still want to harm yourself?" he asked.

"No. I just got drunk and did something stupid. I don't want to hurt myself. I promise."

He sat there taking notes and making noises and looked out into space like he had a crystal ball to read my soul, and then he kept on writing.

Later that night, I woke up with the TV blaring a football game. My father sat at the end of my hospital bed in a Hawaiian button-down shirt, eating a piece of fried chicken. "Hey, Daddy," I said, kicking him with my foot.

"Aimee, you're lucky I didn't have a heart attack when Opal called me," he said. "Do you know how bad you scared everybody?"

"I know. I'm sorry. I just did something stupid. Nobody believes me."

"Well, how many stitches did you get?"

"Twelve."

"You know everybody's gonna know you slit your wrists and think you're some kind of psycho when they see that scar."

"Well, you're one to talk. You got a scar all the way across your chest from where you shot yourself."

"Yeah, but you can't see mine," Daddy said, picking at his teeth with a toothpick.

"Well everybody knows you're crazy whether they can see it or not," I said, laughing.

"This ain't funny, Aimee, you could have died."

"I know it ain't funny," I said, holding up my bandaged arms. "You're funny. We've all been on suicide watch with you since I was eight years old."

"Dammit Aimee, I'm bipolar. You don't know what it's like to go through weeks without sleeping. You don't know the depressions I go through."

"Why did you even come up here, to try and make me feel worse?"

"No, I came up here to check on you and to tell you that when you get out of the hospital, you can come stay with me for a while in Nashville."

I hugged him. "Do you swear I can move in with you?"

"Yeah, but you're gonna have to keep the apartment clean and do my laundry."

"I will, I will! I'm so excited!"

Paw Paw called to check on me. "I love you," he said, then joked, "I'll kick your little ass if you ever try anything like that again."

Opal and Harold visited. Opal looked at my bandages more than she did me. "Baby, we love you so much. Let me pray for you," she said and sat down on the bed next to me and held my hand. "Dear Heavenly Father, we ask that you watch over Aimee, Lord. Please help her to feel better and to know that she can always depend on you and that you know what's best for her. Please let her know how much we love her and please watch over and protect her, Lord. In Jesus' name, we pray. Amen."

Harold brought me a roast beef sandwich from Hardees, a VCR, and two of my favorite movies: *The Breakfast Club* and *Terms of Endearment*. He sat down in the chair beside me. "Baby doll, I need you to promise me that nothing like that's ever gonna happen again." I gave him my word and I kept it, even though I had no idea that in less than a year I'd be in the biggest mess I ever made.

Ty and Jerry and some friends from high school came to visit. No one knew what to say and neither did I. I asked my friends not to tell anybody what had happened, but in a small town, everybody knows everything about everybody else.

When I was released from the hospital, I wanted to kiss the ground and climb the trees. I felt like I was alive for a reason, and as bad as things had been, they started getting better.

It was October, so I had two months to get everything together to move to Nashville. I was terrified that Daddy would change his mind, but he was being nicer to me than ever.

A couple of weeks after I got out of the hospital, Ty came over so we could talk about what happened. We got back together that night. Ty said he had a surprise for me, so we went to our local pet store. He pointed out a little, flat-faced Persian calico kitten. "It's on layaway, but I plan on having it paid off in a couple of weeks," he said. We went to visit my little kitten, who I named Curtis, every few days until he paid off the layaway and I got to

take him home. Even though I knew Ty would never leave Gadsden, he said he would visit me. And Jerry promised he would
come to stay with me as soon as I got settled in. I was happy Jerry had met someone who valued and adored him.

I had been calling my little cat Curtis for a few days before
discovering he was a she, but the name fit her, so I kept it.

***

THE NIGHT BEFORE I WAS LEAVING FOR NASHVILLE,
I rode to Opal and Harold's to have supper. I could see people in
my family and my friends trying to catch a glimpse of my wrist,
but as soon as they saw any part of the scar, they quickly turned
away. Daddy was at Opal and Harold's and he said he had a surprise for me. Everybody was giving me presents.

"Baby doll, I got you a car," he said.

"What kind?" I asked.

"It's a Volkswagen Golf." I had never heard of that, but I was ecstatic.

That afternoon, I rode with Dad over to some guy's house
that had a junkyard behind it. There was a gate, and the whole
back yard was filled with rusted and wrecked cars, some without
doors or missing tires. "Oh, my Lord, what kind of car is he giving me," I thought and then the man pulled through the gate in
a light blue Volkswagen Golf.

It had four doors and a hard roof. It looked about five years
old, but it was the newest, most beautiful car I had ever had. I saw
the guy we were getting the car from yelling at Dad. Then I saw
my dad pointing in that guy's face. "Oh my gosh, I'm not going
to get it," I thought, and I got out of the car to see if I could help
the situation.

"Aimee, get back in the damn car," Dad said. I walked back
and leaned against the passenger side door of Dad's car. He had
won that Volkswagen Golf in a bet on a football game and when
the guy finally gave him the keys, he followed Dad back to where
I was.

"Danny, you need to take this car immediately to a mechan-
ic. She don't need to be driving it 'til you get the fuel line fixed."

Dad threw me the keys. "I'm serious, Danny, she don't need to be driving that car," the guy said, and shook his head as he went back up the steps to his house.

Dad said not to worry about the car, that we could get it fixed in Nashville. He left that night to drive back to Tennessee to his apartment.

The next morning I got up and rode out to Paw Paw's to tell him bye and Mike helped me load up my car. He was a different person. He went out of his way to be nice to me.

Car on Fire

I LEFT FOR NASHVILLE THE NEXT DAY and drove with the windows down and the wind fighting with my hair. "Sweet Child of Mine" blasted on the radio and I had never felt so free. The sky was as blue as a song and the sun was shining down on the highway like the golden door to my dreams. Cruising along Interstate 59, I barely paid attention to the road in front of me. I was busy daydreaming about winning song of the year at the CMA Awards or songwriter of the year at BMI.

Somewhere before Monteagle, Tennessee, I stopped and filled the tank up with gas. I bought a Mountain Dew and a Moon Pie. Everything I had was crammed into the backseat: my watermelon patterned serving tray, the pitcher and matching glasses, my Hello Kitty bath mat, CDs, books, TV, and VCR. I couldn't see anything out the back window.

A couple of miles after I got back on the interstate, a group of guys in a dirty, black pickup truck pulled up beside me hootin' and hollerin' for me to pull over. The more aggressive they became, the more I ignored them. I turned up the radio and focused on the road. There was no way I was stopping the car.

I looked over at the sunburned, shirtless guy hanging out the passenger side window of the pickup, locked eyes with the driver, and sped up to pass them. They pulled into my lane, right behind me, and I slammed on the brakes, almost causing a wreck. I started driving like a maniac, speeding up and slowing down, determined to show them who was crazier. They swerved in front of me and peeled off at the next exit. I looked in the rearview mirror and thought, "Damn, I must look good." My dark hair was a tangled mess, and I didn't have any makeup on.

A few minutes later, a burgundy minivan came up beside me and honked. A man was driving, and a heavyset woman with big auburn hair flapped her arms and motioned for me to roll the window down. I couldn't make out what she was saying, so I tried to get a little closer and almost sideswiped their van.

"What?"

"Your blar on tire," she said.

"What?" I tried to get closer again.

"Your car is on fire!" Her words hit me about the same time as the smell of the smoke. I looked down and saw the passenger side floorboard was in flames, about to ignite the front seat. I tried to slam the brakes, but the back of my ankle burned, and the pain made me jerk my leg up. The brakes didn't work. I kept stomping but nothing.

Everything disappeared, except for one thought: I just filled this car up with gas.

Gas, fire.

Gas, fire.

Explosion.

I could see it all happen. In every movie that I had ever seen when a car caught on fire...boom! A big orange fireball explosion and game over. Any second I'd be dead.

I looked down and my sock was on fire. I kicked my leg and smashed my shin under the steering wheel. Flames leapt across the floorboard and the gas pedal. I stomped the brakes with both feet. The smoke burned my eyes and coated my throat. The fire kept jumping up under my thighs.

"The emergency brake," I remembered and yanked it as hard as I could with both hands. The car slowed and crunched gravel on the side of the pebbled median and rolled to a stop at the edge of a three-foot ditch.

Frozen in shock, I waited to die but my car door flung open and a skinny guy in a red and white striped Kentucky Fried Chicken uniform yelled at me, "Who else is in there?" He looked around to see if anyone was trapped.

"My cat. My cat Curtis," I said as she shot through the window like a fur rocket.

"RUN! RUN!" the guy screamed. He grabbed my hand and pulled me out of the car. "It's gonna blow!" he shouted as we ran fifty feet towards his truck. I grabbed Curtis along the way. "Get in!" he said, and I jumped in the front seat. He moved us a little farther away from the flaming car.

"Shit, I didn't even get my purse," I said.

"Well, you can't get it now," he looked at me like I was crazy.

I had a $50 bill from Paw Paw in my wallet and now I was stranded with no money.

I always wore bracelets on my left arm and I had taken them off because they were hurting from holding the steering wheel. The KFC guy asked, "If you don't mind me asking, why didn't you get out of that car?" He spotted the scar up my wrist and I could see it in his eyes. Dad was right. He thinks I'm a psycho.

"I couldn't move. I thought I was about to blow up. I thought I was dead," I answered his question.

BAM! We both jumped. One of my tires blew. Curtis pounced out of my arms and into the woods along the interstate. Cars were pulling over to get in on the action. There was a crowd now gathering near my car.

"What happened?" a man asked. "I don't know. I'm trying to find my cat," I said, and waded through the waist-high weeds and thick kudzu, worried that she was gone forever. The other three tires popped one by one and then the windows shattered.

"We found your cat!" a man shouted a few minutes after I began my search. When he brought her to me, she trembled, clearly traumatized. Lenny, my hero, the KFC guy, and about twenty strangers, stayed and watched as my car burned.

"I'm gonna be late for work," Lenny said. "Is there somewhere I can take you?"

"Maybe a gas station or something. Somewhere with a payphone."

He lit a cigarette and I asked for one. "Here, take the pack," he said. "You need 'em more than I do," and handed them to me.

As we pulled into a mega gas station and fireworks store called Alabama Tennessee Fireworks World, I jumped out of the truck. I leaned back through the passenger side window and said, "I'm Aimee and I'll forever be grateful. You saved my life. Thank you," and I started to cry.

"I hope you're okay," Lenny said, and drove away.

I wandered into the massive fireworks store and truck stop and as I stepped inside, a woman screamed at me from behind the counter, "Get out! Get out! Go all the way across the street!" she kept shouting and followed me out the double doors. We were outside before I understood what was happening. It was a fireworks store. "Keep going. You've got to be fifty feet away. Put that cigarette out," she said.

Then I noticed the enormous signs posted everywhere. I must have looked like Fire Marshall Bill from that TV show, *In Living Color*; black soot and ash smeared down my legs, a hole burned in the top of my sock, a traumatized cat in one hand, and a lit cigarette in the other. There had to be twenty red and white bold lettered signs, "No Smoking" and "No Smoking Within Fifty Feet." I marched across the pavement and gravel and stomped my cigarette out. I felt the tears coming again and then the humor of what happened hit me. When I walked back in, the woman who shooed me out was behind the counter. "What were you thinking?"

I just looked at her. "My car is on fire down the road."

"Where is your car?"

"It's on the interstate about a mile away."

"Did somebody get the fire out?" she asked.

"No."

"You just left the car burning on the side of the interstate?" She called the fire department and told them someone needed to get there fast.

"Everything I have is gone. I didn't even get my purse. I don't have any money."

"Honey, come sit down," she said. "What can I do to help?" I asked to use the phone and called my dad.

"Is it long distance? Oh, go ahead, just make it quick."

I called him collect. "Daddy, that car you gave me almost killed me!"

"Aimee, what are you talking about?"

"Daddy, that car just caught on fuckin' fire and I'm stranded at a gas station."

"Well, who are you gonna call about it?"

"I'm calling you about it. That's who I'm gonna call about it. "

"Well, baby doll, I can't come get you right now. I've got a lot of money on this Alabama game. We can just tow the car and I'll come get you in a little while."

"You can't tow ashes, you idiot," I said louder than I meant to through the phone. "Come get me now."

"Quit being so dramatic. Did you call your mama about picking you up?"

"I'm eighty miles from Nashville."

"I'll come to get you after the game, Aimee."

"Okay, Dad, just leave me here at some truck stop full of scary-looking perverts," I whispered with anger shaking my voice. I sat down on the curb, starving, with Curtis tied to a shoestring that I'd attached to my belt loop. When it got dark, a guy without a shirt on came over and started talking to me.

The checkout lady stuck her head out the door and said, "Come on in and wait inside. You can bring your cat." I wandered through the aisles and spotted all the racist souvenirs. There were Aunt Jemima cookie jars, and rebel flags on everything. There were personalized key chains, saltwater taffy, and a shelf full of porn magazines.

When it was almost dark, Daddy finally pulled up in his black Z24 Chevy convertible. "Thanks, it only took you five fuckin' hours to get here. If I had gotten raped, it would have been your fault."

We drove to look at the remains of the VW. Peeking in through the windows, I waited for another car to pass so I could see the damage. All my clothes were scorched and my favorite purple velour dress was gone. My word processor, the keyboard, was melted and the screen was charred black. All my hope chest treasures were gone. I had lost everything all over again. Everything except my cat, Curtis, and a couple of boxes with my yearbooks and diaries that I had left at home in Alabama.

"Oh my God, Aimee. We gotta go get a camera. I'm gonna sue Louie's ass off."

"This is your fault. I heard that guy tell you ten times we needed to get this car fixed. That could have killed me."

Daddy drove around on back roads for forty-five minutes,

looking for an open Walmart. He bought a disposable camera and a flashlight, and we went back to the skeleton of the car. He walked out into the interstate to take pictures and almost got hit by a semi-truck.

Nashville

FINALLY, I WAS IN NASHVILLE. It had been eleven years since I lived under the same roof as my father. I romanticized the idea of staying with him when I was growing up because every time that I visited it was like an endless party, but I didn't know how scary his depressions were. All those times he disappeared for months when I was a kid, now I knew why.

Dad's three-bedroom apartment at Royal Arms looked like the picture of insanity. When you opened the door, the first thing you saw was a ten foot tall, taxidermy grizzly bear. It was reared up on his hind legs with razor-sharp claws and big white teeth coming straight at you. It startled everyone that stepped inside. Dad had a pair of Akitas, Moses and Ruth, two, hundred-pound dogs that he never walked.

The sofas looked like a werewolf had shredded them. There was spongy stuffing sticking out of everywhere like a hundred white tongues. Dad also had a potbellied pig named Benson. He named it after some fat guy he didn't like during the Elvis car days. I couldn't believe my eyes the first time I saw that little pig get a running start and dive into Dad's bathtub. He used it like a litter box. I kept Curtis in my bedroom with the door shut.

The apartment looked like Costco after a tornado. The jukebox in the corner lit up yellow and red and had 45s of all Dad's songs, along with his favorites from Bob Seeger, Jackson Browne, and Bruce Springsteen. The dining room table was covered in half-written lyrics, work tape cassettes, and three *How to Train Your Dog* books. Dad's manic purchases were piled high on every counter; baseball cards, an artist easel with watercolors, vitamin powder for milkshakes, a cardboard box with 100 pairs of socks from the flea market, and stacks and stacks of smashed, generic soda cans.

There were boxes and boxes of pornos left over from when Dad sold the video stores. "I thought you burned all these X-rated movies," I said.

"Aimee, that's $10,000 worth of movies. I just burned the boxes."

In the corner was a giant glass jar containing two bull testicles. Dad purchased them from a slaughterhouse. He had wanted to get Garth Brooks' attention when he pitched him one of his new songs. He dropped off the cassette tape with the jar and a note, "You're the only one with the balls to cut this song."

Framed gold and platinum record plaques were leaned up against the wall from Daddy's hit songs. The number one, "If I Had You" by Alabama, and a duet for George Jones and Tammy Wynette, "If God Met You, She Wouldn't Like You" were among the many on display. Dad had at least one songwriting appointment every day. His apartment was a revolving door of songwriters and country music artists.

One morning I woke up to Randy Travis rattling around in the kitchen looking for a coffee pot. "Hey, Aimee, where's your daddy?"

"I haven't seen him in days."

"Well, we're supposed to be writing," Randy said, and I sat down on the couch. He played me a couple of his songs, "On the Other Hand" and "Digging Up Bones." Both were number ones. When he came out in the late 80s, there was nobody like him on the radio, but Daddy said, "Wait and see. He's gonna be a huge star," and he was. I told Randy that I wanted to write songs and he was the first one that didn't make me feel stupid for saying it. So I ran to grab my binder off my bed and just as I sat down to tell him some of my titles, Dad arrived. "Hey Frankenstein," Dad said to Randy and laughed. Dad always aggravated the shit out of Randy. He called him Frankenstein because he said he had a square head.

"He's an idiot," I told Randy.

"I know," he said and we both laughed.

I sat at the kitchen table ten feet away listening to them. I always eavesdropped when Daddy was writing songs. I changed the verses and the rhymes in my head and called out an idea for a line when they were stuck. My dad said, "Nobody would ever say that, Aimee." Any time I tried to talk to Dad about wanting to write songs we got into a fight, and every time we fought, he told me I was tone-deaf. It broke my heart a little bit more, but part of me didn't believe him.

There were two females that Dad wrote with occasionally, but they were both amazing singers who wrote songs for their records. I did not know one single girl songwriter like me who didn't play guitar or sing. "Aimee, I can count the female songwriters in this town on one hand," he held up two fingers, "and they're all lesbians." I don't know what the lesbian part had to do with it or who he was talking about.

Every time he told me I couldn't write, there was a little voice inside me that said, "Yes I can." I left my giant poetry binder on the kitchen table, but he never even glanced at it. "I've got good song titles. You could get lots of ideas from my poems."

"Aimee, I've got my own ideas."

Music City

I WAS SO HAPPY LIVING IN Music City! Nashville! Seven nights a week, the whole town was a jukebox of dreamers, wannabes, and stars. I was in love. Even though Cory and I grew up visiting Dad in Nashville, it was nothing compared to being twenty with my own car, a white Nissan Sentra that my mama gave me to replace the VW. Sometimes I parked and stared at the Nashville skyline. I couldn't believe I lived somewhere with a skyline.

I loved driving down Broadway at night with the windows rolled down so I could catch all the live music pouring out of night-spots like Tootsies, Robert's Western World, and Printer's Alley. Each one was an open door to a different world full of neon signs, cowboys, and honky-tonk angels.

When Dad was manic, it was magic. It was like being with a fourteen-year-old with a million dollars. On the weekends, we went out to Writer's Nights where songwriters sit in a circle in the center of the room, or on stage, and play their biggest hits and newest creations. Almost every time, someone left me breathless with a song. I would say a prayer right then and there that someday I would write a song that good.

We went to concerts. Dad loved seeing shows at the Ryman

Auditorium, the most famous venue in Music City. Daddy always said, "Somebody's gotta be the real deal to play the Ryman. It's the Carnegie Hall of the South." I stared up at the sapphire and ruby stained-glass windows and said another prayer that I'd hear one of my songs there. I would have never imagined that someday I would stand barefoot on that stage and feel the magic of the blonde oak floor vibrate through me as I sang one of the most played country songs of all time.

***

I HAD ONLY BEEN IN NASHVILLE a couple of weeks when Daddy caught me smoking and threatened to send me back to Alabama. Being under the same roof with my father meant doing whatever he said. If he wanted me to spend the weekend babysitting for his friend's kids or to go to Kroger in the middle of the night for provolone cheese, I did it.

The first task Dad gave me was to do his laundry. Dad never did his laundry. He just bought new clothes and I had never seen so many clothes. The tables at Duds and Suds were piled so high that it looked like the men's department at Walmart. I spent over fifteen hours washing and drying his clothes and hung them all on hangers in his closet. Then he came in screaming at me, "You didn't even touch the clothes in the closet."

"What closet?"

"The storage closet." I followed him down the hall and he pointed to a pile of clothes taller than I was. "Aimee, you can't do anything right. I don't even know why I asked you," he said and stormed off to his room.

The next day, I got all of those clothes, put them in trash bags, and dropped them off at Southern Thrift. Then I almost had a heart attack when Dad pulled into the same thrift store parking lot on the way to lunch one day. I saw him gathering shirts that I knew were his; an aqua Hawaiian print shirt, a blue penguin polo. I thought he was headed toward me to cuss me out, but he just said, "They've never had so many shirts in my size. Here, hold these." I watched him buy back his own clothes.

Mood Swings and Acid Trip

DADDY'S MOOD SWINGS WERE getting worse. Worse than I'd ever seen them and I knew I had to find a job so I could save my money and get my own apartment. One morning I sat at the kitchen table with Dad while I went through classified ads.

"I think I'm gonna be a waitress," I said.

"Well, you ought to go see if Brown's Diner is hiring."

"Are you talking about that weird trailer place?"

"Yeah, you've gotta work somewhere that serves meat, cuz everybody knows vegetarians don't tip worth a shit." Brown's Diner was located directly behind a gas station.

When I pulled into the parking lot, the last thing it looked like was a restaurant. It was a double-wide trailer that was somehow connected to a caboose. Walking through the door was like going back in time. There was wood paneling on the walls, ten tables, and five booths. It was full of character, charming, tacky, and a little crazy. Country Music Television blasted from a TV in the upper corner of the dining room. The place was busy, so I stood against the wall waiting to ask for an application. A bony waitress with big glasses marched past me, opened the door behind some customers and threw a handful of pocket change at them. "Keep your damn pennies," she yelled.

Just as I started to ask her again, she shooed me out of the way so a big group of people could come in.

"Forget this. There's no way I'm working here," I thought and headed toward the back door to leave. Then I saw Garth Brooks, and a group of what looked like musicians, pushing some tables together. I sat down at a booth, ordered an iced tea, and eavesdropped and waited.

"Can I get an application?" I asked the waitress. She looked at me like I was crazy and pointed toward the little smoky bar room located in the caboose.

It was filled with men sitting on barstools. The bartender looked like a Hell's Angel with a scruffy black and gray beard and a leather vest. I watched him filling up icy, frosted mugs with the only beer they served: Budweiser draft. I stood under a neon sign next to the register until he noticed me.

"Yeah, can I help you?"

"I wanted to see about getting an application." He started laughing, "What the hell do you want to work here for?"

"Um, Danny Mayo's my dad and he sent me down here to see if y'all are hiring."

"How old are you? You've got to be of age to serve alcohol."

"I'll be 21 on Sunday."

"Terry, give her the damn job. You haven't hired a new waitress since Watergate," a man at the jukebox yelled out. I later learned he was Don Everly of the Everly Brothers, "All I Had to Do Was Dream, Dream, Dream."

I sat down on a barstool and knew within minutes that Terry was going to hire me. "Okay, you can start on Monday."

Betty, the head waitress, trained me. She was in her fifties and her face looked like a roadmap of every bad decision she had ever made. She would deliver cheeseburgers with a cigarette dangling from her lip and dare somebody to say something about it. It took a while for the waitresses to warm up to me, but before long they were like my aunts, giving me advice and telling me everything I did wrong.

Brown's Diner was a song writer's haven. It was about a mile from Music Row and every day at lunch, famous country artists, legendary songwriters, record executives, and publishers flooded in for the best cheeseburger in Nashville. I made a deal with the head waitress, Darlene, that I could wait on her tables as long as I gave her the tips, so when any music people came in, I jumped up to take their orders.

The only problem was, I was the worst waitress in Tennessee. They should have had a plaque on the wall engraved with my name. If songwriters came in, I had tunnel vision. I hovered around their tables trying to soak in every word, compulsively filling their iced tea. It wasn't long until I knew most of the songwriters and artists who came in and before I asked what they wanted to eat, I always asked, "Are y'all writing a hit today?" Garth Brooks said, "If this song's a hit, I'll come back and tell ya."

One of the first people I met about one month after I started working at Brown's was Kenny Chesney. He had a record deal, but the company was closing their doors. We sat and talked about what he was going to do next. He had a song that I loved called "The Tin Man."

Kenny came in a couple of times a week for a free lunch with his publisher, Opryland Music Group. He was a struggling artist and broke, just like me. If he was ever by himself, he always ordered a burger and water, and I slipped him fries and a Coke. We talked about our dreams and our plans, and I always got in trouble for sitting at his table laughing instead of taking orders.

I met other artists before they were famous. When Faith Hill came in, I thought she was the prettiest girl I had ever seen in my life. Everything about her was beautiful, her smile, the dimple in her chin, her big, brown doe eyes. I heard some record label executives talking. They were trying to choose her first single and I knew she was going to be a superstar. Still, I never dreamed we would become close friends and that she'd teach me how to make potato salad and take me on a private shopping spree at Barney's and be there when I learned to snow ski.

Mary Chapin Carpenter came in a few times. She was one of the only female artists getting hits that she wrote on the radio. I stared at her and the two songwriters she was with, I wanted to be one of them so much that it made me physically ache. I was surprised that my passion didn't ignite the red and white checkered tablecloth and burst the table into flames. I wanted to ask them to write so bad I couldn't breathe, but I knew that they would just look at me like I asked to pull one of their teeth.

***

DAD WENT TO JAIL TWICE THAT SPRING. Living with him when he was manic was like "riding a psychotic horse into a blazing barn" as Robin Williams said in the movie *The Birdcage*.

Any time we got into the car, it was like getting into a broken time machine; I never knew where we were going or when we were coming back. We would leave for the grocery store and end up three states away on a riverboat casino, or at the horse races, or broken down on the side of the road somewhere in Kentucky covered in chiggers. It was fun, fun, fun until the cops took my daddy away. I didn't have any choice but to go with Dad because I was his designated driver and get out of jail card. If I lived with him, I had to do what he said or he'd kick me out. If he spontaneously decided to go gambling for a couple of days in a different state and wanted me to join him, I had to call in sick at Brown's and go.

One night we went out to Douglas Corner, Daddy's favorite bar. Then ended up at Joe's Pub in Green Hills. Daddy was buying everybody drinks, falling in love, and yelling at the cover band to play "Tupelo Honey." He stumbled onto the stage with his signature drink, a Seven and Seven, Seagram's Seven mixed with Seven-Up, in each hand. He sang the words and melodies to one of his songs over the music. He never sang in front of anyone unless he was loaded, and his voice always reminded me of a drunk Van Morrison. He had a soulful tone, but he couldn't really control it right.

When we left the bar that night, Dad almost got arrested for urinating on the hood of a red Mercedes owned by Jimmy Bowen, the head of Atlantic Records. The police officers were about to put him in the back of their car when I begged them, "Please let me walk him back to our apartment. We live right around the corner." I was underaged and a little drunk, half carrying, half dragging Daddy down Richard Jones Road while the police car drove slowly right beside us. "We could arrest him for public intoxication and indecent exposure," one of the officers told me. The other one said, "He should go to jail for the scene he just caused."

"We live right here," I said, and pointed to Royal Arms Apartments. Just as I walked over to the stairs that led to Daddy's upper-level unit, the officer said, "You got lucky this time." Daddy turned around and yelled, "Fuck you!" and about that time he was in handcuffs on the concrete before I knew what happened. "You're a damn idiot," I said, watching them put him in the back of the police car.

A few weeks later, the phone rang, rattling me awake at around 4:00 am. Before I could think twice, I answered it. "You

have a collect call from Davidson County Jail. Do you accept?"
My dad came on the line shouting over the automated operator,
"Baby doll, I'm in jail. You gotta come to get me. I have figured
a bunch of shit out."

Less than an hour later, I was sitting on a bean bag chair
eating sunflower seeds in the living room office of a run-down
trailer. There was a pit bull sniffing at my crotch, there was a
two-foot stack of porn magazines on the table beside me, and
Beavis and Butt-Head was blasting on the TV. I waited while Marshall, the bail bonds guy, filled out some of Dad's paperwork. He
was skinny and had a tattoo of Yosemite Sam holding a gun in
one hand and a rebel flag in the other. Marshall's black hair was
short except for a rat tail about the length of a shoestring hanging
halfway down his back. Every time he asked me a question, he
tried to look down my shirt.

When I got to the jail, the clerk told me that Daddy had been
charged with indecent exposure, disturbing the peace, and being
under the influence of an illegal substance. He had taken three
hits of acid and was arrested naked and screaming in some lady's
yard. "Did they bring him up here naked?" I asked.

"No, he was wearing a bedsheet that kept falling off," the
lady snickered. I heard someone on a talk box announce, "Mr.
Mayo is ready to go." The police were the only ones who ever
called my dad, "Mr. Mayo." He walked out wearing a bright orange jumpsuit with "Davidson Correctional Facility" stenciled in
black letters across the back and he had on brown tasseled loafers.
He reminded me of Christopher Lloyd's character flinging open
the door to the silver DeLorean in *Back to The Future*.

When I looked into his brown eyes, they were dilated the size
of dimes. I marched straight back to the window and asked the
lady, "Do I have to take him?"

"He made bail. We can't keep him, honey."

"I don't think he's ready to go home," I said. Daddy came at
me and slung his arm around my shoulder so hard he almost
knocked me down.

"I've been on the edges of the universe tonight, baby doll.
Let's go to the Courthouse Café. They've got the best country
fried ham in town."

I'd seen Daddy wear handcuffs more times than I'd seen him wearing a watch, but I had never seen him zooming on LSD in the middle of a manic spell in a police station. "He's gonna have to return that jumpsuit," the clerk said.

"Yeah, that's gonna happen," I thought.

"I don't want breakfast," I told him. "I want to go back to bed." I knew there was no sense in arguing, so I followed him down the hall. The sun was coming up as we walked into the small restaurant. We sat down at the booth and a waitress came over to take our order. Daddy was holding the menu upside down and talking nonstop. He didn't even know she was there. "He'll have country fried ham and I'll have biscuits and gravy and we'll have two Cokes." A group of four or five police officers came in and sat at a table about ten feet from us.

Every time Dad raised his voice, one of the sleepy, cranky cops looked over at us. He still had on the prisoner uniform, so they didn't know quite what was going on. I picked at my breakfast, wishing I'd never answered the phone as Daddy speared a heaping bite of country ham that never made it to his mouth. It landed in his lap. "I know who the Devil is," he shouted, slamming his fist on the table. He hit it so hard the plates and saucers jumped. "It's James Del Toro." He was the president of a record label who had connections to the mob. "I could just think about somebody, Aimee. Anybody. And BAM, I knew their soul; angel or devil."

"Daddy, can we please eat and get out of here?"

"What the fuck was that?" he yelled, swatting away at what he thought were bats and knocking his Coke over. He couldn't have caused more of a scene if he had fallen on the floor and started having a seizure. He leaned over the table, getting right up in my face, "It's like I woke up from amnesia and remember everything I had forgotten." The waitress approached our table again and cautiously sat down the check. I finally got Daddy out of there and we drove down Broadway heading back to the apartment. Dad kept getting in my face trying to tell me about the revelations he had and made me swerve up onto the sidewalk.

"Put your seat back, Daddy and close your eyes. You're freaking me out." He obeyed for a moment, but then sprang right back up, "I see more shit with my eyes closed," he said. As we pulled up to the apartment complex, Daddy looked over at me and said, "Just so you know, you're an angel."

When he was up, he was like a fireworks grand finale, neon bursting through the darkness. But when it all burned away, all that was left were smoke spiders disappearing into the night. When Dad was down, he was a different person. He spent months in bed in the dark and didn't talk to me except to ask me to bring him a burger home from Brown's, or to pick up some groceries. He didn't leave the bed except to go to the kitchen or bathroom. Every day after work, I was scared that I would come in and find that he had shot himself in the head. I lived in constant fear of him dying by his own hand.

When I flipped on the light in his bedroom and made a trail through the knee-high swamp of newspapers to pick up plates, they looked like science projects covered in moldy food. He started screaming at me, "Aimee, get the fuck out of my room. Call your mama and tell her you're moving back home. I don't want you here." He did that about twice a week, so I would stay away from him until he forgot he was mad.

Somewhere Over the Rainbow

WHEN I TURNED TWENTY-ONE, it was the loneliest birthday of my life. I missed my friends in Alabama and wished I had someone to celebrate with. The only people I knew were Dad's buddies and the servers from Brown's, but they were all a couple of decades older than me. I went to the mall to get a new outfit, then to Davis-Kidd Booksellers. Just as I stepped onto the escalator to go up to the second floor, I saw a couple coming down the parallel escalator. The guy was gorgeous. He was standing behind his blind girlfriend with his arms wrapped around her and as we passed each other, we locked eyes. He yelled out, "I'm in love with this girl!"

It felt like he had hit me in the heart with his fist. I heard her laughing, "Shh, you're crazy," she said. I exploded into tears before I made it to the second floor. I got off the escalator, turned around and went right back down out into the night.

When I got back to Dad's apartment, he was dressed up and eager to introduce me to his companion, a chubby girl with dark hair.

"Hey, baby doll, I want you to meet your new stepmom."

I rolled my eyes. He introduced every girl using the same stupid line. No matter who he was with, he had someone waiting in the wings. He made every girl think that she was the love of his life, the one he had always been waiting for. He was fun, spontaneous, and declared his love for her, but I knew he would break her heart like crackers in soup. Then I'd be left with a crying, raccoon-eyed girl wondering what had happened, what she did wrong, and why he disappeared.

That night I could not deal with watching him and his latest victim, so I walked across the street to Hillsboro High School. It was freezing, and I was shivering, but I made myself walk four miles. Why can't I find somebody who loves me? All I had ever wanted was somebody to love me. To really, really, really love me. But I was thirty pounds overweight and miserable. I thought that if I wasn't such a fat ass, maybe I could find a boyfriend. I spent most nights writing in my spiral notebooks, dreaming about my soul mate. Maybe I was too desperate for love. Maybe everyone could see the flashing neon vacancy sign I wore on my heart. Some nights I wrote songs and sang as I walked. Some nights I lay in the wet grass in the middle of the football field and stared up at the stars talking to God. "Please send somebody to love me. I'm so sick of being alone."

Since I didn't have any friends, I passed a lot of the time wandering around Tower Records. I could stay in there for hours listening to CDs and looking at books. I always rented a video before I left. One night, when I was returning a movie, my heart froze as I looked at the dark-haired guy behind the counter. He had deep brown eyes and dimples. I couldn't move.

Finally, I worked up the courage to ask him, "Is there anything new that's good?"

"Let me see what we got." He walked around the counter and led me down an aisle of movies. "Have you seen *Clockwork Orange*? What about *Blue Velvet*?"

I picked up a box and acted like I was reading it. "Oh yeah, this looks awesome." I followed him back to the register. His name was Zach, and before long I had his schedule memorized. He didn't work on Tuesdays or Sundays, and he worked the day shift on Saturdays. I never rented the movies I wanted to see, like *Pretty Woman* or *An Officer and a Gentleman*. Instead, I always rented whatever he suggested. Every time he smiled at me, I fell a little bit more in love.

But he was moody. Some nights he talked my ear off and walked around the store pointing out movies, and other nights he ignored me completely. Now I was filling all of my notebooks with love songs about Zach being the one I had been waiting for all of my life. I imagined telling him all of my dreams about us dating and moving to East Nashville, the coolest part of town.

I had no idea how to find co-writers, and almost everyone who came into Brown's during the lunch shift was established with publishing deals. I knew from watching Dad that no one professional wanted to write with someone without a writing deal. One problem was that it cost hundreds of dollars to demo songs and most unsigned writers couldn't pay their part. So, most of the music publishers encouraged their writers not to do it. But I fantasized that once I found a boyfriend and fell in love, everything else would fall into place.

I stood around night after night, talking to whoever was working at Tower Video, digging for information about Zach. Marty, one of the other guys who worked there, looked just like Mick Mars from Motley Crue. He always wanted to talk to me. I could tell he had a crush on me. His face looked more like an earring rack. There were piercings everywhere, eyebrow, nose, and tongue. When he talked, he would roll his tongue ring around and it made me cringe.

Marty mentioned that Zach smoked a lot of pot and I knew that Daddy had a giant Mason jar full of marijuana in his sock drawer. So, one Friday night, I took a handful of it and put it in a Ziploc bag. When I got to Tower, I found Zach and told him, "I've got some killer weed if you want to smoke when you get off work."

"Yeah man, meet me in the parking lot at midnight."

I knew his favorite band was Smashing Pumpkins, so I bought

their CD, and had it queued to play right when he opened my car door. I had smoked pot once in Panama City and it was disastrous. I got so paranoid and panic-stricken that I thought my kidneys stopped working and I kept thinking that I was forgetting how to breathe. I waited for him out in my Sentra, then a little after midnight I felt a flutter in my stomach as I watched him walk out to my car.

"Hey, how's it going," he said, sitting down in the passenger seat. "Let's get out of here, where's the herb?" he asked. I tossed the baggie into his lap.

"Where's the papers?"

"I don't have any," I said.

"Well, we need some."

I sat there staring at him because I didn't know where to get them. "Go across the street to the MAPCO," he said. We pulled into the parking lot and I waited for him to get out of the car, but he didn't.

"Okay, I'll be right back," I finally said. I walked in and there was a cop talking to the guy behind the counter. There was no way I could buy papers with him in there. I wandered over to the Slushie machines and when the cop went to refill his coffee, I walked up to the checkout guy and whispered, "I need some papers."

"They're right there."

"What?" I asked.

He pointed, "They're right in front of you on that rack." I looked down and saw the *Tennessean* and *USA Today* newspapers.

"No, no, I need the kind you roll stuff with."

He grinned, "What are you rolling?" He pointed next to him, "What kind do you want?"

"Just the most popular one," I said. When I got back in the car, Zach looked kind of pissed off.

"What the hell took so long?"

"There was a bunch of people in there. Where do you want to go?"

"We need to get the fuck away from downtown, there are cops everywhere."

"I know the perfect place." I drove to Hillsboro High School and parked by the track that I walked almost every night. Zach rolled a joint about as big as his thumb. He took three or four hits, hotboxing it, and then passed it to me. Initially I wasn't planning to inhale, but I was nervous about being alone with him. I took a couple of deep drags off the joint, then passed it back to him. Immediately my body was swimming. I felt warm and buzzy. When I looked up into the sky and saw a giant white steeple glowing in the moonlight, I felt a stab of guilt. "Oh my God, look how beautiful that is."

"What?" he asked.

"That steeple across the street."

"Churches are bullshit," he said. "God is bullshit."

My ears started ringing. Growing up in the buckle of the bible belt, I couldn't believe how sacrilegious he was being. His words were fading in and out, then I heard him saying, "God doesn't exist," and he kept on and on. I started feeling like I might flip out. I took three more big hits from the joint.

"I believe in God," I said.

"Hey, I need to get back. My girlfriend is going to be mad as hell if I'm any later." My heart deflated. It never occurred to me that he had a girlfriend.

"Come on, I gotta go."

He leaned in front of me and put his hand on the steering wheel. Suddenly it looked reptilian; claws shot out and scaly skin moved up his arm. He touched my shoulder and I freaked out, "Don't touch me, I'll come around the car." I walked over to the other side of the Sentra, holding on to it so I wouldn't fall. I gave him the keys, got into the passenger seat, and leaned it all the way back, closing my eyes. When I sat up, we were in the Tower Records parking lot. "Are you okay?" he asked, leaning over and looking at me.

"Get back. Just get the fuck back."

"Listen, you need to get your shit together," he said, and got out, slamming the door.

Sitting there in the parking lot, I wanted to say "ribbit, ribbit" like a frog. I crawled over to the driver's side, but the car was spinning. I knew it was going to be a while before I could drive. After about a half an hour, I walked across the street back to the

MAPCO and bought a bag of Funyuns and a Dr. Pepper.

I got back in my car and thought I'd wait thirty more minutes and then see how I felt. "Knock, knock, knock." I looked up and someone was at the window. It scared the shit out of me. There was a balding transvestite who looked a little bit like David Bowie. He had long hair on the sides that was feathered back and fixed like something out of *The Rocky Horror Picture Show*.

I cracked my window about two inches and told him, "I don't have any money. I just spent my last five dollars."

He threw his hand on his hip flamboyantly and said in a girlish voice, "Honey, I don't want money. I want to sing you a song."

"Okay," I said, crunching a Funyun.

He started singing and I got goosebumps. "Somewhere over the rainbow... way up high... There's a land that I heard of once in a lullaby." He sang so loudly, and opened his mouth so wide, I could see that he only had a few teeth. He was singing with such passion and power. He put every bit of his heart into that song and went up a full octave in the last chorus. I rolled down the window all the way and had tears in my eyes.

"Oh my God. You are awesome! Here..." I tried to hand him my Funyuns.

He shook his head and pointed at his teeth. "Honey, I can't eat those."

Chapter Seven

——

SPACE COWBOY

Space Cowboy

W HEN DUSTIN HITCHINS AND HIS FRIEND, David, walked into Brown's Diner one night that December, I didn't see the detour my life was about to take. Dustin was tall and had reddish-brown hair and blue eyes. I had seen his music video on CMT and heard his song on the radio. He had a publishing deal and a record deal on a major label, and I had a million questions. He always sat in my section when he came in for lunch and was a regular on Wednesday nights when I was the only waitress there. I loved when he came in because he always left me a $20 tip, which was ten times more than I usually got. Brown's was slow that night and there was no one in the dark dining room but us.

When I brought out his sixth beer, Dustin patted the pew-style seat beside him, motioning for me to sit down. I slid in next to him and we had instant chemistry. I was intrigued by every-thing about him and he seemed to feel the same way. "Girl, I could listen to your southern accent all night long," he said, laughing. "Couldn't you, David?" he asked his friend, who barely said a word.

I told Dustin that I was from Alabama, I had moved to Nash-ville to be a songwriter, then said, "My dad's Danny Mayo." I never knew whether or not to tell people who my dad was because I never knew what their reaction would be. People either loved him fiercely or hated his guts. He had helped so many people get record deals and encouraged every new artist he believed in. But he also busted a baseball bat on his publisher's desk when they refused to give him a Number One party for his first number one song. It was pretty screwed up because everybody has a Number One party when they have the top spot on the charts. There was also the time Dad walked straight into Third Coast Bar and broke record producer Bud Marino's finger.

"I know who Danny Mayo is," Dustin said, then told David, "He's one of the best writers in town." Then he sang a little bit of the chorus to "Feed Jake" and started singing Dad's song with the group Alabama: "If I had you, we'd run like gypsies in the wind. We'd be lovers, we'd be friends. Oh, if I had you." He sang, looking straight into my eyes, and it sent shivers down both of my arms with how forward he was being. It made me feel kind of crazy the way he was flirting with me because I rarely got attention from guys, much less a full-grown man. "I love your voice," I told him. I'm sure I was blushing. "Well, as talented as your dad is, I'll bet you're better," he said and took a swig of Bud Light. "We should write a song last week." We both started laughing.

"Well, I mean next week," he smiled. "I've had a little too much to drink, but we should write."

"Fuck yeah, I'm ready to write right now," I practically jumped in his face.

"Well, I've got a confession to make. I've been coming in here a couple times a week trying to work up the courage to ask you out. I'm getting fat," he said and poked at his belly and hit it with his hand. I sat there, not knowing that to say. There was a tingle rushing down my arms and something inside me surged. Nobody had ever asked me out like that. "Aw, a girl as pretty as you? I should have known. You've got a boyfriend."

"I haven't had a boyfriend since high school," I blurted out instantly, feeling like an idiot.

"Do you want to do something this weekend?" he asked, looking straight into my eyes again.

My hand was shaking when I wrote down my phone number on a matchbook. I wasn't sure how I felt about him or even if I thought he was cute, but being from Alabama, I didn't know how to say no. I was in awe of his music and he had asked me to write.

We could probably be friends. I followed him out the side door and said, "I'll call you on Friday and we'll go wherever you want." He was facing me walking backward and then he jumped off the porch and clicked the heels of his cowboy boots. "Woohoo, we're going out!" he said.

Watching him walk across the parking lot, I thought he was going to lose my number before he got home. Cory had come to visit a couple of months earlier and he refused to go back to Alabama. Daddy said he didn't have room for both of us, so he rented us a duplex around the corner from him in Green Hills. I had been setting the alarm every morning, getting up at 6:30 am and dropping Cory off at Hillsboro High, a half of a mile away. It took six weeks before I realized that he was walking in the front door and right out the back. He was in ninth grade, and every day teenage boys were everywhere because we lived so close to the high school. We shared the duplex with a youth minister, his wife, and two toddlers, but our side had turned into a halfway house for hoodlums. My brother and his friends had taken over.

Dustin called me the next day after Brown's and asked me out to dinner. Getting ready, I couldn't believe I had a date. A real damn date. The last time I waited for someone to pull into the driveway and pick me up, it was my senior prom. We had all gone to the dance in a hearse because the only two limos in Gadsden were booked. Dates were different in Alabama. When I was with Ty, we'd just sit in his mom's living room, eating Oodles of Noodles and playing *Super Mario Bros.* on a Saturday night,.

When I saw Dustin walking through the yard, I didn't want to go anymore. It hit me that we were going to be alone, and I didn't want to date him, so I was just going to make an enemy. When he walked into the living room I realized how messy it was. There was a tie-dyed blanket full of cigarette burns covering the couch, and you couldn't see the glass coffee table through the huge, homemade, red, white, and blue bong, and the Mountain Dew cans covered with cigarette ashes. It always looked like we had just been robbed and it smelled like Lollapalooza.

My brother and his friends were either stoned and watching cartoons, or looking out the front window waiting for our neighbors' hot, blonde, teenage sister to walk through the yard. The girl they were lusting after was Reese Witherspoon. I knew who she was from the movie *The Man in the Moon*. Daddy said, "She's gonna be a big-time actress, just wait and see."

Dustin followed me into the kitchen so I could get my purse. Cory and his friends Carlos, Jamie, and Dwight were all fighting over a bag of Cheetos. When I saw Dustin standing next to them under the bright dome light, he looked like their dad. It freaked me out and I really didn't want to go anywhere with him. Dustin's Wrangler jeans were starched stiff as a pelican's beak with creases running down the front. His belt buckle was about as big as a coffee pot and he had on a black Stetson cowboy hat with a teeny-tiny ponytail poking out the back. It looked like a Frito corn chip.

All my brother's wanksta friends froze, mouths open, staring at Dustin like his head was on fire. The music was blasting so violently loud that it felt like the walls were moving. I walked over to the boombox and jerked the cord with so much force that the outlet cover came off. The room fell silent and I felt like I might start crying. My mind bounced around like a jackrabbit on crack, trying to come up with a reason why I couldn't go with him. He had to see the panic in my eyes. Clearly amused, Cory asked, "Where y'all goin'? A rodeo?"

"Shut up," I yelled at him, "and keep that shit turned down or the neighbors are gonna call the cops over here again." Dustin followed me out the front door. I hadn't even said hi to him yet. I had an urge to take off running.

"Y'all have fun now, ya hear?" Cory shouted before breaking into "Friends in Low Places" by Garth Brooks. Then he exploded into laughter. He had also noticed that Dustin wore the exact same flame stitched western shirt that Garth Brooks wore on the cover of his last record.

I followed Dustin to the front yard to the passenger side of his maroon truck, opening my door. No boys I went out with ever opened my door. Cory and his friends watched us, still laughing as we pulled out of the driveway. "I'm sorry, they're idiots," I said.

"Don't worry about it, I got a crazy brother too." The radio was playing one of my favorite songs, "Jealous Again" by the Black Crowes, but Dustin changed the station to some Billy-Bob corn cobb country song. "Where do you want to go for dinner?" he asked as he headed toward town.

"I can't make decisions, you're gonna have to pick."

"Well, what kind of food do you like?" He leaned in closer, trying to get me to look at him. "I'm good with anything," I mumbled. He kept trying to make conversation, but I was too busy cussing myself out in my head to hear anything he was saying. "I heard this place is good." He pulled up in front of Coby's Hibachi Steak House. "Is this okay?" he asked.

"Yeah, perfect," I said and got out of the truck.

Once we were inside, we sat down at the bar. I flagged down the first waitress I saw and ordered a Coors Light. My mission was to get as drunk as possible, as fast as possible. I had only been twenty-one for about six weeks, so I jerked my purse into my lap and pulled out my driver's license, excited to get carded. The waitress never even asked for it, probably because Dustin was so old. I jammed my wallet back into my bag. "Bud Light for me," Dustin said, picking up a menu.

I drank three beers before we were seated at our table. I watched the chef make a fiery volcano and kept drinking. By the time he was done cooking my chicken teriyaki, I was loaded, and the drunker I got, the more I liked Dustin. I hung on his every word as he talked about songwriting. He told me about making his first record and how awesome it was recording at Ocean Way Studios. He asked me all about my songwriting and who I had written with. "Well, mostly by myself. I've got ten thousand titles," I told him. "You'd shit if you saw how many titles I got." We both started laughing.

The chef brought out a complimentary fried ice cream dessert. I took a few bites and kept drinking. About fifteen minutes later, I felt my back begin to lock up and my chest getting tight. I knew what was happening, but I tried not to panic. "Dustin, I'm gonna be sick, I gotta go home," I said.

"What's wrong?"

"I'm having an allergic reaction. There might have been banana in that dessert."

"What's wrong with banana?" He looked at me panicked. "Do I need to take you to the hospital?" He asked the waiter if there was banana in the dessert and he said, "Ancient Chinese secret," and then Dustin kind of pushed him out of the way. "Come on, I'll get you out of here." I had been allergic to bananas, lettuce and avocados since I was in eighth grade. There was something in the chemical they spray on them to keep them from turning brown that made me feel like I couldn't breathe and gave me hideous back pain and pressing stomach cramps.

I cracked the window open and leaned my head back. When the truck came to a stop, I thought I was home, but we were at a gas station. My head fell back. "What is this dipshit doing?"

When he got back in, he slid behind the wheel. "I had to get gas, sorry. Maybe this will help," he said and handed me a box of Benadryl and a bottle of water. "Thank you, but can you please hurry up and get me home?" I heard the desperation in my voice. It felt like the Atlanta Braves were holding batting practice on my back. The pain radiated through me. I dug through my purse for my inhaler, which never eased the pain but usually settled me down. I couldn't find it, so I took a handful of Benadryl, hoping that it would knock me out by the time I laid down. Within minutes I knew that the Benadryl was a big mistake. Not only could I not breathe, but now I was buzzing and felt like a jacked-up space cadet.

I kept my eyes closed and waited to hear the crunch of my gravel driveway under the tires. I couldn't wait to strip down to my underwear, turn the air conditioner on full blast and curl up in the fetal position on my cool sheets. The truck stopped and I sat up. We weren't in my driveway. We were at some weird red brick apartment complex. "Take me home," I said. "I want to go home."

"I'm not taking you back there with all those guys partying and blasting music. You need somebody to take care of you." The crisp, cool air was coming through the window and it helped me breathe a little better. "I just want to make sure you're okay," he said and touched my chin, lifting my face to look at me. My back was hurting so badly that I wasn't sure if I could walk. Dustin leaned over to me saying, "Please trust me. My roommate's in there and I won't lay a hand on you if that's what you're worried about."

"I'm not worried about anything I'm fucking sick as shit," I said. My skin was clammy, and my chest felt like a giant was sitting on it. "Fuck it, where's your apartment?" I asked. "If you're not gonna take me home, I gotta go lie down."

When I stepped out onto the sidewalk, Dustin slipped his arm around my waist to help me as I wobbled up the walkway. I heard a commotion in the bushes beside us and something shot out of the shrubs straight at me. All I saw was a blur of reddish-brown fur, a red mouth, and a flash of teeth. I felt a violent blow from behind as it took me down. I thought some kind of werewolf wolverine thing was about to tear me into pieces. My purse went flying, scattering loose change in all directions, and my face slammed into the concrete. I watched as my lipstick and ink pens rolled off the curb and under cars. I heard a howling scream and then I realized it wasn't an animal at all. It was a wild-eyed girl wearing a fake fur coat that attacked me. She jumped on Dustin's back, latching her arms around his neck and swinging from his shoulders as he tried to sling her off. "Aimee, that's my apartment," he pointed towards the end of the corridor. "Just bang on the door and tell Mitch to let you in," he said, still trying to jerk loose from the girl.

I pounded my fist on the door and I heard someone moving around inside. "I'm Aimee. I'm with Dustin. I'm sick," I shouted. A guy in a baseball cap cracked the door and said, "Hurry, hurry, come on in," and then locked it behind me. "Sorry about that. Brandy's been over here banging on this door all night. Somebody's gonna call the cops over here again if they don't quit doing this shit."

"Can I lie down somewhere?" I asked. Mitch put me on the couch and got me a blanket, then he went to bed. I heard screaming coming through the window from outside. "I knew you were cheating on me, you son of a bitch!" Brandy kept swinging at Dustin and clawed a bloody mark down his right cheek. He picked her up, slammed her hard on the pavement and she hit her head on the concrete curb. "You fucking bitch, you'd better not ever lay another hand on me," he said, and grabbed her by the throat.

Brandy saw me watching from the window and came over toward it. Her hairline around her temple was bleeding and I wanted to go out there and try to help her, but I was afraid she would attack me again. "How old are you, fifteen?" she yelled. "If I was you, I'd run like hell. He's a compulsive liar. He's a psycho son of a bitch, and I promise you, you're gonna be sorry."

The following morning, I woke up with my face stuck to an unfamiliar burgundy leather couch. It took me a minute to figure out where I was. I smelled eggs, then I saw Dustin at the stove. "Wake up, sleepyhead. I made you some breakfast." He put a plate of eggs and toast on the glass dining room table and poured me a glass of orange juice. I just wanted out of there. I looked at the clock on the wall. It was 11:00 am.

"Oh shit, I've gotta be at work for the lunch shift," I said. "I gotta go right now." Then I realized that I didn't have a car. "Can you take me home real quick?"

He turned down my street and I kept one hand on the door handle. I was ready to jump out before he could try to kiss me. When he pulled up in front of our duplex just as I was about to escape, he said, "Let's write one day after the holidays. We can do it down at Sony."

Everything stopped. Oh, my sweet God in Heaven, he really wants to write with me. He just asked me to come to Music Row and write a song. "Yeah, I can write any day that works for you!" I told him. "I'll bring all my titles."

Leaving Las Vegas

I SPENT CHRISTMAS IN ALABAMA, and Mom stayed in bed most of the time. She had torn her rotator cuff, had surgery, and then a couple of months later she had surgery on a ruptured disc in her back. She had been drifting away on a stream of orange, oblong Darvocet ever since. I went back to Nashville after a couple of days.

Dad had just gotten a massive royalty check for the three hit songs he had that year, so the day before New Year's Eve he somehow talked Opal and Harold into driving to Nashville and going to Las Vegas with us. It was a last-minute trip. Dad decided that's what he would give his parents for Christmas, a first-class family vacation to Sin City. The last place Opal would ever want to go. The trip was disastrous and almost deadly.

When my grandparents arrived in Nashville, they pulled into the parking lot of the Royal Arms. Daddy's fleet of cars were taking up every space. He had driven me crazy since he dropped me off at my duplex earlier that day, reminding me to be at his apartment by 7:00 pm sharp to go to the airport. I got there on time, so did my grandparents, but Dad didn't show up until about forty-five minutes later, slinging giant Army-style duffle bags at each one of us. He jerked a can of spray paint out of the floor-board of his Silverado truck and spray painted our initials on each one.

Dad had no sense of the seasons. He looked nuts. He wore coral shorts that were way too short and church shoes with tassels and no socks. He had on a black fanny pack with a bulging zipper that had an orange Walmart clearance tag hanging off it. Even with all of this, when you looked at him, the first thing you saw was the glowing green eyes of the wolf on his shirt.

"Let's go, Mother!" he shouted. "You're gonna make us late!"

"Danny, those bags aren't gonna fit," Opal said with her hand on her hip watching him try to shove them into the trunk.

"Just get back and let me do this," Dad said.

Opal was right, so we had to call two taxis to take us to the airport. When we finally boarded the plane, we were in the last row of first-class, which was a new thing for all of us. I sat in the window seat next to Dad. Opal and Harold were across the aisle, and Cory was directly in front of me. A scraggly looking man with dreadlocks was the last person to board the plane. When Opal saw him, she jerked her purse into her lap, then leaned across the aisle and said, "Look at that man sittin' with Cory. He looks like he ain't got two nickels to rub together. I wonder how he got first class."

"I don't know, Mother," Dad said, "why don't you ask him?" He pretended he was going to tap the man on the shoulder and accidentally shoved him. "Sorry about that dude," Dad said and held his hands up. He had gotten wasted at the bar across from our gate, drinking four or five Seven and Sevens before we board-ed the plane. "My mother wants to ask you a question," he slurred, grinning big.

"How's the weather in Vegas?" Opal asked.

"I'm not a fucking meteorologist," he said under his breath to my brother. Then he looked at Opal and said, "Hotter than here," and turned around and kept talking to Cory.

The flight attendant announced, "Our flight will be approximately three hours and fifty minutes."

"Nurse! Hey, nurse!" Dad shouted. "Bring me two Seven and Sevens." The flight attendant brought him a Seven-Up and two mini bottles of whiskey. By the time we hit twenty thousand feet, Daddy was trashed, Opal was crying, and Harold was breathing heavy and clicking his dentures like he always did when he got nervous. Cory and I gave each other a "Holy shit" look and started laughing just as Daddy and Opal started to get into it.

"Las Vegas is no place for kids, Danny."

"Mother, you're so selfish. You don't even care about taking a vacation with your grandkids."

"Danny, you know I hate gambling."

"Yeah, but there's other things to do. You could go to the shows. You just want to ruin the trip for everybody."

"Danny, no I don't."

"You're just afraid somebody from church will find out you went to Vegas."

"No, it just breaks my heart because you could have bought a mansion and put Aimee and Cory through college with the money you've lost gambling."

"Shut up, Mother. What I do with my money's my business."

"You're just gonna lose it all."

"You want to talk about losing money. You've been sending Jim Bakker a check every month for the last fifteen years, paying for all his cocaine and hookers."

One of the happiest days of my Dad's life was the downfall of the TV evangelist of Praise the Lord Ministries, Jim Bakker. Every time he and Opal got into an argument, he harped on mistakes made in the past, grabbing weird, random events trying to make a point, and he always raised hell about Jim Bakker.

I couldn't stop laughing.

"Would you two just shut the hell up?" Harold said.

Daddy ordered two more drinks when the flight attendant walked by. His flirting was slowly becoming harassment. After downing the drinks, he wanted two more. Opal sank low in her seat, staring out the window with a hopeless expression on her face. Daddy unbuckled his big, black fanny pack and held it up. "If you can guess how much money I got in this bag, I'll give you a thousand dollars," he said to Cory and me. His voice was so loud that everyone was staring at us.

"How close do we have to get?" Cory asked, turning around ready to play.

"Within a thousand."

"Okay, fifty thousand," Cory guessed.

"Eighty thousand," I said.

"No, there's $330,000 in this bag."

"No there's not," Cory said.

Dad unzipped it to show us and dumped bundles of cash into the aisle. "Shit, Aimee. Get down there and get that money."

There were stacks and stacks of one hundred dollar bills in the little, yellow wrapper bands. I was on my knees looking under seats and strangers' shoes trying to put it all back in the fanny pack. I had never seen so much cash. It looked like he had robbed a bank.

Harold was really nervous now, smacking his dentures double time. "Danny, put that damn money up. You're gonna get us killed."

Dad thought that was hilarious and got even louder. "I've got $330,000 right here." He waved a handful of cash around and dropped half of it.

If you want to make a group of people extremely nervous, just start throwing around gasoline or money. The commotion drew two of the flight attendants to our seats. "Is everything okay, sir?" one of the women asked, staring at the pile of cash in my Dad's lap.

"Give me two more," he ordered and waved his glass at her.

"I'm afraid we're gonna have to cut you off," she said.

"Where's my waitress, the other one, the pretty one?"

"I'm the head attendant on this flight, and you're cut off," she snapped.

"Nurse, nurse!" Now he was up, headed toward the back of the plane.

"He's headed for the bathroom, Cory. Go help him," I said.

"I don't want to."

We watched as Dad swayed back and forth, holding on to the tops of the seats. We hit a little bit of turbulence, and he started to fall, then grabbed a bald man's head to regain his balance.

Dad was still yelling, "Nurse!" when the plane landed. "I want to talk to your boss," he said to the head flight attendant as we were exiting the plane. Cory walked beside him holding his shoulders.

"I'm sorry," I told her. "He's afraid of flying. Please don't have him arrested," I pleaded.

"Well, he disrupted this whole flight."

"I know we did, but my grandparents are with this. Please, just let us take him to the hotel."

"Hey, Captain, how much for that hat?" Dad reached toward the pilot like he was going to pull the navy and gold cap from his head.

"Oh my God, Cory, get him off this plane," I said. He could barely make it up the jetway. I stayed back and saw Harold struggling to get Opal's bag down from the overhead bin. The underarms of his short-sleeved, button-down shirt were drenched in sweat. I reached into the seat pockets for my notebooks and magazines when I noticed something under Dad's seat.

The black fanny pack, full of money, was sitting on the floor. "Miss, can I help you?" a voice said, scaring me so badly that I jumped. The flight attendant stood behind me with a trash bag.

"I'm good," I replied and stuffed the fanny pack into my neon backpack. I raced to the restroom and sat in the stall staring at all that money. Dad will never know it's gone, I thought, and took out a bundle of cash and flipped through the rest. Each label said $10,000. I could buy a washer and dryer and get my transmission fixed. I looked at Benjamin Franklin's face and decided that this could be retroactive child support. I hid a grand in the zipper pocket of my backpack.

There were eight or nine stations at the baggage claim and my grandparents still hadn't found their suitcases. Opal was crying again telling Harold, "I told you we shouldn't have come on this cotton-pickin' trip."

"Mother, shut up!" Dad was still yelling at her as he tried to lift his bag then fell back on the luggage carousel.

Cory and I watched him being pulled by the conveyor belt

alongside the suitcases until he finally got enough balance to roll off onto the floor. One of his loafers came off and made the full trip around. "Let's go to the hotel," I said while Cory was trying to help Dad get his shoe back on.

We walked out to find a long, black limousine parked at the curb and a man in a black suit holding a sign that read, "Mr. Mayo." We never traveled like this, so I didn't know what was going on. Dad walked over to the driver, but he was slurring so much that the chauffeur couldn't understand him.

Cory and I got into the back of the limo. Opal didn't say a word, just stared out the window with mascara smeared under her eyes. I waited until we got to the strip before I asked Dad, "Where's all that money?"

"Oh my God, stop the car! Stop the car!" he banged on the window to talk to the driver.

Then I pulled it out of my backpack. "You left it under the seat on the plane."

"Give that to me," he snatched it from my hands.

We pulled up in front of the Golden Nugget Hotel and Casino. Every valet and bellhop there knew Dad. They had provided the limousine that picked us up and gave us parlor suites. The rooms had floor to ceiling windows, a spiral staircase, a dining room table, and a jacuzzi tub in the marble bathroom. It was pure luxury, which Opal usually would have loved, but she didn't want to do anything but go to bed.

Cory followed me to our room, dropped his duffle bag on the floor, and disappeared. Dad was in the casino gambling. I walked across the street and played bingo. I spent the night at a folding table with a group of chain-smoking grandmothers while Frankie Avalon and Frank Sinatra crooned in the background. I laughed thinking about that joke: *How do you get an old lady to say, "Fuck?" Yell, "BINGO!"*

When I got back to our suite, I couldn't figure out if it was 6:00 am or pm, thanks to all the lights on the strip. I didn't see Cory again until 11:00 pm the next night.

"Where in the hell have you been for two days?" I asked.

"Circus Circus, the coolest place on the planet. There's arcades, rides, carnival games."

"Oh my God, Cory," I said, staring at a big, black dolphin tattoo on his forearm. The second I saw it, I knew it was real because it was already infected. "Who gives a fourteen-year-old a tattoo?"

"It's badass," he said. He had been drinking.

"Yeah, it's badass infected. Do not let Opal see that tattoo."

"Where's Dad?"

"He's probably still down there playing craps. He never leaves that table."

Cory and I found him in the casino. "Can we have some money?" I asked. "We're starving."

Dad pointed to a desk. "Go over there and get a voucher."

"I'm sick of that stupid buffet. We want to go to McDonald's."

"Aimee, I'm not giving you any more money when you can eat for free."

I could tell by his mood that he was losing. He looked at Cory, "What the fuck is that on your arm? It better not be real."

"Okay. It's not real," Cory said.

"Who gave you that? I'm gonna find them and kick their ass," Dad said, rolling the dice again.

"I'm not listening to this shit," Cory said. "You've got two tattoos." I only knew about the one that Dad had on the back of his right shoulder in black stenciled letters, "Feed Jake," after his song.

"And you've got that stupid tattoo on your butt," Cory said.

"What? Daddy? Gross."

"Yeah. He's got red lips tattooed on his ass and the words 'Your name.'"

"That's stupid. What does that even mean?"

"Haven't you heard him tell some stranger, 'I'll bet you twenty bucks I've got your name tattooed on my ass?'"

"He's an idiot." I gave Cory two hundred dollars.

"Where the hell did you get that money?"

"I won it playing slots." I didn't see Cory again until the following night at the hospital.

I wanted to get Opal and Harold out of the hotel room, so I booked us tickets for the Lance Burton magic show. He pulled silver dollars out of the sky and turned scraps of paper into doves.

After he had been on stage for about ten minutes, a parade of topless women came out. It doesn't get much more awkward than sitting between your grandparents staring at a bunch of nipples.

"How vulgar," Opal said, and we hurried to the cafeteria.

***

THE FOLLOWING MORNING, Cory and I went to find my dad. He had not slept since we had arrived and had been in the casino the whole time. None of us had seen him for more than a few minutes.

"Daddy, you got to go pack," I said. "We've gotta leave for the airport in one hour."

From the look on his face, I could tell something was really wrong. His eyes were red like he had been crying. "Aimee, do you have any money?"

"What? Why do you need money?"

"Can you just give me twenty dollars if you have it?" His voice sounded broken.

"Daddy, where's all that money you brought?"

He didn't have to tell me. I could read his face. "All of it? Did you lose all of it?"

I didn't know that Opal was standing behind me listening to us.

"No, Danny. No! You could have bought a mansion with that money. It just makes me sick," she said. "I knew this was gonna happen. There's Harold. I'm gonna go tell him I'm ready to go."

I gave Daddy two, twenty-dollar bills and watched him walk back toward the craps table.

A couple of minutes later, two men ran past me. There was a lot of commotion and a crowd gathering in front of the reception desk. I thought it was a fight, and then I saw the back of Opal's blonde head. She was on her knees on the floor. Harold was lying in the center of the crowd. I could see his bare chest as paramedics positioned defibrillator pads, sending electric shocks to my grandfather's heart.

An hour later, Harold was in surgery and I was trying to comfort Opal in a hospital room. Cory sat in the waiting area. It was hours before Dad got to the hospital, then he just walked up and down the hall outside Harold's room. "I can't go in there, Aimee."

"He just got out of surgery, you've gotta go in there and see him."

"I can't," he looked through the crack in the door. "If something happens to him, I won't make it," Daddy said.

We were all praying that Harold didn't die in Vegas. "Dad, you need to go in there and be with Opal," I told him. It was one of the first times I had ever seen him cry.

"Aimee, I'm not gonna be going back to Nashville for a while. You're gonna have to move back to Alabama."

"There's no way in hell I'm going back to Gadsden."

"Well I don't care what you do," he said. "That band Tupelo Road's gonna be staying at my apartment while I'm gone." Dad disappeared that night and left Opal stranded in Las Vegas.

Whirlwind Romance

THE DAY AFTER CORY AND I RETURNED TO NASH-VILLE, Mom and Mike came to get him. The landlord said that Dad was a month late on the rent and gave me two weeks' notice to get out. Dustin called and asked, "Do you want to meet me downtown at Sony at 2 o'clock tomorrow and write?"

"Yes! I can't wait!" The next day when we got to Sony Publishing, all the writer's rooms were taken, so we went and had a few beers at the Longhorn Steakhouse. Dustin forgot his guitar, but I wanted to write, so we went to Daddy's apartment because I knew he had a couple of guitars. The guys from the band Tupelo Road had already moved in.

That night, I wrote my first song in Nashville, sitting in my Dad's living room. I had stacks of notebooks spread all over the couch and on Dad's big, tree trunk coffee table. I pulled out all my favorite lyrics that I had been working on. The one he liked best was a poem. I had almost all of it and Dustin started singing. He made it sound like a song instead of just words on a page. From the first line it sounded like it belonged on the radio. I was wonderdrunk. I fell in love with his voice first. It was like smooth whiskey that made me feel fuzzy and warm inside. That song would get recorded by a platinum-selling country star two years later, but by then I'd be a different person.

We spent the next ten days together and wrote seven or eight songs. We went out to dinner or a bar every night. Dustin paid for our meals and took me to Gilly's, one of the biggest country bars. We would order a bucket of beer and I liked Dustin when I had a buzz. At every honky-tonk we went to, the house band begged Dustin to get up and sing. He usually played three or four songs; two of his and covers by either Merle Haggard or Keith Whitley. Girls were always hanging all over him, asking for autographs. His popularity made me like him a little bit more. We had been hanging out and going out for a week and a half when Dustin got on stage and announced on the microphone, "I wrote this next song, 'Waiting for You,' for that pretty little brunette right there," pointing at me. "I love you, Aimee."

"What the fuck just happened?" I couldn't believe that he told me he loved me in front of a room full of people. Everyone in the bar was staring at me while he sang the song. When he walked back to our table, he sat down and said, "You're so beautiful and I'm so in love with you. I couldn't hold it in anymore." That kind of flattery was something I had never experienced before. Someone declaring their love for me in a crowded room full of people.

I had to get my TV, bookshelves, and the rest of my stuff out of the duplex. I was starting to panic. I didn't know where I was going or how I would move all my stuff. "I've got my truck, I'll move you anywhere you want," Dustin offered. Reality hit when I tried to rent an apartment. I couldn't afford even the cheapest place I looked at, so I bought a copy of the *Tennessean* and circled some of the roommate want ads.

The first guy looked kind of like a fifty-year-old Fred Flintstone. His apartment smelled like onion rings and sour feet. He blocked me in when he showed me the spare bedroom. I crossed him off the list and went straight to the next potential roommate. She was a kindergarten teacher, about thirty years old and she gave me a four-page application. "I've got to get up at 6:30 every morning, so I can't have anyone in here who doesn't go to bed by

10," she said. Sometimes I didn't go to bed until 7:00 am, so that wasn't going to work.

My third and final option was a lady who was more masculine than most men. She had short, brown hair and tight jeans with chains on them. She lived in East Nashville and locked the door with a key after I walked into her house. She was about fifty-five years old and her yappy little dog, part terrier, part terrorist, followed me through the house, growling and barking. He bit me when I tried to open the bathroom door. "He'll calm down in a minute," she said. I was out of options and ready to sign the lease. But when she found out that I had a cat, she said it wouldn't work out.

I didn't care if I had to sleep in my car, there was no way that I was going back to Alabama. The thought of pulling into that driveway and taking my stuff to my old bedroom made me want to throw up.

That night, Dustin came over with an apartment finder magazine. He threw it on the couch. "I'll get you an apartment anywhere you want and then after I have my next single, I'll buy you a house anywhere you want." I had only been dating him for two and a half weeks, but I thought, I can always move out if I don't like living with him. "Okay, let's do it!"

Nightmare Texarkana

THE FIRST NIGHT IN OUR two-bedroom apartment at Stoneridge, I had a horrible nightmare. Dustin was standing over me with red-ringed eyes, pressing a butcher knife into my throat. I bolted upright in bed. I stared at him in the dim light. Shadows distorted his face and I felt like I didn't know this man at all. His receding hairline kind of looked like horns. He'd never been anything but wonderful to me, so I didn't know why I had this dream. Why would I dream something like that?

A couple of weeks after we had been living together, Dustin went to a meeting at Sony Records and came home drunk. "They don't want to sign me. They passed."

"What do you mean?" I asked.

"I mean they're not gonna make a record on me. The label doesn't want to sign me."

"What, how?" I couldn't believe it. "They're stupid. You'll get another deal."

"Yeah, I will," he said. "And they're gonna be sorry."

My first visit to Texarkana, Dustin's hometown, I was a nervous wreck. We made the twelve-hour drive and, on the way, we stopped at McDonald's for breakfast. He ordered biscuits and gravy for me and got himself a sausage biscuit. A couple of minutes later, he spit something out of his mouth and started yelling, "There was a fucking bloody Band-Aid in my biscuit!"

I started laughing and he came at me like he was going to hit me, then tried to play it off like he was joking around. "It ain't fucking funny, I could have AIDS." We didn't talk for about an hour before he apologized. "Okay, it is kind of funny." When we pulled into his mother's driveway, his two sons were waiting, jumping up and down in the front yard. They barreled into him, both hugging him at the same time. I sat in the truck, worried they were going to hate me.

The older one came over and said, "Hi, I'm Blaine." He kept his head down, but he looked almost just like Dustin. Then the younger boy came over and said, "I'm Robbie." He had a sweet face and I could tell that he liked me immediately by the way he smiled and talked to me. Blaine was right up under Dustin, just wanting to be with him as Dustin headed toward the porch. "Come on in and meet my mom," he said.

The living room was like a shrine to Dustin. There were a couple of pictures of his four siblings, but about fifteen of him. There were black and white, 8x10 headshots of him everywhere.

"Hey, Mother, this is Aimee, the girl I've been telling you about," Dustin said and put his arm around me as we walked into the kitchen.

His mother didn't say a word and the room turned as cold as a popsicle. She hugged Dustin and turned back to the stove. "I'm making black-eyed peas and cornbread, your favorite."

I sat down at the table.

"Can we play football, Daddy?" Blaine begged, holding a ball.

"Sure buddy, let's go. Come on, Robbie," he said, and they walked into the backyard. The room was silent for a couple of minutes, but then I said, "Blaine looks just like his daddy."

"Well, Dustin needs to spend more time with his kids. I don't know why he's always gotta bring some girl home with him."

That meant he must have brought his last girlfriend, the one that tackled us from the bushes. Dustin said she was a psycho who was stalking him that night. "His divorce isn't even final," his Mom said. I almost choked on my sweet tea.

"I thought he'd been divorced for two years."

"Yeah, well, he just moved his stuff out three months ago," she said.

Dustin came in and yelled, "Come on! We're going to my brother's real quick." We drove about a mile down the road and pulled up in front of a trailer. There was a sunburned guy sitting at the picnic table out front. He had blondish-red hair and freckles. He didn't look anything like Dustin. Bobby reminded me of Howdy Doody. He was five years older than Dustin, with a beer belly and tattoos all over. Bobby opened a blue cooler of beer, handed Dustin a Keystone Light, then they sat down at the table to catch up.

Bobby's wife, Brenda, came out and the screen door slammed. She had short black permed hair. Dustin said she was in her mid-thirties, but she looked fifty. She was missing one of her front teeth and the first words she ever said to me were, "Bobby's sorry ass knocked my tooth out and he can't make enough money to get me a new one."

"They just got here, Brenda," Bobby sighed, and gave me kind of a hopeless smile. He didn't seem like he had a mean bone in his body. Brenda pulled me inside their trailer and said, "If we didn't have three boys to raise, Bobby'd be dead already." It sounded like she was only half-joking.

The last stop on our trip to Texarkana was Dustin's Aunt Gwen and Uncle Lou. I was expecting another witch like his mother, so I was happily surprised when a redhead with a big grin walked over and handed me a Long Island Iced Tea. We drank a few together and she showed me the quilts she had made, explaining the detailed stitching. Dustin tried to help his uncle fix his truck. Before we were leaving, Aunt Gwen said, "Dustin, remember when you fell on that electric fence out there and had to get all those stitches under your arm?"

I froze. Dustin had told me that the scar came from a broken beer bottle in a bar fight. What a weird thing to lie about.

When we got back to his mom's, his soon-to-be ex-wife came over to pick up the kids. I got up to say hi to her, but Dustin told me to stay in the house because she was a bitch and might try to start something. I watched them talking in the yard and then she loaded up the boys and left.

I waited until the drive home to ask Dustin why he didn't tell me that he was still married. "We've been separated for two years," he said.

"Well, what about that scar under your arm? You told me it was from some guy at a bar."

"Yeah, but I was just embarrassed because I fell on a fence. I didn't want you to think I was a wimp."

***

ABOUT A WEEK AFTER we returned to Nashville, Dustin said he was recording three of our songs. The day we drove to Studio 19 on Music Row, I was so excited I felt sick. I sat at the soundboard next to an engineer and watched through the big, glass windows as Dustin talked to musicians from the vocal booth. He had headphones on, and when the band kicked in and I heard them bringing our song to life over the speakers, my heart inflated like a balloon. I almost couldn't contain the joy I felt.

After the band had recorded a couple of takes, Dustin said, "Aimee, how's it sound?" The engineer told me to hit a little, red button so that the band and Dustin could hear me talking on the feedback.

"I love it, except for that banjo."

"What about the banjo?" Dustin asked.

"There's just a lot of it."

He started laughing, "Okay, Barry, kill that banjo."

I hit the button again, "Can he play steel guitar instead?"

"Okay, Barry, can you play steel guitar instead?"

"Who is she?" one of the musicians asked Dustin.

"I wrote the song with her and I think she's right, we don't need that banjo."

Everyone who came in and out of the control room just talked over me and around me and acted like I wasn't even sitting there. Like I was someone's daughter or wife. I asked the main engineer if I could tell Dustin something else and he ignored me, turning knobs on the mixing board. I listened to our demos a thousand times, every time I got in the car, over and over. Dustin said if he got to make another record, he would record all three of our songs.

Magic 8-Ball

DUSTIN AND I HAD BEEN TOGETHER ABOUT SIX weeks when we went out drinking with his sister one night. She got drunk and told stories about their dad and she told one about him throwing a chair at their mother at the dinner table and scaring all the kids.

When Dustin and I got home I asked him about it, and he said, "My dad was one of the best men that ever lived."

"Yeah, it sounds like it," I said sarcastically.

Dustin came toward me in the corner of the room. "You don't say shit about my dad."

The next thing I knew, Dustin had me up against the wall, pressing his elbow to my throat. It felt like he was crushing my windpipe. I couldn't breathe. I don't know if he saw the horror in my eyes or just decided to let go.

"Get the fuck away from me," I tried to yell, but it burned my throat. I backed into the bathroom and locked the door. I looked at myself in the mirror and there was a red splotch down my neck. "What the fuck just happened?" I was shaking. "Oh, my God. How did that just happen?" I was too shocked to cry.

After about twenty minutes locked inside, I thought Dustin had left. Then I heard him slide down the bathroom door. I looked for something to hit him with in case he busted the door in. He was making a weird noise and then I realized that he was sobbing. When I opened the door, he was still on the floor backed up against our bed. He crawled toward me and wrapped his arms around my legs, looking up at me. "You know I would never hurt you," he said, hugging my legs tighter."

"You just did."

The tables had turned. I felt a tremendous power over him. He was the victim now.

"What the fuck is wrong with me?" he said, and hit himself on the side of the head with his fist. His voice was like a child's. "You're all I have and you're gonna leave me. Please don't leave me." He was crying in a way that I had never seen another person cry. There was snot pouring out of his nose and his whole face was wet with tears. He was shaking like he was hyperventilating. Something about the way he was crying scared me just as much as being choked. "Just lay with me here, please. Just lay here and let me hold you," he said and took my hands, pulling me toward the bed. "You've got to forgive me, please." He lifted my chin to kiss me and I jerked away. He kissed my hair and pulled me to him again.

I laid there, silent. My throat was throbbing and it hurt when I tried to swallow. I waited for his breath to fall into a steady rhythm. When I was convinced he was asleep, I counted to five hundred just to be safe, and then I slipped out of bed. I threw my clothes and make-up into a TJ Maxx bag and ran as fast as I could to my car and took off for Gadsden.

On the three-hour drive to Alabama, there was almost no one on the interstate. I was alone with the night and my thoughts. Sixty miles into the drive, I started feeling sorry for Dustin and almost turned around.

I shouldn't have said that about his dad. This is my fault. No, he hurt me. I kept going back and forth. I stopped at my favorite truck stop at 4:00 am to get a coffee to keep me awake.

The whole drive, my mind was playing, rewinding, and replaying how he attacked me. I had always thought if someone hit me, I'd go fucking crazy and hurt them. When I heard those stories about Maw Maw being beaten black and blue, I always thought she was kind of weak for not fighting back. I realized how wrong I had been. She was strong. She was doing what she had to do to survive with an eighth-grade education and five kids in the 1950s.

The black sky faded to indigo blue. It was still littered with stars. When I crossed the state line, I held my feet up off the floor-board and made a wish, "God, please show me what to do and please help me stay in Nashville."

You could always see the crazy coming the closer you got to my hometown. The billboards along the interstate were warning signs that just got weirder and weirder: *Fairview Madison Guns ... Vasectomy Reversal ... See Rock City ... Cumberland Heights Rehab ... Hot Babes Direct to You.* I passed a crooked homemade sign nailed to a telephone pole that screamed *REPENT* in dripping red paint.

The second I entered Gadsden, I felt myself fading into who I was when I lived there. My self-confidence disintegrated. I remembered the hopelessness and how trapped I had been. Then the fear hit me, "What if this piece of shit car breaks down and I'm stuck here?" I drove toward Mom and Mike's house. The streets were lined with churches and bars. My hometown always seemed like it was caught in a tug of war between Saturday night and Sunday morning.

I pulled into the driveway just as the sun was coming up. Mike was in the kitchen making a pot of coffee, about to go to work. He greeted me and said, "I got up early because the phone was ringing off the hook. Dustin was looking for you."

Mike tried to say "I'm sorry" once about what happened and all the beatings, but it was so awkward and heavy emotionally that I just wanted away from him when he did it. He apologized to Cory, too, more than once. I had forgiven Mike for the bad years in middle school when he was so abusive to us. Mike had been in my life for over a decade, and what makes somebody family are shared experiences, good and bad. For years he had been trying to make up for the early years with Mom, and he would continue to for the next three decades.

But there was still anxiety in the air when we were in a room alone together. When I came home, Mike went out of his way to be nice to me, checking my oil and tire pressure, asking if I needed gas money to get back to Nashville. Throughout my twenties he had been the only person in my life who acted like a parent. When my car broke down on the interstate on my way back to Nashville, he drove two and a half hours to pick me up and tow my car. He paid to have the radiator fixed, then turned around and drove two hours back to Gadsden. In some uncomfortable, unexplainable way, I loved him.

It was hard being back in that house. I never knew what to

expect when I opened the door at the end of the hall. Mom had one surgery after the other. Two operations on her back in the last few years. I went home for all her surgeries, but half the time she was on so much pain medication that she didn't even know I was there.

This time she was better. She was sitting upright in bed in a floral, flannel nightgown and said, "Hey, baby, I didn't know you were comin' home." She reached her arms out for a hug. She smelled like linen and vanilla, like she always did. I laid down beside her on the bed and felt the familiar comfort of Mom's worn sheets and handmade quilts. It had been a while since I had talked to her because no one ever answered the phone when I called. "I'm so happy you came home, baby."

I drove out to see Paw Paw and take him lunch. The minute I walked into the house, I wanted to run back out. He was sitting alone in the living room. It smelled like dirty diapers and cigarette smoke filled the house. I could tell by looking into his eyes that he was so happy to see me. I felt sorry for him. He was trapped alone in the prison of time, haunted by how he treated my grandmother.

I sat down on the couch to talk to him and I felt the tears coming. That house was nothing but an empty egg without my grandmother in it. Paw Paw laughed and told me that he had been listening to the neighbor's phone calls on his police scanner and that they were as crazy as hell.

Then I drove back to the house that I had grown up in. The rules had completely changed. No smoking cigarettes had become no smoking pot on the porch.

My step sister Leah lived in my old bedroom. When I knocked, she was hanging out with her boyfriend, Mohammed from Saudi Arabia, and his friends. Her room smelled like a nightclub from their exotic cologne and cigarettes.

"Hey girl, look at this diamond watch Mohammed gave me." We hung out for a while and laughed and laughed. Cory stayed gone the whole time I was there. I talked to him for about four minutes on the porch before he disappeared with his friends. "I'm worried about Cory," Leah said. "He stays gone for days and nobody knows where he's at. Becky's always in bed and Daddy stays upstairs with the door shut. He's depressed."

Dustin called nonstop until I took the phone off the hook again.

I drove up the mountain to see Opal and Harold, and Dustin called their house too. Harold was still recovering from his surgery. My great-grandmother, Mimi, had moved in with them. She had dementia. As soon as the screen door slammed, Opal came running straight at me and kissed me right on the lips. "Okay, baby, sit down. I've got some pot roast in the freezer."

There was no way in hell I was getting out of there without eating, so I sat down on the edge of the fireplace by my great-grandmother who was sitting in the recliner. "I've missed you," I told her, and gave her a big kiss on the cheek. "Do you know who I am?" I asked.

"Yeah, you're Linda," she said.

"No, it's Aimee. Remember, I stayed with you all the time when I was little and walked to the dime store and you made me fried shrimp all the time." Memories welled up in my heart as I held her hand, her waxy skin and veins like a map of everywhere she had been, the light brown callus on her index finger from holding a cigarette for half a century. Now, Mimi's mind wandered through time. Sometimes she was a schoolgirl on her first date with my great-grandfather T, other times she was at the hospital where she worked as a nurse, demanding that someone draw blood or take blood pressure.

Now she leaned over and whispered, "I gotta tell you something." I got closer. "Get me the hell out of here," she said, and I busted out laughing. Then she looked at me again and grinned like a Cheshire Cat. She leaned in towards me again and asked, "How old am I?"

"You're 89 years young," I said.

"Damn, that's old!" She shook her head and seemed as shocked as if I had just walked up to a nineteen-year-old and told them that they were ninety. She had a small book, a little paperback that she kept in her lap, Angels by Billy Graham. She had always cussed like a sailor and only went to church when somebody made her.

"She loves that book. It makes me so happy she's getting closer to the Lord," Opal said.

I flipped through the book and it broke my heart. There was handwriting everywhere on the pages. It read, "Danny is my grandson. His kids are Aimee and Cory. Danny's wife is Becky." She didn't remember my parents were divorced. "Beth is my granddaughter. Her kids are Vanessa and Blake and her husband is James." It's so hard to watch people you love get old.

Harold was asleep in the recliner next to us, snoring with his dentures hanging out.

"Okay, Mimi, I got a question for you," I said. I asked her, "Do you think I should go back to Dustin, my boyfriend? We got into a fight and I don't know what to do." Staring into her eyes, I waited for the answer. I knew I was in trouble because I wanted her to say, "Yes." I was playing Magic Eight Ball with my great-grandmother and in that moment, I knew I was going back to Dustin. He might have hurt me, but at least I'd get to stay in Tennessee.

I called him that night and said I'd be coming back to Nashville sometime the next day. When I walked back into our apartment the following night, Dustin grabbed me in his arms. "I've missed you so much, baby. I realized how much I loved you while you were gone." He had a dozen red roses on the counter and had cooked my favorite: chicken and dumplings. He had cleaned the apartment and shampooed the carpet with a vacuum thing he rented from Home Depot. It still smelled like chemicals from the cleaner.

After dinner he said that he had a big surprise for me. In the hall outside our bedroom, he dropped down on one knee. I thought he was looking for something and then I realized what was happening. He opened a small, black box and I looked at the diamond ring because I couldn't look at Dustin. He would see the panic in my eyes.

An awkward silence swallowed the room. We'd only known each other for two months. The last thing on Earth I wanted to do was to get married. The smell of the chicken and dumplings mixed with the eye-burning chemicals on the carpet lingered in the air along with my answer. But I couldn't find a way to say maybe in the magnitude of the moment. So, I nodded my head and Dustin slid the princess cut, almost one carat, diamond ring onto my finger.

Chapter Eight

———

DON'T STOP BELIEVIN'

White Trash Wedding

NOTHING REALLY CHANGED for me being engaged. When I stopped at the store, I still chose *Billboard* over *Bride* Magazine. I had never been one of those Cinderella girls that daydreamed about the fairy-tale wedding day. I had spent more time planning my funeral, choosing the songs that I wanted to be played, and what I wanted to be carved into my headstone, "Here lies an award-winning songwriter."

I did love having a diamond ring, though. Every morning I cleaned it with toothpaste or Windex, and at work I always made sure to hold my waitress pad so it was showing. If someone asked when the big day was, I usually said, "Oh, we're probably gonna wait at least a year. We haven't been dating that long." To me, marriage was like the moon, this glowing idea somewhere out there, far, far away.

No one in my family was excited about the news that I was engaged. When I called Opal, who lives for bridal showers, she just said, "Oh hun, promise me you'll wait at least a year. Dustin can't have kids and someday you're gonna want children."

I had always imagined my life with kids. "Well, he can have his vasectomy reversed," I said.

I called Mom, "Oh, baby, that's good. I never had a wedding. We're gonna have so much fun planning it together."

My parents had both only met Dustin a few times. He had been home with me for one of Mom's surgeries and a couple of weeks later when we went to check on her, but we didn't stay long. Dad was still spending most of his time in Florida, but the three of us had dinner once and had been out to a couple of songwriter nights when Dad was in town.

When I called Dad to tell him the news, he said, "Oh Aimee, I don't even want to hear it." He thought I was playing a joke on him, but once I convinced him that I was serious, he said, "Well, that's stupid. You don't even know him."

"You knew Mom for ten days when y'all got married."

"Yeah, but I loved your mama."

"Well, I love Dustin."

"Aimee, you're stupid if you marry him," Dad said and hung up on me.

If I had imagined a fantasy wedding, it would have been about three thousand light-years from what I was about to get. A couple of weeks after Dustin popped the question, I came home from my Friday lunch shift to find Dustin slinging socks and t-shirts into a camouflage bag on our bed.

"Where are you going?" I asked.

"A wedding."

"Who's getting married?"

"We are," Dustin said, and a huge grin spread across his face.

"What are you talking about?"

"I booked us a chapel in Gatlinburg. We're getting married tomorrow at 2 o'clock."

"Yeah, right," I laughed. But the look on his face, along with the feeling in the pit of my stomach told me he was serious. "Are you drunk?"

"No, I'm ready to make you my wife," he said, coming around behind me and locking me in his arms for a long hug. "We're gonna leave tonight around 7. I got us a cabin at Honeymoon Hideaways."

"Dustin, I just can't just run off and get married. What about my mom and Opal?"

"We can still have a wedding later if you want. I'm tired of waiting."

"Waiting? We've been engaged for fifteen days. I'm not ready."

"Well, you're ready to live in my house and let me pay all the bills, and I'm ready to make you my wife," he said, holding a cigarette between his teeth as he folded a button-down shirt.

"You've been married. I haven't."

"Aimee, I might have been married, but I've never loved anybody until I met you." Our argument continued until he gave me an ultimatum. "You can either pack your shit for Gatlinburg, or you can pack your shit and go back to Gadsden."

"I don't even have anything to wear," I said.

"I'm wearing jeans and a nice shirt."

I had two dresses in my closet, one that I wore to Maw Maw's funeral, and one that I wore in my high school Homecoming parade. I drew it on a piece of paper and Mama made it without a pattern on her Singer sewing machine. It was metallic blue and fuchsia, short in the front and longer in the back, with puffy sleeves.

I slung my hot rollers, caboodle full of make-up, clothes, and shoes in a bag, and we headed out. When we pulled into Honeymoon Hideaways, Dustin was exhausted, and I was in a stone-cold panic. There was no way I could sleep.

After he went to bed, I snuck outside and sat in a gazebo, freezing my ass off and chain-smoking. I walked in circles staring up at the moon through the fog. "I don't know what to do, God. Please show me what to do. How can I get out of this? What if I'm about to ruin my life?" I asked. Then I calmed myself down. People get married all the time. People get divorced all the time. If I'm miserable, I can leave.

The sky was the color of a ripe peach when I went in to lay down.

Three hours later, Dustin was waking me up to get ready. Looking at myself in the bathroom mirror, I didn't know whether to laugh or cry. I had packed in such a rush that I had forgotten almost everything I needed. My hair was a rat's nest and I didn't have a brush. My leopard bra straps were showing, I didn't have a razor and my eyes looked like ghosts with no mascara. Driving to the chapel I hardly heard a word Dustin said. Outside it felt like the dead of winter; it was March and it was freezing. There were gray, slushy sidewalks and bare branches on the trees. It looked like the world was dying.

Dustin dropped me off in front of the little steps that led up to the log chapel. It sat on a tourist-filled street, sandwiched between a Ripley's Believe It or Not and an old west photoshop and fudgery . Couples in sloppy sweat suits crowded around a corn dog stand. The cold, wet air smelled like smoked sausage from another vendor who was parked on the curb. I felt a wave of nausea, followed by intense stomach cramps as I walked up the pathway. In the window, a sign read, "No blood test.

No waiting period. Ordained, Christian minister." A couple burst out the front door, blushing with love and holding hands. They didn't even see me as they walked past. I almost stepped on something in the slushy mud in front of the steps. I couldn't tell what it was at first, so I leaned down to get a better look. It was brilliant blue, and as I got closer I saw it's twisted black beak, the white ring around its eye, and it's dead wings. "Oh, my God, it's a dead bird. This has to be a bad omen."

"What are you doing?" Dustin yelled as he came up the sidewalk.

"I'm looking at something."

"You're supposed to be inside filling out the paperwork."

"I know, but look."

"Get away from that thing unless you want to get rabies." The second I stepped inside the chapel, a lady with teeny-tiny teeth and short, black hair that looked like a Brillo pad said, "Come on, come on, come on. We've got to stay on schedule. Groom, you go to the left, and bride, you come with me." As we walked into the pink painted parlor, she said, "You can put on your dress and get ready. We're gonna be going out in about ten minutes."

"This is my dress. I just found out we were getting married last night." She looked at my bra straps and shook her head, then she handed me a clipboard. "Okay, fill this out. These are the three packages." I chose the cheapest one: the simple "I Do for Two."

"You don't want that one. It doesn't even come with pictures."

"Yeah, well, I don't really want pictures. I don't even want to be getting married," I said under my breath.

"Did you fill in your blood type?"

"I don't know it."

"Well, you are eighteen years old, aren't you?"

"Yeah, I just turned 21." She studied me for a second like she didn't believe me.

"Okay, just give me your license." She handed me a bouquet of artificial flowers and led me to where the ceremony would take place. She ran up front to a Sanyo keyboard and sat down and began playing "Here Comes the Bride." Dustin was already down front, standing between two plastic pillars at the entryway. My legs were shaking and I couldn't make them stop. My throat got tight and my arms were numb. She played the wedding march for a couple of minutes and then started again, nodding her head at me. I took my first step and the world went silent.

Walking down the aisle, I looked at the empty rows of pews, the flickering of candles littered everywhere, and the water-stained, vaulted, popcorn ceiling. Monstrous urns were cascading with fake ferns. It looked more like the Rainforest Café than it did an altar. Dustin stood perfectly still next to a man who looked like a redneck Michael Myers from the movie Halloween. Dustin had his hat off, and I looked at his receding hairline, then into his eyes. They were misting like he might cry. I was glad he took my hand because I felt dizzy.

"We are gathered here today..." The minister was so loud that I jumped. He continued to raise his voice like he was performing a ceremony at St. Patrick's Cathedral marrying Princess Diana. It was so dramatic that I dropped my head down and stared at the mauve-colored carpet. Dustin kept tapping the center of my palm, trying to get me to look at him, but I knew better. Something was happening inside me like an avalanche about to break free. I closed my eyes and fought it as hard as I could, giggling silently at first. I pried my lips shut, cupped my free hand over my mouth, and tried to pretend that I was crying. I knew that everyone could see my shoulders shaking. Dustin caressed my hand to comfort me.

The minister asked, "Are you okay, Annie?" I didn't correct him. I just kept my head down and nodded. Then I heard it. It was as if a barking seal sound escaped from my lungs, followed by a snort. Dustin realized I was giggling and gripped my hand tighter. He was hurting my fingers. I tried to look up at him, but his scolding eyes and the furious expression on his face just made everything funnier.

As the minister recited the passage from Corinthians, "Love is patient. Love is kind," he reached the words, "Love is not easily angered." Hearing that while worrying that Dustin was going to break my hand with his bone-crushing grip, I lost it and exploded into loud laughter. There was no camouflaging the hyena-like cackle that echoed off the walls of the empty chapel. Suddenly everything was hilarious; Dustin's stupid, starched western shirt, the shouting hillbilly preacher, the jungle of plants in the room, and the look on the face of the lady with the teeny-tiny teeth. I was helpless with hysterics and bent over, clutching my stomach, trying to catch my breath. Dustin was mortified and getting madder by the moment as the vows proceeded.

The minister continued to call me Annie and I continued to stare at my feet. I didn't look up when Dustin said, "I do," but I heard the anger in his voice as he made the promise into my hair.

When it came time for me to say my vows, I felt every atom inside me refusing and radiating the word 'no.' Then I heard a tiny voice that didn't even sound like mine mumble, "I do."

When we walked out of that chapel, I didn't feel any more married than I had when we walked into it. In a way, since the minister kept calling me Annie, I didn't feel like I had said 'I do.' Annie did.

Twice as Hard

I MADE THE BIGGEST MISTAKE of my life twice. That May, a couple of months after the Gatlinburg wedding, Dustin and I got married again in Gadsden. This wedding was as much for my family as it was for me. All my life, Mama had looked forward to helping me plan my wedding since she never got to have one. We went shopping and picked out a white, off-the-shoulder dress. I designed my tall veil with dramatic netting around my face. We bought navy fabric and Mom made all the bridesmaids dresses.

My flower girl was a long-time patient of my mom's. She was in a wheelchair and had a basket full of rose petals in her lap and a giant smile on her face. While planning the wedding, it was easy to see it was going to be a disaster. Every phone call I made to my friends, Dustin listened on the other line. He refused to let me invite Jerry, and when my friend, Stephanie, asked, "Does Ty know you're getting married?" Dustin went batshit and told me she couldn't be a bridesmaid. Three days later, he made me call Stephanie and tell her we couldn't be friends anymore.

"Aimee, I'm worried about you. And Dustin, you psychotic piece of shit, I know you made her call me and I know you're on the phone right now. You can go fuck yourself," she hung up. The next day I called her from a payphone and told her how much I loved her and she pleaded with me not to go through with it.

Opal threw me a bridal shower and invited everyone from her church. I opened presents for over an hour. Mom looked beautiful in her beaded ivory suit and her dark hair was cut in a long bob with bangs. Mike, Cory, Uncle Kelly, and Paw Paw all wore dark gray suits. Everyone was there but Maw Maw. I was breaking the promise I made to her again. Dustin and I fought all the way to Cedar Hills Baptist. The last words we said to each other pulling into the parking lot of the church were, "I hate you, you fucking bitch."

"Well, I promise there's no way you could hate me as much as I hate you," I screamed at him and slammed the door.

Mom curled my hair and helped me do my make-up. I couldn't hide the hopelessness I felt. When I started to cry, she knelt beside me and asked, "Baby, what's wrong? You know you don't have to marry him if you're not sure. I'll go out there right now and tell everybody. It doesn't matter."

I cut her off. "Yes, it does."

"I can tell everybody out there to go home and it will be okay, I promise you it will."

"Mom, I'm already married. We've been married for almost two months."

Minutes later, Dad stood at the entryway with his arm locked in mine. "Baby doll, we ought to just run out the door and down the street."

"Yeah, well I would, but I'm already married." For once I shocked him.

What I remember most from that day was coming down the stairs of the church with people on both sides of us throwing rice. We were headed towards Dustin's truck. Aunt Debbie had decorated the tailgate with cans hanging off it and wrote "Just Married" in white shoe polish on the windows. It was freezing outside, and just before I climbed inside the truck, I saw Jerry. He was standing across the street, shivering in a black leather jacket with his hands in his pockets. His long, golden hair was blowing in the cold wind and his breath was smoke. He just wanted to see me in my dress.

Green-Eyed Monster

A FEW MONTHS AFTER we were married the second time, Dustin evolved into a different person. Now that I was his wife, I was just another possession to him, like his teal green Chevy pickup or his black acoustic guitar. His monstrous love, which had seemed so romantic in the beginning, was now just a monster. In the early months his jealousy flattered me. I felt lucky. All I had ever wanted was for someone to love me. To really, really love me. In the past I'd always felt like I loved the most and I was always the one begging somebody to stay, so I tolerated his jealousy and made excuses for it. His first wife cheated on him and broke his heart. It was that bitch's fault he was like this. "I'm loyal as a tick and in time, he'll learn to trust me," I thought.

From the beginning, Dustin had an insatiable curiosity about my past. I found myself telling him things that I had never told anyone. I told him about the night when I was sixteen and the guy assaulted me in his cheap motel room instead of giving me a ride home. He wanted to know every detail about every ex and every confession would come back to haunt me.

We couldn't go anywhere without getting into a fight. If we went to dinner, the waiter was flirting. If we went to a bar, the night usually ended with Dustin threatening to break a beer bottle over some confused guy's head. If we went to a movie, I had to research multiple newspapers until I found out the names of the characters the actors were playing. I learned that lesson the hard way. When we were sitting in the theater watching the movie *Speed* with Sandra Bullock and Keanu Reeves, the character's names were Jack and Annie. We weren't in the movie for fifteen minutes and Dustin said, "Let's go."

"What?" I asked, confused.

"Come on. We're leaving."

"Why?" He stood up and gripped my forearm.

"I said let's go, you fucking whore." I just thanked God we were in the dark and then I followed him out of the theater like a stupid baby duck.

When we watched TV, I waited for a name to come up that would set him off like a Chinese rocket, ruining the night. Dustin destroyed the VHS tape of my graduation because Ty was in the background. That was so heartbreaking because that was the only video I had of Maw Maw. He took a Sharpie to my high school yearbooks, blacking out my life before I knew him. When he found out that my cat, Curtis, was a gift from Ty, suddenly the cat was a problem.

"I hate all the fur all over my clothes," he said. He started complaining nonstop about the cat. Her personality changed and she started hiding in the laundry room behind the dryer. I was afraid that he might hurt her, so I gave her to one of my mom's friends.

Dustin was even jealous of my father. On the rare occasions when Daddy was in Nashville, I had to make excuses why I couldn't go to dinner or a movie with him. Dustin would show up at Brown's Diner every day I worked and sit there drinking and scowling at anyone who looked at me. "I saw you over there flashing your tits at that guy in the back booth," he said.

Waiting tables under his watchful eye made me a jumpy wreck. When one of my few friends, like Kenny Chesney, came in, I ignored him, hurrying away from his table instead of saying hi. It didn't take long for the bartender, Terry, to ban Dustin from Brown's, and from that day on, Dustin relentlessly begged me to quit. "We don't need the money and I thought you moved here to be a songwriter," he said. "You need to focus on writing songs." And how in the hell was I supposed to write with anybody when I could only write when Dustin let me?

Music business parties were always the worst. Every single one of them was followed by a three day, knock-down, drag-out fight. The BMI Awards were the biggest celebration to honor composers. They were kind of like the Academy Awards for song-writers. It was their night to shine. I looked forward to the BMI Awards more than I did my birthday. All the hitmakers, famous artists, and publishers of the top fifty, most-played country songs of the year received awards. I had gone to the BMI Awards with my dad and it was bliss. When the day of the show came, Dustin tossed me the checkbook.

"Here, baby, go get you a dress for tonight." He was always generous, but I had to find something that he would actually let me wear. I picked out a dress I loved. It was royal blue with hot pink sequins, and a frilly, short skirt. It looked like something my high school hero, Cyndi Lauper, would have worn, but on the drive home I worried he wouldn't like it, so I made one last stop at Dress Barn. I had only been in there with my mom, and most of the clothes looked like grandma dresses, but there was a red suit hanging in the back corner that appeared professional and dignified.

I got back to our apartment and Dustin asked to see what I had bought. I went into the bathroom, put on my favorite dress and came out. "Spin around," he said. "Well, you're not wearing that one."

"This is the one I like." I twirled around some more.

"Well, we're not going to a whore convention," he said. "So, you can take that one back."

"What's wrong with it?"

"What else is in here?" He rattled the bag.

"There's a suit." I went into the bathroom and put it on. In the fluorescent light, I realized the fabric was more of a maroon than red. It was made of thick, brocade fabric with five ornate brass buttons down the front. I busted out laughing because I looked like some kind of confused newscaster. "Come on, let me see it," he yelled. I walked out with a crazy smile that said, Can you believe this shit?

"Yeah, that's the one."

"I'm not wearing this anywhere."

"Well, I don't give a shit. Just be ready to go at six."

I put on the suit and tried to convince myself that I looked older and like a businesswoman. My self-esteem was at an all-time low. I had gained over twenty pounds and gone up two sizes in jeans. I was miserable. I didn't buy clothes I liked anymore, I bought clothes Dustin approved of; nothing that revealed too much leg or too much cleavage. Even if I had worn a burka, Dustin would still be wondering who I was looking at through the small eye slits.

When our truck pulled up in front of the event, it was lit up like a Hollywood premiere. The valet guy opened my door and reached for my hand, but I knew better than to let him grab it, so I jumped out of the truck. We walked up the stairs and there were so many lights and camera flashes as everyone stopped Dustin to talk. As I walked the red carpet, I was in a dream. I followed Dustin over to a table where women sat with index cards. They pulled out a red ribbon with a gold medallion and put it around his neck. I stared at it like it was My Precious from Lord of the Rings. Dustin was in a good mood since he was getting an award for a song he had written. At the cocktail reception in the lobby, I ate a couple of chocolate-covered strawberries and killed three Coors Lights to give me the courage I needed in case I got a chance to talk to any of the female music publishers.

When we walked into the ballroom, it was overwhelming. I absorbed the buzzing opportunity in the air. Everyone that was anyone in the country music world was under that white tent. It seemed a thousand feet high and music royalty was in the air. Glasses clinked, champagne and red wine poured as we made our way through the room to look for our table. I passed Kris Krist-offerson from the original A Star is Born movie and my all-time favorite country music songwriter. I ached to talk to him and tell him how much I loved "Me and Bobby McGee" and "Sunday Morning Coming Down." To tell him how much his songs inspired me. But I kept walking.

Once we were seated, I had a perfect view of the stage. Francis Preston, the president of BMI, walked around the stage in pearls that hung down to the ground. "And our next song is "Chattahoochee," written by Alan Jackson and Jim McBride. It was recorded by Alan Jackson. The music blasted over the speakers.

I watched each songwriter climb the stairs to collect their awards. They all had a red ribbon around their necks and posed for pictures with the producers and publishers. I wanted to be one of them so badly that it physically hurt. After Dustin received his award, he went to work the room. He was still in pursuit of a new record deal and a couple of labels were interested. I scanned the crowd until I found the two women publishers I wanted to talk to; Karen Conrad, who owned AMR Publishing, a company my dad had written for, and Kelly Ellis from Blue Sky Music. "Hi Karen, it's Aimee Mayo, Danny's daughter. I've been writing songs for over a year and I wanted to ask if I could come play them for you."

"Well, call Ron at the office and we'll see if we can set something up, okay, hon?" I tried to keep her attention, but she turned back to the stage.

Kelly Ellis blew me off when I tried to introduce myself. About two-thirds of the way into the show I had to go to the restroom, but couldn't find Dustin. I walked through the tables and didn't take my eyes off of the stage, until I ran straight into Dolly Parton. Oh. My. God. I stared at her, stunned. She seemed like a Barbie doll with her big dimples and tiny waist and she smelled like cotton candy and hairspray.

She put her hands up to cradle my face and said, "Oh, honey, you look so pretty, but you gotta watch out where you're goin'." I felt the graze of her long fingernails on the sides of my cheeks and I heard her little signature little "hee hee" laugh as she walked off.

It may have been October, but the summer hadn't let go yet. I was burning up in my suit as I stood in line for the bathroom. All the girls wore strapless gowns and short, black dresses and I felt like an idiot in my maroon suit. Loretta Lynn was behind me in line and my heart was beating like a bass drum. I turned around and said, "I love you. Go in front of me."

When I came out of the bathroom, I ran straight into one of my dad's oldest friends, Woody. His arms were outstretched and he was headed straight for me, but Dustin's golden rule was no hugging men under any circumstances. He instructed me to shake hands instead. But it would have been more natural for me to walk up and kick Woody in the shin than to stick out my hand. So I covered for myself by saying, "No, no, don't get too close. I've been sick."

"I don't care, girl," he slurred as he wrapped his arms around me. "How's that crazy daddy of yours doing?"

"I don't know. I haven't seen him in about three months." Dustin walked up, holding his award plaque, and I could tell by the look in his eyes that it was going to be a bad night. He couldn't hide his anger, and when Woody stuck his hand out, Dustin shrugged him off. "Come on. We're leaving." Dustin led me away before I could say goodbye.

We hadn't even seen who won 'Song of the Year' or 'Songwriter of the Year' yet. There was a big surprise performance coming up and I was hoping it would be Tim McGraw. I did not want to leave. "Now," Dustin said and grabbed me harder by the arm. I stared at the stage, looking back over my shoulder as he led me through the tables, bumping chairs and knocking into arms, spilling drinks. As we walked out, I tried not to cry. I looked back at the stage and swore to myself, someday I'm going to walk up those steps.

At the end of a long hallway on the way to the exit, Dustin shoved me. "Go get in the truck, you fucking whore." I tried to catch myself, but I fell in front of a group of women who were sitting on the marble floor in their ball gowns with their shoes off, talking and smoking. I tried to play it off, but Dustin glared at them and put his arm around my waist. He was nice as we walked through the lobby, and I thought that he might be calming down when he smiled to get my coat. He said goodbye to everybody, and we waited for the truck. I asked, "Can we please go back in and see who wins?" The valet opened the door and smiled at me. Then he took my hand to help me into the truck. "Yeah, hold her hand. She'll probably let you fuck her too," Dustin snapped at him.

He drove straight to Rafferty's Restaurant and went into the bar while I waited on him in the truck for about an hour. When he came out, he was blind drunk. "You're too drunk to drive," I said and took the keys. He chased me through traffic and out into the center of the intersection, tackling me to get the keys. We rolled around in the middle of the grassy median. A woman shouted from the Rafferty's parking lot, "Get off her! I'm calling the police!"

Moments later, a couple of guys pulled up and one of them got out of a Corvette and came over. He stood above us and looked like the Incredible Hulk, except he was black with a tight white t-shirt. He reached down and helped me up while Dustin kept yelling. "Mind your own fucking business."

"Somebody needs to teach you some manners," the guy said in a low voice. Then I heard sirens and saw two police cars flashing their lights. "Are you going to be okay?" the guy asked.

"I'm okay, thank you," I said, trying to catch my breath. He walked across the street to get in his car and an officer headed toward him.

"He was trying to help me!" I yelled at the cop.

The officers motioned for us to get out of the median and I ran to the sidewalk. Dustin followed.

"Yeah, I saw the whole thing," the woman from Rafferty's said. She was shaking.

"Okay, what happened?" the officer asked. "He chased her and jumped on her and started beating the hell out of her," the lady said. "I've never seen anything like the way he was hitting her. And then he started choking her. I was too afraid to try to break it up. "

"I didn't hurt her, officer. It was just a misunderstanding," Dustin slurred. My blazer was ripped at the shoulder and two of the brass buttons were gone, so I tried to hold it shut. Dustin looked like a drunk Woody from Toy Story. He couldn't control his legs. "Look at her, she's okay," he huffed to the woman.

She got right in his face and I loved every syllable she said, "You were trying to choke her out."

One of the cops looked at me and asked, "What do you want us to do?"

"He's just drunk. Everything's okay, can I just take him home?"

A Bible and a Bud Light

THE DAY AFTER THE AWARDS SHOW, Mike called. He said, "Tomorrow your mama's having another surgery on her back. The doctor said he might have to fuse her spine."

I started packing and told Dustin I was going to Alabama.

"We can't go until Sunday," he said. "I'm playing the Red River Grill this weekend." Red River was a restaurant that had an outdoor bar and deck where Dustin performed with the house band a couple of times a month.

"Dustin, I'm going. This is a more serious surgery than last time and Mama needs me there." After going over the rules of what I could and couldn't do while I was in Gadsden, Dustin finally gave in. I made it to the hospital while Mom was still in surgery. Dustin kept me up all night at the hospital. He called every thirty minutes, making sure I was there. I spent more time on the phone with him than I did caring for my mom.

Driving back to Nashville, I was running on fumes and no sleep. I pulled in the driveway at 4:30 am and I hoped Dustin would be in bed, but he was waiting for me in the dark in the living room. He started drilling me the moment I walked in the door. "Who'd you see? Where'd you go? Who all did you talk to? Who came up to the hospital?" He asked me the same questions repeatedly for hours, tearfully begging me to tell him the truth.

"I didn't see anybody. I was at the hospital."

"Well, that's a lie," he said and took a big swig of Bud Light. "You're telling me you didn't go anywhere but the hospital?" I went through each step of the two days I was there.

"I saw Opal and Harold. Dad's living there again, but he wouldn't come out of the bedroom. I took Cory to Baskin Robbins to get ice cream. I repent," I said sarcastically.

"I know there's something you're leaving out and if you'll just tell me the truth, I swear to God I won't be mad at you," he said. "I'll forgive you if you'll just tell me the truth."

I talked to Jerry on the phone for almost two hours. He still lived in Birmingham, but there was no way in hell I was going to tell him that. Confessing nothing, I sat on the bedroom floor with my arms around my knees. This went on until I felt like I was losing grasp of reality. His questioning eyes were strained and bloodshot, and my brain felt like a French-fried tater tot. Dustin got me so confused and sleep-deprived that I felt like I was lying when I told the truth. My thoughts were so unclear. I almost believed I had done something wrong. He would interrogate me until I felt like a criminal. I had been awake for forty-eight hours and he would confuse me until I felt like talking to someone was cheating on him.

Dustin stormed out of the bedroom and came back with the dusty King James Bible. I knew it was going to be an all-nighter. He had a bible in one hand and a Bud Light in the other. First, he started reading and slurring the words, "Wives obey your hus-

bands as you obey the Lord. The husband is the head of the wife."
Then he grabbed my hand and placed it on the textured, burgundy leather across the gold words and held it there.

"Do you swear to God on your mother's life that the only places you went are where you told me? And that you didn't see anybody or talk to anybody else?"

"I'm not doing it," I said and pulled my hand back.

"Aimee, you'd better put your hand on this bible right now."

"She's in the hospital and there's no way I'm doing that."

"Then you're lying," Dustin shouted at me and punched the wall. Our bedroom already looked like a battlefield. The bed looked like a fucked up unicorn since he had knocked all the posts off but one. The other three sat propped in the corner of the room like vampire stakes. It was easy to see something was wrong with our marriage the minute you walked into our apartment. There was a Johnny Cash poster hanging waist level in the hall, and a full-length mirror hung too low on our bathroom door. They were there to cover the fist-shaped holes.

I thought about making something up so he would shut up and let me go to sleep, then right about that time I remembered....

"Okay, I went to Walmart with my Aunt Debbie to get Mom a nightgown and some toiletries my second day there."

He stood up, trying to walk in two directions at the same time. "I knew you were out whoring around. I knew you were lying to me. Who'd you see?"

"Dustin, I went to Walmart. You act like I pulled a three-day gang bang on the Dallas Cowboys."

East of Eden

WE WENT BACK TO OUR regular pattern. I ignored Dustin for a few days, and he apologized, promising that things would be different. He painted this watercolor dream of how wonderful everything was going to be if I gave him one more chance. Sometimes we went weeks without fighting. For my twenty-second birthday, Dustin bought me smiley face pajamas, a Nintendo, Super Mario Bros., Gorilla house shoes and a ceiling fan. He made me a birthday cake from scratch. Dustin could be great when he wanted to be. I tried to make myself believe that he could change if I just loved him enough and helped him.

But if he couldn't change, I had to get away from him. Twelve hours a week at Brown's Diner wasn't going to get me very far. Every day I prayed obsessively that Karen Conrad from AMR Publishing would call and ask me to come to her office on Music Row and play her songs. It had been almost two months since I had seen her at the BMI Awards. The only time I was happy was when we were writing and that was all at Dustin's mercy. He knew how bad I wanted to join in when he had a co-writer come over. Sometimes he let me and sometimes he didn't. It just all depended on how I was behaving.

That December, a phone call came that was the best Christmas present I could ever ask for. Decca Records called and asked to put a song on hold that we had written called "Story of My Life." There was a new band, East of Eden, that they had just signed. A hold is when an artist or producer asks you to hold off on playing the song for anyone else while they decide if they want to record it on their record.

Dustin had a showcase at a bar where he played with a live band, and he performed for three different record labels. Warner Records was interested in signing him and he was like a different person. As wrong as everything had been, things started going right. If I had a hit song, that would be my golden ticket to get the hell away from him.

I called Karen and told her about having a song on hold and asked her if I could come to AMR and play it for her and Ron. She said yes! The following Tuesday I left two hours early for my meeting. I drove in circles around Music Row until it was time to go into AMR Music Publishing. They shared the same office as Polygram Publishing and Mercury Records. I walked into the lobby and there were so many framed platinum records that it looked like the walls were covered in aluminum foil. I rode the elevator up and waited for Karen to come out and get me. Instead, a guy around thirty years old came out and said, "Come on Aimee, Karen's waiting for you." It was Ron Stuve.

I knew him from when Dad had written for Karen. I walked

into her office, but I was so excited that I didn't sit down for the
first couple of minutes talking ninety to nothing. I looked at her
sitting behind her large, ornate desk. She reminded me of Paula
Abdul. She was as classy as it gets. "How long have you been
writing songs, Aimee?" she asked.

"Since I was eight."

"Well, your dad called me the other day and told me you had
a song on hold with East of Eden. He played me the demo over
the phone twice. He's so proud of you." My heart stood still thinking about Daddy telling her that I was writing. I didn't know Dad
had even listened to the cassette I left for him at Opal's. "Your
Dad says you're pretty talented, so I think I need to hear these
songs," she laughed. When she hit play on the first song, it was
"Story of My Life." She listened and nodded her head. "Yeah, I
know that one. I want to hear some new songs."

She hit the intercom button and said, "Ron, come back in
here, please." He walked in and sat down on the arm of a chair.
"I like that purse," Karen said. "Show it to Ron." I held it up.

It was silver and looked like a little boom box. "I got it at
Walmart," I said, and then felt stupid for saying it, so I kept on
talking. "I mean, all I want to do is write songs. That's all I've
ever done and that's what I'm gonna do. You have no idea how
bad I want to write for y'all." I had to force myself to stop talking.
Karen reached across her big, oak desk and picked up my cassette.

She took it out of the plastic case and before she put it in the
stereo, she said, "And these are your new songs, right?"

"Yes."

She listened over the loudspeakers and I tried to watch her
and Ron's facial expressions. All of a sudden, everything seemed
wrong with the songs. I sat there taking them apart. I shouldn't
have said that. Oh my God, this title isn't strong enough. This
melody sucks.

"Okay, who did you write this next one with?" she asked and
paused the tape, not saying anything about the first song.

"I wrote all these songs with Dustin."

"Do you plan on continuing to write with Dustin?" Ron
asked.

"Oh yeah, for sure."

"Do you play guitar?"

"No, I mean, I try to play a little, but I'm not very good."

She pressed play and the next song came on. She said nothing again and listened to the last two songs on the cassette, then handed it back to me. I was heartbroken. She didn't even want to keep it. "Does Dustin have another record deal? He's such an amazing singer," Ron said.

"Well, he's talking to a couple of labels and there's one that's really interested. They're probably gonna sign him in the next few weeks."

"Do you think you're gonna get some songs on his next record?"

"Yes, we've got a few he wants to record."

They asked me about writing with Dustin twice, so I felt like the only thing they cared about was that Dustin was a co-writer on the songs. "What about your dad, will you write with him?" Karen asked.

"I don't know if I could write with him, he's crazy," I said, and she laughed.

"Well, Aimee, thank you for coming in. Maybe you can come back in a couple of months and play us some more songs."

"Blue Sky Publishing might want to sign me," I blurted out. "We're setting up a meeting for me to play them songs." I had talked to the owner one day when I wrote there with Dustin and one of their signed writers. I was hoping Karen might be concerned that she could lose me, but that plan backfired.

"Oh, they're a great company. Pat's a wonderful publisher," Karen said, getting up from behind her desk. When I got to my car, I dropped my head on the steering wheel and cried so hard I made myself sick.

South Wind Street

THAT FEBRUARY, DUSTIN TOOK me to look at a three-bedroom, brick, two-level house in a high-end subdivision. I loved the sunny, manicured lawns and the garage door opener. I couldn't wait to put my clothes in the walk-in closet and take a bath in the oversized jacuzzi tub. We went on a shopping spree to Sprint's Furniture. He let me pick out all new things: a cream-colored leather sofa and loveseat, a new bedroom suit. As bad as things were at Stone Ridge Apartments, they were nothing compared to the hell I had coming at 402 South Wind Street.

I never met any of our neighbors. When kids skipped down the sidewalk selling Girl Scout Cookies, they never knocked on our door. On Halloween, our candy bowl sat untouched on the front porch. Women stared, but never spoke, and I knew why.

The day we were moving in, Dustin found a five by seven photo of my high school boyfriend Ty and I at my senior prom. He attacked me in the driveway. I was carrying a cardboard box full of picture frames when he came up behind me and kicked me in the lower back. The box flew from my hands, shattering glass everywhere. I barely caught myself, scraping the palms of my hands bloody and pink. I sat back on my knees. "What the fuck is wrong with you?" I screamed.

"I told you to get rid of this shit." He shoved a photo in my face. "You've probably been talking to him the whole time we've been married, you fucking whore."

"Get the fuck away from me," I said. The next thing I knew, my face was against the concrete. I heard something shuffle beside me and looked up. Standing ten feet from me was a teenaged girl. She was in a purple and yellow cheerleading uniform. She was frozen in shock at what she had just witnessed. We locked eyes. I'll never forget the way she looked at me if I live to be a hundred years old. She was frightened by Dustin, but equally repulsed by me. Seeing the look in her eyes showed me to myself. I was a pathetic victim. She threw her gold and purple pompoms into the back seat of her mom's Volvo and sped away.

The houses in our subdivision were so close that if I stood between them, I could touch both. There was more privacy living in our apartment. I knew everyone heard the screaming. Helen Keller could have heard the screaming. When I thought my life couldn't get worse, Dustin told me his mother and sons were coming to live with us for a while. My heart dropped into my stomach. His mother was an ice-cold bitch and we had been allergic to each other from the moment we met. Dustin didn't come with baggage, he came dragging a whole damn airport, but I tried to see the brightside; maybe he wouldn't be so scary violent with his kids living here.

Within a week, Annalise took over most of the wifely duties. She cleaned the house, cooked every meal, bought the groceries, did the laundry, and glared at me if I got near the oven. The only time I cooked was when Dustin specifically asked me to make something he wanted. The only things I knew how to make were spaghetti and red velvet cake. I didn't feel like the woman of the house. I felt like a trapped kid. I felt grounded all over again. But to my surprise, I loved Robbie and Blaine living with us.

As fucked up as Dustin was, he was a good father. Most weekends he would take them fishing or hunting. I ignored Annalise and she ignored me. I stayed in our bedroom with the door locked. I grew close to Dustin's younger son, Robbie. We played Tetris every night on the computer, and he let me put make-up on him and dress him up. Dustin and Annalise were horrified. Dustin stormed upstairs, yelling at me when he saw it. "Get that shit off his face."

It wasn't long until the whole house smelled like Annalise. We fell into some weird family dynamic where I was like one of their kids and the boys were my stepbrothers. When Dustin stayed out late, we ate dinner in silence; forks scraping plates, meatloaf that tasted like embalming fluid. I was closer in age to Dustin's boys than I was him and I felt more like their sister than their stepmother. Everywhere we went, everyone thought I was one of Dustin's kids. When we went through the bank drive-through, all piled up in the front seat of the truck, three lollipops always came back in the plastic container. When we ordered at a restaurant, the waiter always asked, "And for your daughter?"

One night, Dustin came in from the studio where he had been recording all day, kicked off his ostrich-skin boots by the front door, and slung his black Stetson cowboy hat on the side table. I sat on the ottoman in front of the TV watching the live footage of OJ Simpson in his white Bronco being chased by the police. Dustin plopped down on the leather couch behind me. "Go fix me something to eat," he said.

"I will in a minute."

"Now." He kicked the ottoman with his foot.

"I'll fix you something, honey," his Mom chimed it.

"No, Aimee can do it," he said. I saw the smirk on Annalise's face without turning around.

"I'm watching this, let your mama do it," I said.

With no warning, Dustin flew at me and yanked me off the couch by my hair. Then he gripped it tighter and dragged me across the living room, dropping me in the middle of the kitchen floor. He was tearing open the brown, wooden cabinets. Dustin started throwing pots and pans and small appliances at me. The electric can opener hit me in the chin, striking it numb. I could tell it was bleeding. I felt pathetic cowering on the floor and covering my head. When I looked up at Dustin, his face was red and I could see every tendon in his neck. I glared at him. My hatred was strong enough to glow in the dark. I saw the wooden knife block on the counter behind him and I heard a voice in my head say, "Grab it. Grab it." I saw a flash of myself grasping the biggest butcher knife and stabbing him over and over in the side of the neck. I imagined the blood spurting and soaking through his white t-shirt.

That's when I heard sniffling on the stairs. His sons were there. They had witnessed it all. The side of my head was burning raw with pain. "I fucking hate you, Dustin," I screamed.

He jerked me up by the hair again, gripping it like a cowboy would hold a rope. "When I tell you to do something, you get up off your fat ass and do it," he said through gritted teeth. "Do you understand me?" He tightened his grip with each word. I didn't care what he did. There was no way I would say yes, I understand.

What happened next was the biggest shock of all. His mother walked into the kitchen and stepped over me like I was a piece of lint. She picked up a Calphalon skillet and started frying him a BLT. "How can you do that in the fucking aftermath of what just happened, you crazy witch?" I wanted to scream, staring at her boxy rear end and hearing the bacon sizzling.

Getting up off the floor, I walked to the back door and slammed it as hard as I could, stepping out into the night. I dropped down to my knees in the backyard and I felt the wet grass and mud soaking through my jeans. I stared up at the three anemic stars in the Nashville sky and started to cry. *HOW IS THIS MY LIFE? How is this my life? How did I make such a mess out of my life? God, please get me out of here before he kills me. I'm begging you.*

Losing Myself, Grapefruit Moon

THE FOLLOWING MORNING, I woke up earlier than usual and I saw something out of the corner of my eye. *Where did that brown wig on my pillow come from?* I wondered. Just as I was leaning down to look at it, I realized, oh my God, that's my hair! I felt a ringing in my throat and ran to the bathroom. I was scared to look in the mirror. I thought all my hair was going to be gone. When I finally worked up the courage, I stared at the softball-sized patch of bare, pink scalp. It was the color of a school eraser. There was no way in hell I could hide this. Somebody was going to see it.

My head was so tender that I could barely get my shirt on. The last thing I wanted to do was go to Brown's Diner and wait tables all day, but the thought of staying in that house with Annalise made me want to throw up. I got dressed as fast as I could and headed to work. I was terrified that somebody was going to pat me on the head, or hug me and accidentally tug at my hair. the way when you have an injury and people are almost magnetically drawn to it. I was a zombie going through the motions. When I got off work, the heavy dread of going home set in. I sat at the bar and had three beers in frosty cold mugs. It was April and warmer than usual.

I walked around the corner to the MAPCO that shared the same parking lot with Brown's Diner to get some cigarettes. I heard the little bell on the door jingle and a giggling group of girls came in. They walked past me and headed into the aisle with the coolers of refrigerated drinks. I couldn't stop staring at them. I was twenty-two and they were close to my age, but I felt like their grandmother. They were living in an alternate universe, arguing over peach or strawberry wine coolers. They jumped in front of me, laughing. They were wearing cut-off, blue jean shorts, tank tops, with their tan legs and toe rings, and glitter nail polish. I longed to be one of them. Then I caught my reflection in the glass door of the refrigerator. Standing there in my pastel prairie dress, I looked like I had escaped from a Mormon cult.

They smelled like summer and flirted with the clerk. "What are you girls getting into tonight?" he asked.

"You'll never know," the blonde one said, and their laughter hung in the air and stabbed me like a thousand knives.

I held my head down, trying not to make eye contact. My heart felt like it was being squeezed so tight that it was going to burst. I watched them jump into a black Jeep with a Belmont College bumper sticker on the back, and they wandered out into the night, happy and free.

Driving home from Brown's, the night was balmy, and the moon was in that phase where it looks a hundred times its normal size. Like it's almost sitting on your shoulder. It looked so big. It looked like I might run into it with my car. For months I had been desperately praying and hoping that God would get me out of this marriage. That a door I could not even see would open and I could walk through it into the life that I was supposed to be living. I tried to make myself believe that someday this would all be a bad dream. A glitch in time. A distant memory. But I was stuck in reality.

I pulled the car over in the parking lot of Blockbuster Video, a half of a mile from our house. I felt myself beginning to crack. I didn't know how I fucked up my life so fast. I was dependent on him financially. I felt myself fading away. I had lost all of my hometown friends because Dustin wouldn't let me talk to them, and now I was losing myself completely. My internal dialogue had turned into Dustin's words.

Something about that giant grapefruit moon made me stop and realize that this was my one and only life and I was wasting it. I've been throwing it into the trash can like an empty bottle of nothing. I've been morphing into some version of a pity case that Dustin has created. Not the person who God made me. Not the person who I had always been. And definitely not the person I wanted to be. Where was that little girl with the unbreakable spirit? Who drew detailed dream houses and filled thousands of pages of diaries and spiral notebooks with plans, poetry, and dreams? Walking in circles, aimlessly in the moonlight, I talked out loud to God: *Just tell me what to do and I'll do it. Please show me what to do. I need help. I'm not strong enough to do this by myself."*

Places I've Never Been

I SWORE TO GOD AND MYSELF that no matter what I had to do, I was signing a publishing deal and getting away from Dustin. The boys decided that they wanted to move back to Texarkana with their mom. They said it was because they missed her, but I knew it was because of what had happened. Dustin asked his mom to go back too, so that we could work on our marriage.

The only things that kept me going were my second meeting with Karen to play her new music, and an appointment with the publisher, Blue Sky Music. The people at Blue Sky liked all my songs, but lost interest when they learned that I didn't sing, play guitar, or the piano. The owner of the company said, "Well, I just don't understand how that would work." And that was the last I heard of them.

My second meeting with Karen and Ron at AMR was shorter than the first. I played them two new songs that I had written with Dustin. Karen closed her eyes and nodded her head as she listened, then asked, "Can you write something by yourself? Just so we can get a feel for *your* voice as a writer?"

"And maybe write something with someone besides Dustin?" Ron chimed in. "I've got a couple of writers I think you'd be good with," he said.

"For sure!" I answered, even though I had no idea how I was going to pull that off. I drove straight home and went through all my binders and picked two of my favorite lyrics. I sang stuff until I found a melody I loved and finished a song by myself called "I've Always Been Alone."

Dustin still felt guilty about the hair scalping episode and I had ignored him for weeks, but that night I made spaghetti, cleaned the house, and told him that I wanted to work on being a better wife. After dinner I told Dustin that Karen wanted me to write a song by myself. I asked him if he would help record it. I needed him to sing and play guitar on the work tape. The only way I could record it by myself was acapella, and there was no way in hell I was doing that. I had enough problems. If they found out I was tone-deaf, they would never sign me to a writing deal. For the next week, I was on my best behavior to avoid upsetting Dustin. I did everything I could to make him happy.

Then I got a phone call at Brown's Diner one afternoon that wrecked me. It was from Jerry. He had to call me at work because he knew that Dustin wouldn't let me talk to him. Jerry told me that he had cancer. He told me the kind, but I didn't hear anything past the word 'cancer.' He was twenty-one years old. "I got diagnosed about six months ago," he said. "And the doctors don't think I'm gonna make it much longer."

I felt hysterical, but I tried to sound hopeful. "Have you been to more than one doctor?"

"I've been to three." His voice sounded weak. It was almost a whisper. "I love you, Aimee, and I hope I can see you sometime soon."

"I love you too. And I'm gonna find a way to come to Birmingham and see you." I promised him. Later that night, I couldn't stop crying and Dustin asked, "What's wrong with you?"

"Jerry called me at work today at Brown's and..."

"What the fuck is he doing calling you?" he said.

"He's got cancer and it's really bad."

"Well, don't think if he dies, you're going to that funeral," Dustin shot back.

I hated him in that moment, more than I had ever hated anything. It took everything inside me not to tackle him and beat the shit out of him, but I was too afraid. I had never hit him back. I went to bed.

That night I stared at him with red hot hatred watching him sleep. I hated his stupid, big, black cowboy hat. I hated his freckled shoulders, his long, knobby toes, his receding hairline. I hated his bow-legged hips and his stupid starched shirts, the way he wore his baseball cap too high on his head. I hated the way he piled his jaw full of Copenhagen and how it looked like he had a mouth full of monkey shit. I hated his beady, blue eyes. I hated the gurgly sound he made in the back of his throat when he slept. I hated the way he said my name and all the dumb ass shows he liked on TV. I hated every pore on his face, but I needed his help.

I knew I couldn't see Jerry until I was closer to getting a writing deal and I hated myself for not leaving after what Dustin said about Jerry. But I hated myself even more for sleeping with him. I felt like a pathetic piece of shit, but I had to have those work tapes. They were my only ticket out of that house.

One morning the following week, we sat down at the kitchen table and Dustin said, "Okay, let me see what you got." Then I gave him the lyrics and hummed the verse and chorus to the song I wrote on my own. I also played him a song called "Rain King" by the Counting Crows and told him,

"I want it to feel like this vibe and tempo."

Dustin listened and figured out the chords on the acoustic guitar, and then we recorded a work tape on the boombox. It sounded like a completely different song with his voice on it. Dustin really liked another idea I had called "Places I've Never Been," and he came back from writing that day and said, "I told Tony and Reese about your idea and they like it. They said they'd finish it with you."

They were two of Dustin's closest friends who worked with him weekly. I had been around them a lot, but they were both older, established songwriters and they would have never written with me unless he asked them to. I don't think Dustin would have let me work with them unless it was his idea.

A week later, I walked into Sony Music thirty minutes early and waited in the lobby until Reese came to get me. "Come on back, girl," he said, and we walked into Tony's office. When I sat down, Tony said, "Dustin told us your idea and I think it could be a great song."

They sat in leather chairs, but I sat cross-legged on the floor so I could spread out all my lyrics and notebooks. I gave them the lyrics I had and they did the rest. I didn't get a word in. The song needed a second verse, which they wrote, and then they worked on the music and melody. Forty-five minutes later, the song was done. They had written hits, so I had to trust that they knew what they were doing on the second verse. "Okay, it was good to see you, girl," Tony said, and they both got up, letting me know it was time to leave.

"Sorry to run you out so fast. We've got a demo session at 2 o'clock," Reese said. "We'll let you know if we put this song on it."

"Can I get a copy of the work tape real quick, so I can listen to it?" I asked Reese, and he sat down and played it on acoustic guitar. It was wham-bam, thank you, ma'am, and I was out the door. But I loved the song.

Bite

I LISTENED TO THE WORK TAPE over and over on the drive home and my heart was like a jumping bean every time I heard it. Mama was the first person I called. I played her the song over the phone and told her, "You're where I got this idea and lyric." She and my Aunt Lana had won a trip to Jamaica and when they came back, they couldn't stop talking about how much they loved it. That's where the first line came from:

I've never seen the sunset in Montego Bay, but I get a chill when you look at me that way

And then the chorus:

You take me places that I've never been. I've traveled the world in your arms and back again.

Mom made me play it for her three times. "I'm so proud of you, baby. I love that song and I bet you get a publishing deal with that one."

Dustin came in around 11:00 pm and I was still on the phone with Mom grinning ear to ear. I jumped up and hugged him. He smelled like whiskey and smoke. I sat back down on the floor with the boombox.

"Dustin, I can't wait for you to hear it. Even Tony and Reese think it's a hit!"

He stood next to the wall holding on to it to steady himself while he took off his cowboy boots.

"Well, it turned out better than I thought it would. You're lucky I got them to write with you," he said.

"I'm playing it for Karen and Ron tomorrow at 1:00 o'clock and I'm hoping they're gonna wanna sign me when they hear this song."

"Aimee, they're not gonna sign you. They never were. They're just being nice because of who your dad is," he hiccupped. "And because you're married to me and they want songs on my next record."

"What record? You don't even have a record deal," I came back at him.

"You'd better shut your fucking mouth."

"Well, why would they keep calling me back over there if they didn't like my songs?"

"You can't do shit without me. You can't sing your songs. You can't play guitar. You can't do anything and nobody would write with you anyway."

"Well you wanted to write with me. You loved my ideas and lyrics," I said.

"Yeah, I wanted to get in your pants. That's the only reason I ever worked with you."

"Ron has a couple song writers that he's gonna set me up with. Some guy named Sam and..."

"That ain't gonna happen," Dustin said in a cocky voice coming towards me. "I'm not having my wife running around all over town in and out of rooms with men."

"If they set me up with people, I'm gonna have to write."

"You can work with any girls you want to."

"What girls? I don't even know any girl songwriters." There were a few women writers, but they all had record deals. "There's no way they're gonna sign me if I can't write with anybody!"

"Well, if you think you're going to sit in a room all day alone with a man, you're crazy."

"If I get a writing deal, I'm gonna write."

Dustin took my smoky gray cassette out of the boombox and started pulling the ribbon out of it. "Uh, oh. How are you gonna play it now?"

"Stop! I hate you!" I tried to grab it.

"Aimee, I've tried, and I've tried to break your spirit, but..."

"Shut the fuck up!" I jerked the work tape from his hands and screamed again, "If I get a writing deal, I'm gonna write!"

It took me a minute to realize what was happening next. Dustin took my head, shoved it into the carpet, and then I felt a red-hot ring of fire. I thought he was cutting my face with something. When I saw his eyes as big as golf balls looking at my face, I started screaming, "What did you do? Oh, my God!"

"I'm going to end up killing you, Aimee. It's going to be your fault because of your fucking mouth."

"Did you just bite me in the fucking face? I'm calling the police." I ran towards the phone on the bedside table and he jerked the cord out of the wall. "You're a monster!" I screamed at him.

He fell to his knees in front of me and wrapped his arms around my thighs and started into his psycho cry. "I don't know what's wrong with me. I can't believe I just did that to you. I need help. I know I need help." He was sobbing.

Kicking loose from him, I ran to the bathroom, where I always went to lick my wounds. Looking at myself in the mirror, there was no way I could go play the song for Karen and Ron, even if I had it. There wasn't a lie I could make up about a human bite mark on my face. Teeth marks tell the truth.

Finally

FOR THE NEXT TEN DAYS I didn't leave the house. I was too embarrassed and humiliated for anybody to see me. I had to cancel all my shifts at Brown's Diner. I stayed in bed in the dark. One morning the phone rang, and it was Reese. He said, "Hey, girl! We demoed our song with a full band and it's a bad mother fucker. You need to get down to Sony and pick up the copy I left for you at the front desk."

My face was starting to heal. There was a light blue bruise that made a perfect circle with a bluish-red blood clot about the size of a marble in the middle. I covered it with concealer. That day I sat in my car and listened to the demo of our song, "Places I've Never Been." The sun was shining through my windshield like a halo. I drove straight around the corner to AMR. I didn't have an appointment, but I was so excited for Karen and Ron to hear it. I walked in and went back to Ron's office and knocked on the door.

"Hey girl, we were just talking about you this morning. It looks like Southern Eden is going to record your song. I talked to the producer last night."

"I just picked up this demo at Sony a few minutes ago and I just couldn't wait to play it for y'all. Have you got five minutes to listen?" I asked.

Ron popped it into the stereo and after he listened, he said, "Come on in here," and we walked into Karen's office. "You gotta hear this new song Aimee wrote," he said. Karen turned the song up almost as loud as it would go.

When it ended, she started it again. "I love it," she said. "Who'd you write it with?"

"Tony and Reese over at Sony."

"I can get that song cut," Ron said.

Karen stood up and said, "We've got something we want to tell you."

My mind was electric. I was praying the whole time she was talking. "Does that sound good to you?" Karen asked.

"What?" I asked.

"We want to sign you."

"To a writing deal?"

"Yes to a writing deal," Ron laughed.

"Can I sign it today?"

They were both laughing. "No, it's got to be drawn up by a lawyer."

"I don't need a lawyer. I know I want to do this." I jumped up and hugged Karen and Ron. This is the best decision you ever made. I'm gonna work harder than anyone in this building." I started to cry.

"There's no crying allowed." Ron threw his arm around my shoulder and said, "Come on, I'm heading to a pitch meeting, and I'll walk you out."

The phone on Karen's desk was ringing. She called out, "It's gonna be wonderful. I'm excited!"

I didn't hear a word Ron said as we walked down the hall and got on the elevator. So many emotions were exploding inside me. I wanted to run out of the building screaming with joy, but I controlled myself until I got to my car. When I sat down in the driver's seat, I kicked my legs like an excited preschooler and yelled, "Yes, yes, yes, yes, YES!" I rolled down the windows and sped around the corner in the parking garage.

I slammed on the brakes, almost hitting a man in his mid-fifties. He had on khaki pants and a plaid, purple and white shirt. He jumped out of the way and I could tell I scared the shit out of him. Then I heard Ron yell from across the parking lot, "Don't kill the best damn songwriter on Music Row on your first day!"

It was Bob McDill. He was the most successful songwriter in Nashville. He had written two of my favorite country songs; "Good Ol' Boys Like Me" by Don Williams and "Everything That Glitters Isn't Gold" by Dan Seals, along with over thirty other number ones. I was mortified when he stepped to the side and waved his arm for me to drive by. I motioned for him to go and he shook his head. He wasn't moving until I was gone.

I was buzzing, buzzing with adrenaline and I drove around aimlessly trying to decide who I would call first when I got home. I almost caused a head-on wreck going the wrong direction down 16th Avenue. I decided to pull over until I calmed down. Sitting in the Burger King drive-thru, I ordered a chicken sandwich when I noticed Dustin's truck go by. There was a blonde sitting right up under him. I swerved out of the line and started chasing him. When he saw me in his rear-view mirror, he sped up. I kept on his tail down a back alley of Music Row. He pulled into the parking lot of his publishing company and I saw the girl jump out and she ran in the back door of the building. I blocked him in. "Who the fuck was that?" I screamed.

"That's a new artist on Capitol, Joey Hendricks."

"You're a fucking idiot if you think I believe that."

"Well it's true."

"Then why did you take off when you saw me?" I asked.

"I didn't even know you were behind me," he argued.

"Well guess what? I just got a writing deal, so I don't really give a shit." I peeled out of the parking lot slinging a tornado of gravel. When I got home it was almost dark. I stood in front of the bathroom mirror. I stripped down and saw myself for the first time in a long time in the reflection of the mirror. The bruise from the bite was trying to disappear and the old bruises up and down my arms had turned brown.

I got in the bathtub and tears broke through from somewhere deep inside me. It was one of those big cries. The kind that you know is going to change your life. Two years of torment and I let it go. I let it all go. I thought about all the abuse the women in my family endured. I thought about Maw Maw and how she lived her life. I found myself thinking about my great-grandmother (Paw Paw's mother,) even though I had hardly known her. She always wore a faded, floral house dress. She was round like a little ball and wore her hair in a white bun. She had spooky eyes and as a child, she kind of scared me. Through the years I heard stories about her husband, my great-grandfather, and the hell he put her and his kids through. He was a deacon at church and the devil at home. She ran away, the only place a woman could in those days—in her mind.

I went under the hot water and held my breath as long as I could. When I came up out of the water, I knew. I was leaving. One way or another, I was leaving. I put on my smiley face sweat suit and started packing a duffel bag. I was getting the last of my make-up when Dustin came upstairs. "Where do you think you're going?" he said.

"I'm leaving you," I smiled.

He came towards me, trying to block me in the bathroom. I shoved him out of the way and headed for the door, when he backed me against the wall and said, "You're not going any-where."

I got in his face. "Do you know why you don't have another record deal? Because everybody knows you're a wife-beating psycho. I'm done listening to anything you say. I'm leaving."

He slid open the double closet doors and pulled out a shotgun.

"Come on, do it. I dare you," I laughed. "Shoot me, I'm beg-ging you."

"Aimee you'd better back up," he said. The more he threat-ened me, the more I laughed.

He pointed the gun at my head, and I walked closer to him pressing my forehead into the barrel of the gun, pushing it hard-er and harder into the cold muzzle. I looked straight into his eyes and said, "Pull the trigger. Nothing would make me happier than knowing your redneck ass was rotting in prison. You think people don't know you hit me? You think people don't see the bruises? Everybody at Brown's knows. You'll be locked up by midnight."

"Get the hell out of here. Get the hell out of here before I hurt you, Aimee," he said.

I grabbed the duffle bag and ran to my car. Pulling out of that driveway, the pavement was glittering like metallic silver and the sky looked like a mirror. I rolled the windows down. My first night away from Dustin, I slept in my Nissan Sentra in the parking lot of the Krystal fast food restaurant on Charlotte Avenue. I was scared about sleeping in my car all alone, so I chose somewhere that would be open all night. So that someone would hear me if I screamed.

——

Chapter Nine

FREEBIRD

Free Bird

THE NEXT WEEKEND AS I DROVE, I looked at the sky as much as I did the highway. The stars seemed to shine like a divine invitation to a new beginning. I had cracked open the oyster of life and could finally see the glowing pearl inside. That night, with the fresh air coming through the window on my skin, I had never felt so free. Like a nightingale, a dolphin, a comet, I could go anywhere, and the thought overwhelmed me. I turned twenty-three and finally, for the first time in my whole life, I was free. It was like waking up in a new world. All my life I had been controlled by men, and now I was in control. I could wear what I wanted, watch what I wanted on TV, talk to whomever I wanted, stay on the phone as long as I wanted, eat what I wanted, say what I wanted, and go where I wanted to go. It was like I had been released from an emotional and psychological jail cell.

I went to see Jerry to tell him how sorry I was. Part of me had avoided it because I didn't want his illness to be real. The first thing I did was apologize, and as usual, he was trying to comfort me. Knowing that he had cancer, it was almost unbearable trying not to talk about it, but he didn't want to talk about the chemotherapy that he was about to start. He told me, "I'm so glad you're away from that asshole and I love you."

My first night out with my girlfriends Laurie, Stephanie, and Brooke, we went to celebrate that I was free. I scanned the restaurant before we sat down and I kept one eye on the door, afraid that at any moment Dustin would sneak up behind me and strangle it all away. I had to relearn what normal was.

Mice City

BACK IN NASHVILLE, I had to find an apartment, fast. I had zero credit history. I'd never had a phone bill, water bill, or credit card in my name. Everything was under Dustin's or Dad's name. I had $280 and my Nissan Sentra with the schizophrenic transmission. By law, I was entitled to half the royalties of every song that Dustin had written during our twenty-two months together. If I took him to court, I could get more than enough money to put a down payment on a house. But as much as I needed the money, I wasn't asking him for a penny. I didn't want him to support me in any way. I wanted a clean break so that he had no control over me.

There were these beautiful Spanish twins, Adele and Adelaide, who always hung out in the front room bar at Brown's Diner. They had long, dark, waist-length hair, tan skin, and turned every head when they walked in. I didn't know them that well, but when they found out that I didn't have a place to live, they insisted that I stay with them.

One day I was working at Brown's when they came busting through the door and announced, "We found you an apartment! We found you an apartment and it's right around the corner from us." They gave me the address. It was about a mile from Brown's Diner. When I got off work, I drove straight to Murphy Road and spotted the house.

It was a bungalow that didn't quite fit in with the rest of the homes on the street. There were so many cement figures crowding the front yard that it looked like some kind of statuary store. Walking to the porch, I passed cherubs, fairies, and gnomes, and as I walked up the steps, a breeze passed by, tinkling a dozen wind chimes.

I tapped on the door and an old woman answered. She had wiry, white hair that stood on end like a Troll doll. The panic on her face was like an alarm clock ringing. Then a man who looked about seventy-five years old came up behind her and he glared at me like he was mad that I knocked on their door. "Is the apartment still for rent?" I asked.

"Let me find the key," he said, annoyed.

I followed him down the steppingstone pathway to the back of the house. The backyard was just as crazy as the front. Rainbow glass, sun catchers, and birdhouses were hanging from the trees. The ground was littered with broken statues. There was a seahorse fountain spurting rusty water, and right beside the back door stood a cement frog in a tuxedo holding a little tray. "How much is the rent?" I asked.

"Three hundred dollars and that includes utilities." I tried to ask more questions, but the man couldn't understand my accent and I kept having to repeat everything. We went down a few steps as birdseed crunched underneath our feet. He had a ring with about thirty keys on it and he finally found the one to the little, blue door. When we walked inside the apartment, I busted out laughing. This was the weirdest place I had ever seen. The man had to duck to get under the doorway. The ceiling was no more than six feet high. I could reach up and touch it with the palm of my hand.

The kitchen had a brown stove and an ugly, mustard yellow refrigerator, and a dirty linoleum floor that looked like it might have been yellow in the 1960s. There was a step down to the next room, which was about the size of a grand piano. It had shag carpet the color of orange sherbet and a dingy, beige loveseat. I peeked into the bedroom and the full-sized bed took up the whole room. It had a bedspread that looked like Betsy Ross had sewn it just after she made the American flag. The bathroom was about the size of a phone booth and looked like something you might see at a haunted campground. The shower had green slime growing out of the drain and a dirty, plastic shower curtain.

"I love it. I'll take it," I said.

"Well let's go get an application so we can run a credit report," he said, and my heart sank. As I followed him back around the house he asked, "Where do you work?"

"I'm a songwriter." That didn't impress him. He rolled his eyes and shook his head.

Everyone in Nashville was a songwriter and most couldn't

make a living doing it. I followed him to the front door and told him, "I really need an apartment."

"Well if your credit's good we'll need $300 for a deposit and the first month's rent."

I didn't have enough money for the deposit and I didn't know what was going to happen when they ran a credit report. The man pointed for me to sit down on the front porch swing and wait. He told the Troll-haired woman what I said. I could hear them through the screen window.

"Let's just wait for someone else who can pay the rent," the woman said. I was about to start crying when something shot up the wheelchair ramp beside me and scared the shit out of me. It was Lonnie. I knew him from Brown's. Everyone in the neighborhood knew him. He didn't have any arms or legs and he shot around the sidewalks in his wheelchair so fast, it was nuts. Somehow, he drove the wheelchair with his shoulder. He was one of the peppiest and most positive people I had ever met. He always got three burgers and fries when he came to Brown's to pick up his to-go order, and we usually talked while he waited.

"What's up?" he asked, surprised to find me on his porch.

"I'm trying to rent the apartment, but I don't think I'm gonna get it," I said, fighting back tears.

"This would be the perfect place for you to live. It's so close to Brown's," he said in his chipper voice.

"Do you live here?" I asked.

"Yeah, hang on a minute," Lonnie said and flew in the open door. "I know her. She's nice. You should rent her this apartment," he told his parents. And that was all it took. I was in.

My first night in the apartment I realized that there were no windows, but I kind of liked it because it made me feel safe, like I was in a little cave. I sat on the loveseat, flipping through the channels on the TV. It was such a liberating feeling not having someone watching over my shoulder, not being scared of what might come on and start a fight.

Just as I settled on *Star Search*, something fuzzy grazed against the side of my foot. I tried to talk myself into believing I hadn't felt anything. Then I saw something dart across the floor behind the cabinet TV. I jumped like a jackrabbit onto the brass armrest of the loveseat. Then I saw another one...and another one.

There were mice everywhere. I stayed on top of the small sofa for about fifteen minutes not knowing what to do. Then I dove three feet to the bed, and I laid wide-ass awake listening to the crunching of wrappers and movement coming from the kitchen. I didn't sleep a wink listening to the mice running through the walls. I was terrified that I was going to wake up with a mouse nesting in my hair.

I started to cry and then I felt myself laughing. I had survived living with my bipolar, emotional terrorist dad who almost blew me to smithereens. I had survived my stepfather, who kept me a prisoner in my bedroom, beat me, and made me eat puke, and I had survived Dustin, who bit me in the face and aimed a loaded shotgun at my head. I could deal with these fucking mice.

Moving Out

I WAITED A COUPLE OF WEEKS to let things cool down before I went back to the house on South Wind Street. Mike and Uncle Kelly drove up to Nashville to help me move the last of my things. My hands were shaking as I turned the key on the brass doorknob. I was scared that Dustin might jump out and attack me. He had given me his word that he wouldn't be there. I hadn't seen him since I left and I didn't want to. Dustin refused to help pay for the divorce and I couldn't afford to pay for it, so Daddy did. I just wanted it over.

I packed up my cookware and dishes from the kitchen, then went upstairs to get the rest of my clothes and books. There was a red bra hanging on the towel rack next to the sink, and a curling iron and toothbrush that I had never seen. A *Cosmopolitan* magazine sat on the bedside table, along with an ashtray full of brown, filtered cigarettes with pink lipstick. Just like the ones I had found in the ashtray of Dustin's truck while we were together. He had already moved some other girl in, and I found out later that they had been having an affair for months.

I turned around with my box of books to find Dustin standing in the doorway, blocking me in the bedroom. "I need to go through that box first and make sure you're not taking anything of mine," he said. He came towards me. I backed up against the wall.

Mike walked in and he was covered in sweat. He asked, "Is this the bookshelf we need to move?"

"Yeah, that one, and there's one more downstairs," I told him.

Dustin walked back over to the doorway. "Yeah, well, you won't be taking that one. It's mine," he told Mike.

"Dustin, I bought that with my own money. You know I had it before I moved in here," I said.

Mike picked it up and headed towards the door when Dustin stepped in front and said, "I told you, you're not taking that anywhere."

Mike stepped closer to Dustin and looked up at him. "Move out of my way or I'll move you myself."

"You need any help up there?" Uncle Kelly asked from the foot of the stairs. We packed up the last of my stuff, and a few days later, Dad paid for my divorce.

Living on a Prayer

THE WAITING ENDED and the wonder began. At least that's what I was expecting to happen. I was living my dream, writing songs all day, every day. My first songwriting appointment was with a guy named Sam. He suggested that we meet at Bongo Java, a coffee shop close to Music Row. I got there an hour early with my leather briefcase that was about the size of a microwave. Dad had bought it for me at a pawn shop. I found us a table. I had never drank coffee, but I didn't want to seem like a kid, so I ordered the only drink on the menu that I had heard of, a cappuccino, and I got a blueberry muffin. I was crazy nervous and ordered another cappuccino. I sat flipping through my three-inch binder full of titles and lyrics. By the time Sam arrived, I was so jacked up on caffeine, I could barely stay in the chair.

"What are you wanting to do today?" he asked.

"Write a big ass hit," I said.

Sam was laid back, a little too laid back, and he was in no hurry to start writing. He had thin long brown hair and a goatee. We sat there and talked for about fifteen minutes. He was from Cincinnati and had just signed his first publishing deal a few weeks earlier.

"Let's go write," I said. I was ready to go, go, go. We walked around the block to his duplex and sat down at a Formica table at a 50's style booth in his kitchen. I spread pages and pages of lyrics all over the table and started throwing out ideas. "I've been wanting to write something, kind of like in the vibe of Van Morrison's 'Into the Mystic' meets 'Islands in the Stream' by Kenny and Dolly. I love that groove. Just a song that sounds like something you'd hear on the beach in the Bahamas. You know, something with a summer night vibe, outdoors, twinkly lights, and just the right amount of a peach Bellini buzz. You know, just a song about that fuzzy high feeling of new love. And I got another title, 'I Ain't Wearing a Dress.' Kind of like 'Fist City' by Loretta Lynn. You know, if you mess around with my man, I'll kick your ass. Never mind, never mind. I don't know if that even makes sense. Oh yeah, I got one more idea that I think could be cool as shit. 'I Don't Love You Anymore.' It's kind of talking about when you break up with somebody, even though they hurt you and cheated on you, and you don't want to be with them anymore. You kind of have to go through that reprogramming yourself to live after them. To quit thinking about them. Just how you don't stop loving somebody all at once. It takes a little time to get them out of your system. And I got one more idea that..."

"Hang on a minute," he said. "Let's figure out what we want to do first."

"Write a big ass hit," I answered again.

"Let's do that breakup idea," he said. "I've got a piece of music that's perfect for it." He grabbed his acoustic guitar, played a verse and a chorus and hummed along. I liked it, but the chorus sounded just like the verse. Sam played it over and over and each time I heard a melody that jumped a half an octave in the first line of the chorus to make it more dynamic. In my head, I kept hearing melodies all day, but there was no way I was singing anything I heard out loud. I was terrified of being off-key and for him to find out my secret; that I was tone-deaf. Sam didn't care what the lyric said as long as it rhymed and fit into his melody. He had to leave at 3:00 pm, so we jammed in the words. It wasn't great, but at least it was finished.

I drove straight to AMR to let Karen and Ron know that I wrote a song with Sam. Ron had set me up with him. I became overwhelmed every time I opened the double, glass doors to walk into the brick, four-story building that we shared with Decca Records and the other publishing company, Polygram. AMR was on the third floor. At twenty-three, I was the youngest signed songwriter in the building, and the only female. Dolly Parton and Loretta Lynn wrote all their hits, but for most of the 90s, ,female artists like Faith Hill, Marina McBride, and Patty Loveless, recorded songs written by other people. There were five signed songwriters at AMR, and Bob Regan and Ed Hill were the veteran hit makers at the company. I hung on their every word and listened to every song in their catalogues.

When I went to Karen's office to play my new song for her and Ron, Ed Hill was there. He was playing the demo of a song that I loved. I stood at the door and ached over how powerful and emotional the song was. The chorus melody soared and it was so hooky that you could sing the chorus by the second time it rolled around. "It Matters to Me" was the name of the song and it would go on to be a number one hit for Faith Hill. After he was done, Karen said, "Come on in, Aimee. Did you get a song today?"

"Yeah, but I'm not playing it now." I slung the cassette into the trash can next to Karen's desk.

"Who's that girl singing the demo?" I asked.

"It's Sara Evans. She's a new artist on RCA."

"Can you get me a day to write with her?" I asked Ron.

"I don't know if she writes, but I'll work on it," Ron said.

I overheard Ron in the kitchen telling Karen, "I'm having trouble getting Aimee any good appointments. Everybody just asks, 'Is she making a record? Has she had any songs cut?'"

Ron made my schedule and I wrote with anybody and everybody who would write with me. Every day I showed up at 10:00 am and wrote with someone I had never met. Sometimes I had a double or a triple and raced from one writer to the next. Half the time I wrote on Music Row at a publishing company and half the time I worked at my co-writer's apartment. Most of the people who Ron could get on my schedule were brand new and hadn't written more than a dozen songs. Even though I had just signed my deal, I had been writing nonstop for fifteen years.

Living my dream wasn't quite like I had imagined it. Most days I sat across from someone I had just met, I threw out song titles, lyrics, poems, and ideas that they rejected. Most of the writers I worked with summed me up the second I walked in the door. They looked at me like a young girl who didn't know what she was doing. Appointment after appointment, none of the songs sounded like I wanted them to. I had been spoiled rotten writing with Dustin and his friends.

After we were divorced, when I ran into songwriters who had worked with Dustin, they'd walked right through me like I was a ghost. I knew some of their wives and kids, and had dined with them a dozen times. They ignored me when I said hi. Dustin now had two songs on the radio and he was about to sign his second record deal. They all wanted songs on his album.

I had been signed at AMR for two months when Ron called and said, "I've got some bad news. "I froze in panic.

"Southern Eden got dropped from Atlantic Records today."

"What does that mean?" I asked. "What about my song?"

"Well, the song isn't coming out. The band lost their record deal. I mean, I guess they could get another one, but the lead singer's in rehab, so it doesn't look good. Sorry about that, Aimee. I know it's hard to hear."

The two biggest reasons they signed me were because my song, "Story of My Life," had been recorded for a major label release and because I would be writing with Dustin, which was never going to happen again.

That night I laid in bed in a stone-cold panic. What would happen if I lost my writing deal? I heard Dustin's voice in my head over and over, "I never thought you could write. I just wanted to get in your pants." Then I heard my dad, "You don't play guitar, you can't sing. Why would anybody write with you?"

My inner critic started up next, "You don't know what you're doing You're an idiot for ever thinking this could work." Things are always worse at night. Self-doubt, fear, and all their friends kept me up all night. I was in a battle between faith and fear.

A Gun and a Shovel

I RAN INTO DUSTIN in the lobby of Starstruck Publishing. It scared me for a second because I didn't know how he was going to act. He walked over to me and smiled, then asked, "Can I talk to you for a minute?" I followed him outside. There were song-writers hanging out in the lobby and in the back parking lot, so I felt safe.

"Do you remember that song we wrote 'Heroes'?" he asked. "Well, I finished it. It only needed a couple of lines and it is so good. I've got the work tape in my truck if you want to hop in and hear it real quick. Everybody that's heard it loves it," he said.

I climbed up into his truck and left the door open, just in case. "Aimee, I know I was wrong and I feel so bad about how I treated you. I hope that you find someone who treats you the way you deserve." He played the song "Heroes" and I couldn't wait to get a copy so I could turn it in. Then he asked, "Can I play you an-other song I wrote about you? It's gonna be out on the radio soon. Hell, all my songs are about you." He played it and it was so well-written, and so much better than anything I had written in the last few months.

I got out of the truck and he followed me to my car. "You know, there's no reason we can't be friends. And we can still write sometimes if you want to," he said. A couple of days later he called and asked where I lived, saying he would drop off the cassette. When he came in, he had a twelve-pack of Bud Light and his guitar. "I've got something I want to run by you. I started this song the other night after I saw you." He sat down and started to play, "You may wish that you and I had never met. Or swear you can't forgive and won't forget. And I won't blame you." He kept singing. I wanted to write, but I didn't want him back in my life again.

Dad had moved back to Nashville and rented an apartment from his friend Woody. It was right around the corner from where

I lived. I never told anyone about the abuse from Dustin, maybe because I would have had to admit it to myself. Cory was the only one who figured it out. One day, Dad, Cory, and I were eating at a seafood restaurant and when Dad reached across the table to get the ketchup, I jumped and blocked my face, cowering in fear of being hit.

"What did you just do?" Dad asked. "What's wrong with her?" he looked at Cory.

"I think Dustin was hitting her," Cory said.

My dad threw forty bucks on the table and got up and went out to his truck. When we climbed inside the truck, Dad said, "I'll kill that son of a bitch if I ever see him."

A couple of weeks later, Dustin called and gave me the best news of my life. Our song, the first one we ever wrote together, was recorded by one of the biggest artists in country music. I was so happy and grateful. I proved to myself that I could do it. I had a song on a platinum-selling country artist's album that went on to sell almost two million copies. That meant I could keep my writing deal for at least another year.

The second time he came over ended with three cop cars in the backyard. Dad drove by and saw Dustin's truck and the next thing I knew, all hell was breaking loose. Dad was pounding on the door and shouting so loudly that someone called the police.

Dustin put on his boots and he was headed through the back yard to go to his truck when Dad walked over and slapped him in the face knocking his cowboy hat onto the ground. "You better get the fuck away from my daughter and stay away from her or I'll fucking kill you," he said looking Dustin straight in the eyes. The cops were coming over now, ready to arrest somebody. In front of all the neighbors, my landlords and three policemen, Dad got in his face again and said, "All it will take to get rid of you, buddy, is a gun and a shovel and I got both."

Surprise!

THAT SPRING, DAD CELEBRATED the biggest hit of his career, 'Keeper of the Stars' performed by Tracy Byrd. It went number one and won Song of the Year on TV at the Academy of Country Music Awards. Dad and his two co-writers on the song didn't fly to L.A. for the televised award show because no one thought that they had a chance in hell of winning after Dad called the president of the ACM board and told him to stick the award up his ass when he found out that they nominated him, but then charged him four hundred dollars for tickets to the show.

When Dad was in town, he always stopped by AMR since he was a signed writer upstairs at Polygram in the same building. Every time he came into Karen's office, he got into my business. I had only been signed at AMR for a few months when I was playing Karen and Ron a new song and Dad walked in. He stood at the door listening. "Aimee, that song's all messed up. That's not the right title. You should call it 'One of These Days' instead of 'One of Those Nights'."

I was furious with him. I had enough insecurity about keeping my writing deal. When I turned around, he looked flat out crazy as usual, standing there wearing women's sunglasses. I said, "I'm not gonna listen to anybody who's got their shirt on inside out," and Ron started laughing.

I loved it when Dad came to town because he took me out to eat and to a movie a few times a week. And then when Cory came up, we went to the horse races and to a gambling casino boat in Metropolis, Illinois. I worked Sundays at Brown's Diner for some extra money and one night, Dad called me at work. "Meet me at Pancake Pantry in the morning. I got somebody I want you to meet."

"Who?"

"Her name's Lydia. She's five. Bring her a present."

"I'm not going if you don't tell me who she is."

"She's your little sister."

"What are you talking about..." and he hung up on me. The next morning, I wasn't sure how I felt or if I even believed him. I scrambled around Eckerd's drug store and settled on a Strawberry Shortcake coloring book and a pack of crayons. At Pancake Pantry, I sat at the table with Dad and waited on my surprise sister and her mother to walk through the door. Millions of questions raced through my mind while Dad casually read *USA Today*.

When they walked in, Dad waved them over and I froze. I had no idea what to say and no time to think of something before her mother walked over to me.

"Hi, I'm Madeline. It's nice to meet you, Aimee. Just so you know, I haven't told Lydia that you're her sister or that Danny's her father. I don't want to confuse her." Madeline radiated wealth in her Chanel loafers, a diamond the size of a doorknob, and mysterious perfume. She was a little overweight, so I assumed she got with my Dad at one of the fat farms.

Lydia bounced over to the table and it was like I looked at a childhood photograph of myself. She had big, hazel eyes, tangled, brown hair, and was a tomboy. My mind worked a genetic dot-to-dot and connected our similarities. We both looked a lot like Dad. She had his hands and my brother's pigeon legs. Something about her mannerisms reminded me of my grandmother, Opal. My heart melted when I saw her eyebrow arched just like mine when she got excited. When I gave her the coloring book, she screamed, "I love Strawberry Shortcake!"

"Me too," I smiled.

Lydia had beautiful, olive skin, the kind that would take me all summer and a gallon of baby oil to get. My favorite thing about her was the cute little speck above her lip. "Wow, I've always wanted a mole like that," I smiled at her again. As a teenager, I wanted a mole so badly that I called a plastic surgeon's office. "Do you have a procedure where you could put a mole on my face? You know, like Cindy Crawford?" I had hoped that the answer would be yes, but the surgeon just said, "You want us to put a mole on your face? No, we don't do that."

Lydia danced around in her seat and dumped everything out of her little plastic purse. "Where's my bubblegum lipstick?" she asked as she went through her collection of Bonnie Bell lip gloss.

"What grade are you in?" I asked.

"I'll be starting first grade in two weeks." She had a lisp from the space where her front teeth used to be.

"What's your favorite thing to do at school?" I asked.

"Painting and singing. Oh, and I like playing kickball too."

After an hour of small talk, and way too many silver dollar pancakes, it was time to say goodbye. Madeline stood up and said, "We're headed back to the hotel. I promised Lydia she could swim before we head home."

I gave Lydia a hug and my Smackers Dr. Pepper Chapstick from my purse. That was the last time I ever saw her. Dad paid the check, and I waited until we were outside to confront him.

"Why in the hell did you never tell me about her?"

"Aimee, I don't have to tell you everything about my life. I have other kids you don't know about. It's none of your business."

First Demo Session

I THOUGHT I'D NEVER write a good song again until I met Bill Luther. I could not breathe listening to him sing. His voice just grabbed me by the heart. He sounded like Bryan Adams meets Bob Seger, but better. I sat there staring at him, stunned by how much I loved his voice. "If you don't like that, we can try something else," he said, then got up and sat his guitar down.

"I am in love with your voice."

"Really?" he looked at me trying to decide if I was telling him the truth.

"Yes really, you just blew my mind."

Ron knocked on the door and stuck his head in. "Patty Loveless is looking for a positive, up-tempo. She's cutting next Friday." I soon learned that everyone making a record was looking for a positive, up-tempo song. That's what all the labels wanted. It's what the producers wanted and what the album needed. They were the hardest to write and the hardest to find.

I was so into the ballad that Bill and I were writing. It had a vibe like Jim Croce's "Time in a Bottle," but we shifted gears and started an up-tempo female song called, "Not This Time."

After we finished the song, we played it for Ron and Karen. "Way to go guys," Ron said. "Ed has his demo session tomorrow, but he needs one more song to fill it, so let's get it demoed and we'll have it in time to play for Patty Loveless."

Bill and I were ecstatic. This was the first song they had agreed to let either of us demo. Every publisher was picky about what songs they were willing to pay for to be recorded. The next day I arrived at Ruckus Room Studio at noon so that Bill and I could go through the lyrics and get our production ideas together. We were scheduled to record at 12:30 pm. I asked a guy in the kitchen, "Do you know if Bill Luther's here yet?"

"Yeah, he's been here since around 10 am," the guy said. When I found Bill on the back porch, he had had about five cups of coffee already. We sat on the front step and went over the lyrics line by line. Then we came in and stood by the door to the control room. At 12:25 pm I stuck my head in. "Hey, are you guys almost ready?" I asked.

Ed was behind the engineer at the mixing board. He was frustrated, running his hand through his dark beard. "Okay, let's do it again," he said to the band. Just before they started playing, he looked over at me and said, "Sorry, we're running a little late. We've had some technical problems with the microphone outputs."

"Okay," I said, and walked back out to the lobby. Bill was sweating and pacing in full-on panic mode. We watched the clock and the door. Finally, they called us into the room at 12:45 pm. The engineer played our work tape over the loudspeakers for the band while they stood with clipboards charting the song with the Nashville number system. It was a secret code that all the studio musicians knew.

"Is that you singing on the work tape?" the engineer asked Bill. Bill nodded. "Cool voice, dude. Come with me." He took him into the vocal booth and helped him get his headphones and microphone adjusted. We had a full band, drums, bass, electric guitar, acoustic guitar, fiddle, and piano. They were all playing our song. It sounded like it was going off a cliff. The piano player and fiddle player dominated the whole track, and the drummer changed the groove to a shuffle.

About halfway through, I tapped the engineer on the shoulder. "I need to talk to Bill and give the band some notes." He turned the volume down on the mixing board and said, "Let them finish this take, and you can tell them."

"Yeah, but the groove is all wrong and we've only got seven minutes to get this recorded."

After they played the song all the way through, they all started talking on their mics and we could hear them in the control room.

"I think we nailed it," the bass player said.

"I can do one more," the drummer chimed in. "I've got a couple of fixes."

I hit the red talk button on the console and it fed a high pitched screech into everyone's headphones. "Can y'all hang on a minute?" I asked the engineer. "Where's the vocal booth?"

"Right through there," he pointed.

I ran inside. "Bill, this sounds terrible."

"What's going on?" he jerked his headphones off.

"I hate how they're playing it."

"What's wrong with it?"

"Everything. Who's playing that piano? I hate what he's doing and I asked them not to put a fiddle on here. They turned this song into a shuffle. It's not a shuffle."

"I can't hear anything they're playing while I'm singing. I'm just trying to stay on the right key," Bill said. He was sweating and gulping down water.

"Bill," I grabbed him by the shoulders looking up at him, "do you like how this sounds?"

"Aimee, it's 1 o'clock. These guys gotta be in another studio at 2."

"Well, this song's getting more fucked up by the second. We gotta do something!"

Then I heard, "We can all hear you," coming through one of Bill's headphones. Every musician, the engineer, everyone in the studio heard every word I said through Bill's microphone. When I walked back into the control room, it was dead silent. Then the drummer counted them off, "One, two, three, four," and they played it again the exact same way they did the first time.

"It'll be all right, trust me. These are the best musicians in town. They know what they're doing," the engineer told me. In my mind, I had heard our song like Dolly Parton's "Nine to Five" and now it sounded more like the televangelist Jimmy Swaggart had a head-on collision with "The Devil Went Down to Georgia."

When the song ended, they were all back on their mics talking. "Yeah man, that was the one." They started packing up their instruments. I sat down behind the mixing board on the brink of tears and the engineer said, "You can mute anything you don't like."

"Well, you can't mute the whole song," I said under my breath.

Ron wanted us to put this new female singer, Misty Myers, on the demo. Her voice was good, but Bill's voice was a million times better. It took almost three hours for her to learn the lyrics and she kept singing it out of tune. Around 5:00 pm, Bill had to head out for his night job. He had two other jobs; he worked at a TGIF restaurant, and on the weekends he answered phones for JC Penney's catalog orders.

I recorded background vocals with a different singer who kept asking me to sing what I wanted her to do. "Just sing whatever you think it needs," I said, and sunk down into the leather chair at the mixing board. Then I waited for a couple of hours for the engineer to mix the track and vocals. I left with the CD around 1:00 am. I was psychologically and emotionally exhausted, and I hated the song.

My Team

RON SENT ME TO THE BLUEBIRD CAFE to check out a new writer who was the bass player for a famous country artist. The Bluebird Café is the most famous songwriter club, probably in the world. That night there was a new songwriter showcase where four people sit on barstools on stage and take turns singing their original songs. I wasn't knocked out by Bobby Barns, the guy who I was there to see. His music was too country for me with too many clichés, but the third guy in the lineup that played that night was Chris Lindsey. I loved his music. He had more of a rock 'n' roll flavor to his voice, and I could tell that we had a lot of the same influences.

He played acoustic guitar on the first few songs and each one was better than the one before. I knew instantly that he was the guy I wanted to write with. For the last song, Chris switched to piano and played a song called "A Place in the Sun." That song hit me straight in the heart. The lyrics described exactly where I was in my life. I was looking for the one person who I believed was out there somewhere:

Long ago, far away
I felt your lovin' glow upon my face
Was it a dream or just a promise made
What is my destiny?
Someday I'll find a way to shine
Leave all these rainy days behind
I know there's got to be
Someplace warm and bright for me
I'm runnin' out of places I can run
Lookin' for a place in the sun

After the show, I stood at the bar and waited for Chris to unplug his guitar and get packed up. When he walked over to pay his tab, I was surprised that he was over six foot, five inches tall. Chris' chestnut brown hair was sticking out in all directions. He had a dimple in his chin and glasses. He looked down at me and smiled.

"Hi, I'm Aimee. I loved your songs,"

"Thanks."

"I'm a new writer at AMR."

"We should set up a day to write," Chris said and threw his guitar case over his shoulder.

Chris had his publisher call the next day to set up a writing appointment for a couple of days later. We wrote together for the first time on February 19, 1996. My diary entry for that day was:

February 19, 1996

> *Got up this morning went to API and wrote with Chris Lindsey.*
> *We had an awesome day and wrote a song I love called, "I Know*
> *What You Like."*

And then at the bottom of the same diary page, it said:

> *"I know there's someone out there that I'm supposed to be with. I'll*
> *just have to wait until the day that they find me or I find them."*

When I made that diary entry, I had no idea that Chris was the guy who I had been waiting for all my life.

***

CHRIS TOLD ME ABOUT another new writer, Marv Green, who he worked with sometimes.

I met Marv at a party that fall. He was a sandy, blonde-haired California boy with a lot of girlfriends. Right off the bat, we were competitive with each other. "I've got a song on hold for this new artist, Mark Wills," he said.

"Yeah, I've heard he's good. I've got a song on hold with him too." We went back and forth with our stats and about thirty minutes later, we were sitting cross-legged in Ronna's living room, playing a song on her stereo. There were a dozen songwriters there taking turns playing their new music, but our songs were the best ones. I think Marv had to think about writing with me. I'm not sure if he had ever written with a girl before, but Marv was my third steady co-writer.

Bill, Chris, and Marv. They were the first people who I wrote with that I truly felt magic come into the room. When I wrote with them, I didn't find inspiration, it found me. It was like plugging into a universal outlet. I discovered my muse, and so had they. When we wrote together, something extraordinary happened; I was feeling instead of writing. I learned that my subconscious was better than my ego could ever be. When I let go and just followed the words flowing through me without worrying if they were good enough, or if anyone would like them, everything changed. When my muse entered the room, I never knew how long it would last. We all felt it. It was palpable that something bigger than us was happening.

I hate the act of trying to write a song. I hate thinking about a song. I like to feel it, and the faster, the better for me. Some songwriters like to agonize over every word and torture themselves and the people they're writing with, but that has never been my process. Some of the best songs that I have ever been a part of happened in less than thirty minutes. We couldn't write the lines down fast enough. My dad used to tell me that, but I didn't believe it until I experienced it. For me, I could always write better with people I felt close to. People I could open up with. People who wouldn't judge me in any way.

Sometimes you have to say a lot of insane or stupid things to find your way to the incredible or spectacular. I have written the best songs with people who I'm not embarrassed to cry in front of because sometimes that's what a song is: crying out.

I read a quote once by Robert Frost that is really about books, but I would say it applies to songs as well, "No tears in the writer, no tears in the reader." When you get honest, people know it. People feel it at a subconscious level. I had written with dozens and dozens of songwriters trying to find people that inspired me. You never know who you're going to have chemistry with, but I had found my team.

Tears, Fumes and Faith

BEFORE LONG I FELL INTO A WORKABLE ROUTINE. I found a way to share the apartment with the furry kingdom that lived in the kitchen. I kept my groceries in the refrigerator: Peach Pull 'N' Peel Twizzlers, Ragu spaghetti sauce, noodles, and Coca-Cola. Every night I slept in my clothes and shoes. Sometimes at night, I closed my eyes thinking about my favorite Disney movie, Cinderella and the scene where the mice are singing and sewing her that ball gown. But all these mice were doing was stealing my groceries.

I never got out of bed at night unless I felt like my bladder was going to rupture. If I had to go to the bathroom, I stood on top of my bed and jumped the three feet into the bathroom, landing as hard as I could and stomping, hoping to scare off any mice nearby. I peed holding my legs out in front of me so that they didn't touch the floor. Then I stood on the seat and dove back onto the bed.

I tried to convince myself that the mice were just hamsters with less fur and longer tails. But they were just as scared of me as I was of them. That's what I told myself, but the fright of seeing a mouse bolt out of the wall like a jack-in-the-box scared the shit out of me every time.

Falling asleep in blue jeans, a t-shirt, bra, and socks, and my flowered Doc Marten combat boots, I was still worried about waking up with a mouse running up my thigh. My ivory cotton sheets looked like white cheetah print. They were splattered with spots of ink and smudges of mascara that dropped in tears of inspiration and exhaustion.

All I did was write. My apartment looked like a scene from the movie, A Beautiful Mind, but with words instead of math. There were songs everywhere; on the top of to-go boxes, napkins, receipts, the back of my checkbook. I hung positive quotations everywhere:

> *What we believe we become.*
> —Oprah
> *It always seems impossible until it's done.*
> —Nelson Mandela
> *When you want something, all the universe conspires to help you achieve it.*
> —Paulo Coelho

On Saturdays I went to the downtown library and paged through volumes of poetry books, quotation books, and the reference books that you couldn't take home. In the days before the internet, I absorbed Rumi, E.E. Cummings, and I revisited old friends like Emily Dickenson and Sylvia Plath. I filled pages with thoughts and quotes and lyrics, until all the words looked the same. At closing time, when they started turning down the lights, I always checked out the limit: twenty-five books, five music CDs, and three movies. The librarian, Larry, helped me carry all my materials out to the parking lot and loaded them into the back of my Sentra.

I believe if you want something bad enough, that it will give up its secrets. Why would God give me a dream and put it so deep inside my heart if it couldn't come true? What would be the point?

So, every night my bed was an island of quotation books, love poetry, lyrics, work tapes, my boombox, and spiral notebooks. I wrote out the lyrics to the top one hundred songs of all time to see what they had in common. I dissected the weekly top ten country songs, made lists of all the nouns, analyzed the opening lines, the length of the chorus, the lyrics, the melody, the tempo, the timing. Okay, the verse should be thirty seconds and the channel to lift up to the chorus, fifteen seconds. Then I hit the chorus. The beat of a ballad was the same tempo as a resting heartbeat.

I read all of the *Songwriting for Dummies* books and tried to follow their advice. I learned to be careful who you listen to and not to take advice from anyone who hasn't done what it is that you're trying to do.

Then I found a copy of the book *Songwriters on Songwriting*. It was the only book about composing that ever taught me anything. There were interviews with dozens of writers, including two of my favorite songwriters: Paul Simon and Paul McCartney. Everyone in the book had a different method. I wanted to know what makes a tune get stuck in your head and figure out why some songs you never get tired of. The ones that grab you by the heart every single time. What was the magic formula?

The one fantastic thing about being broke and afraid to get out of bed after dark, was losing thirty pounds. I had not been that thin since before I went through puberty in eighth grade. When I went to the mall with my friends, Melissa and Regina, I watched them buy clothes at Ann Taylor in the Green Hills Mall. They were so successful and able to pay forty dollars for a shirt. I tried on blue jeans and stared in disbelief that I fit into a size four. I didn't recognize my body in the dressing room mirror. I had to hang the jeans back on the rack. I couldn't afford them, but I could zip them. The stress of not having enough money to pay the rent or go out to eat with a group of people was hard.

The brakes on my Sentra sounded like an airplane landing the way they screeched and scraped every time I stopped. But what I hated most was when my car would break down on a busy street, blocking traffic like a Beluga whale. I never had the money to tow it. Chris was who I always called, and he helped me figure out what to do.

A couple of times a week I snuck into music business parties. Whether it was a showcase for a new artist trying to get a record deal or a Number One party celebrating songwriters, there was usually an open bar and free food, and I came home with a purse full of shrimp cocktail or lobster ravioli. It was chocolate fountains and champagne, or Oodles of Noodles. I was either starving or feasting. I didn't have health insurance, car insurance, or insurance of any kind.

My transmission was jacked up and I had to count pocket change from the ashtray in my Sentra to pay for gas. I usually fell asleep with a pen in my hand and highlighter spots all over me. I always had ink on me somewhere. I didn't know how to make it happen. All I knew was that it had to happen. Passion was my biggest resource. I didn't have anything to fall back on. I had to make it. I was running on fumes, tears and faith.

Chapter Ten

———

AMAZED

Owner of a Lonely Heart

I WAS HAPPY DURING THE DAY while I was out and about writing, but the nights were endless. I was so lonely. It seemed like everyone I wrote with had someone to go home to. Someone who loved them. Every day after I was done writing, I was alone, and felt as lonely as I had ever been. When you're by yourself, it feels like you're going to be alone forever. It seems like looking out into the infinite blue and seeing nothing in the distance. But somehow, I was still in love with love and believed that I would find my soulmate.

I still don't understand how I got myself into that mess. With Dustin, I saw the signs. There were red flags flying like at the Talladega 500, but for some reason I ignored them. Occasionally I had a nightmare that he was after me. I'd wake up in a cold panic at the realization that I could be his battered wife, held hostage for the rest of my life. I realized that with each person you're with, you become a different person, and had I stayed with him, I would have been his victim. That could have happened.

It had been six months since my divorce, and I wanted to try to fix myself. When I wasn't looking for song titles, I was highlighting self-help books: *Codependent No More* by Melody Beattie; *You Can Heal Your Life* by Louise Hay; *Love Signs* by Linda Goodman. I filled my journals freewriting, looking for titles, writing pages and pages of stream of consciousness. My OCD was in overdrive again.

In the deepest part of my heart, I believed there was someone out there who I was meant to be with. I made a promise to myself that never again would I be in a relationship with someone who tried to control me. Never again would I dim my light hiding in the shadows. If someone really loved me, they would want me to be everything I could be. I never wanted to be with someone again who was so full of insecurity that they wanted to stomp out my dreams.

I wrote volumes of poems to my soulmate. I believed that he was out there somewhere waiting for me. I planned my life out on paper so clearly that I could see it. I imagined being married to someone who loved me as much as I loved them. Every spiral-bound notebook had pictures of the same dream house that I had drawn since I was a child. I imagined a house full of kids, laughter, and noise, where we wrote poetry on the walls and made music and memories. It was the house that I wished I'd grown up in. It had a red, ruffled roof and there was a pool, a tennis court, and a little stream with a bridge that ran along the right side with a weeping willow tree.

I filled my diaries with passages like these:

What I want in a husband: Someone who's my best friend, who makes me laugh, who laughs at me, who I can count on, who is always there for me and puts a little light around me and thinks I am the best, the coolest. Someone who supports me emotionally and helps me keep grounded. Someone I could hold hands with and pray with, someone who I can say anything in front of. Someone who wants to make a promise, a commitment, and stick it out for the rest of his life, good times and bad. Someone who kisses me every day and shows me they love me. Someone who wants to have a strong, Christian family and raise our children in a loving and crazy-fun home. I want love you can't deny and you can't control. I want unforgettable moments and passionate kisses. I want to be wrapped around your little finger and have you in the palm of my hand. I want tangled hair and sleepy smiles and half-asleep conversation. I'm waiting for you to come and make my dreams come true. I have waited all my life for love like this. To find my soul in a kiss.

***

MAX WAS MY FIRST BOYFRIEND AFTER MY DIVORCE.
What attracted me to him most was that he had such a gentle
nature. He was like the anti-Dustin. He was tall with dark, curly
hair and he always had a tan and a koozie in his hand. On our
first date we went to the Mix Factory Club in downtown Nashville and slow danced to Cheap Trick on the roof. On our second
date we went to see Tom Petty. We went on road trips and to the
river on his boat. It was always a party. Max was always drinking,
so there was no intimacy. I could only get so close to him.

After we had been dating for about ten months, I found out
that he had been seeing his ex-girlfriend, Jen, the whole time. He
had spent Valentine's Day with her and was snowed-in at her
house for four days. Chris would always say things to me like, "I
don't know why you're with him. You deserve so much more than
that."

Chemistry

CHRIS AND I HAD INSTANT CHEMISTRY from the first
day we worked together. Our songs were different and deeper
than anything I had ever written with anyone else. I could tell
him anything. Chris and I wrote a couple of times a week and it
wasn't long before I realized that I worked better under pressure.
Every demo session I had I booked at County Q studio, with an
engineer and a full band with an acoustic guitar, electric guitar,
steel guitar, piano, bass player, and drummer. Knowing that I
had to have five songs or my publisher would be out $3,000 forced
me to finish songs. It also freaked out Karen and Ron, as well as
most of my co-writers, but I created great songs that way.

Chris was the one person who I could call at 7:00 pm the
night before a demo session and say, "I've gotta write two songs
tonight or I'm gonna be in deep shit with Karen and Ron."

It was too much stress for most of my songwriter buddies, but
Chris was always game. He came over in faded denim overalls
with paint splattered all over them from his other job of rehab-
bing houses. We stayed up until 2:00 am writing under the gun,
but loving every minute of it. Some days, if we didn't feel like

writing, we went to an Indian buffet or a Mediterranean restaurant and sat there half the day laughing and talking.

Sometimes we snuck off to a movie. I had never been so comfortable around someone. I had never experienced what was happening between Chris and me. He brought out something in me, encouraged me, and made me believe in myself like no one ever had. Chris was the first person I was comfortable enough to sing in front of. "I think I'm tone-deaf," I told him.

"Well, I don't know where you got that from. You have almost perfect pitch," he said. Chris loved my voice and encouraged me to sing, and for some reason I did. He talked me into singing one of our demos. Terrified to sing in front of the engineer and musicians, I bought a six-pack of Coors Light and killed three beers before I went into the vocal booth. I had not sung on a microphone since I was in middle school. I made it through the song "We Live in our Own Little World" with Chris at the mixing board and the engineer producing my vocal. My publisher loved it.

Chris, Bill, Marv, and I played a songwriter show at Douglas Corner Café and the crowd seemed to love the whole show. From then on, we wrote many songs that I sang: "Happy," "Liar," "Trunk Full of Junk," and they started making their way around town. After hearing one of our demos, a songwriter at AMR said, "Your voice is crazy. You sound kind of like Cyndi Lauper with a southern accent meets the Chipmunks."

When Martina McBride heard some of my songs, she told Joe Galante, the President of Sony Records, that he should sign me to a record deal. She was the four-time winner of the CMA 'Female Vocalist of the Year.'

But the biggest surprise with singing came a few years later. I got a phone call from John Kalodner, a legendary A&R (artist and repertoire talent scout) for Atlantic Records based out of L.A. He was responsible for signing Peter Gabriel, Phil Collins, AC/DC, Foreigner, and lots of other rock music artists. He offered me a record deal and I could not believe that I turned it down, but I had a big reason.

One evening I came in from a long day of writing and a little, grayish-brown mouse was sitting on my yellow stove. He had a green rotini noodle hanging out of his mouth. We made eye contact, but he didn't scurry away. I stared into his pink little eyes and he looked at me as if to say, "Bitch, this is my kitchen!"

As I walked a little closer, he didn't budge, holding his ground with my noodle. I slammed my fist on the stove and he disappeared too quickly for me to see where he went. That was it. I was hungry and I had had enough. "I tried to play nice with you little bastards," I said and kicked the cabinet. "I'm moving."

My next apartment was another basement apartment on Bowling Avenue. It was the bottom floor of a three-story building. There were six real apartments above me, and the community laundry room was right outside my door, but it was a million times better than the mouse house. I gave the property manager Chris' number and he pretended to be my landlord, saying that I had always paid my rent on time and had never been a problem.

Before long I had a roommate named Julie Reeves. She was a badass singer from Kentucky and a new artist on Virgin Records. She sang demos during the day and usually brought home toilet paper, coffee, and paper towels from different studios in town. We couldn't afford cable, so Chris showed us how to unhook our neighbor's cable from the box in the basement by my door so that we could watch CMT and see Julie's video.

We always had to set the alarm to make sure we remembered to hook it back up every morning so that the businessman who lived upstairs wouldn't call the cable company to report something wrong. I hung canvas on the walls and wrote quotes everywhere. This apartment was the launchpad to my dreams.

I was in that room full of quotes the first time I heard one of my songs come on the radio. It was "Places I've Never Been" by Mark Wills. I had to hold on to the support beam to keep from falling. It was so overwhelming. I jumped up and down for an hour afterward. That song would go on to be my first hit. It went to number three on the *Billboard* chart.

Chris and I were always together. He was my best friend, my favorite person to talk to, the funniest person I knew, and the first person I wanted to call when something good happened. Chris looked at me in a way no one ever had. And he took care of me. If I had a flat tire, or if my kitchen sink pipes burst, he was always right there. We were spending more and more time together and I felt like I could talk to him forever. I was closer to him than I had ever been to anyone. There was only one problem, he was married.

Three Chords and the Truth

EVERYTHING I HAD BEEN TRYING TO DO writing songs was wrong. Instead of telling the truth, I had been trying to guess what the artists might want to say themselves. I wrote up-tempo after up-tempo because that is what the record labels said they wanted, and that is what every artist was looking for. All the pitch list ever said was positive, up-tempo or 'big hit' songs. No shit, Sherlock! None of my songs that were up-tempo were very good. Maybe one out of twenty. It wasn't my sweet spot. I loved love songs and life songs and story songs. Not 'get your butt in the bed of this truck and we're going out tonight' songs.

One day during a writing appointment I told Bill, "Let's just write what we want to write. Let's just forget what everybody's telling us to do." We wrote a song called "Closer to Heaven" and when we played it for Karen and Ron, they wanted to record it with a different singer. There was no way anybody would sing that song better than Bill.

"How can y'all not let Bill sing these songs? This is crazy."

"He doesn't remember the melodies," Ron said. "He changes the melody every time."

"So, change it back. He's gotta sing these demos." I had to test my feelings, so I took the song to my friend, Melissa, and we played it for a new artist, Mila Mason. I played the work tape for her on a jam box with Bill singing, playing the acoustic guitar on a cassette. "Oh I love this," she said. "Who's that singing?"

"That's Bill Luther."

"I love his voice."

"Me too," I said. A few months later, Mila Mason recorded that song, "Closer to Heaven," and it was a single for her.

I started taking pages of my diary and poems to our writing appointments. Bill and I wrote a song called, "When I Find You," and another song called, "Something Real." They were both callouts to my future someone I was looking for. Once we stopped trying to make stuff up and started writing from the heart, everything changed. We started getting songs cut.

From then on, I started writing what was in my heart. I didn't care or listen to what was on the pitch sheet. My songs followed right along with my life. My longing for love and believing it was out there, the ache I had always felt for someone to really love and know me. I wanted a witness to my life.

Harlan Howard was a songwriter who was more famous than most of the country artists in Nashville. He was famous for the quote: "All you need to write a country song is three chords and the truth."

I wrote that song, "Three Chords and the Truth," with Sara Evans and another co-writer, Ron Harbin, who I hit it off with. It was released to radio as a single and the title track to Sara's first album.

Birds and Dolls

I NEVER KNEW WHAT TO EXPECT when I went back to Alabama to visit. It was heartbreaking how many surgeries Mom had. She ruptured a disc lifting a patient at the hospital and things went downhill from there. Every time she almost recovered from one injury, something else happened: multiple back surgeries, a torn rotator cuff, a full hip replacement, and having her spine fused. We spent three consecutive Christmases in the hospital. It's so hard to watch someone you love in pain and to feel helpless to help them. She had been in bed for almost a year.

When I tried to surprise her on Mother's Day, her eyes were glazed over and she sat in bed talking to herself. All she wore were pajamas and she had run up $10,000 worth of bills on her Master Card from the Home Shopping Network collecting porcelain dolls. There had to be seventy of them lining the shelves that went all the way around the room. There were cheerleaders, brides, Indian princesses, Victorian dresses, umbrella carrying weirdo shit. They all had scary eyes, thick eyelashes, and black, patent leather shoes.

Along with the dolls, Mom had started collecting birds. All

kinds of birds. There were seven cages in the living room full of parakeets and canaries that she forgot to feed. They were going ballistic as soon as the sun came up, and if Mike hadn't fed them, they would have all died.

My mom had vanished. I didn't know who I was looking at anymore. When I stared into her unfocused eyes, I couldn't find her. When I tried to talk to her, she nodded off. Most of the time I'm not even sure if she knew I'd been home.

Dad's mental illness spiked after Harold died. He was in and out of the psychiatric hospital and needed to be cared for. He moved back into his childhood bedroom at Opal's. They still fought like he was ten years old. I never knew what to expect when I drove up the mountain to Opal's to see Dad. He was on lithium and a flea market of psychiatric medications. He didn't know my name. He was so lethargic that his eyes were half shut and he slurred his words. I couldn't stand to be around him for long.

There were notebooks all over the bed; a diagram of a base-ball field, pieces of short stories, lyrics, and a book he had been working on called, God: An Autobiography. I wanted to shake him loose to bring him back. Some visits, though, he was his usual, vivid, wild-eyed self, yelling at Opal to make him some fried chicken, and trying to teach Opal, Cory, and I how to play Spades and demanding we play cards at 2:00 am.

I never knew what to expect with Cory either. He had raised himself from the age of thirteen and he seemed bound for preach-ing or prison. Now he was nineteen and looked more like Brad Pitt's little brother than he did mine. Cory was usually gone somewhere, stoned with his friends. I hadn't seen him in a few months when I went home, and he had cornrows in his hair and his lip pierced.

That visit Cory and I went to the Gadsden Mall to buy some tennis shoes. We stopped at Baskin Robbins for a slushie on the way out. We sat in my car and I heard a blast that I thought was a shotgun, and there was glass in my hair and freezing, red goo dripping down my face. I thought it was blood for a second. Then I realized a rabid teenage boy had busted out the passenger side window. He was halfway in the car, hitting Cory in the face.

"Holy shit!" I screamed and slammed the car in reverse. I backed out and slammed on the brakes, then hit the gas going about thirty miles an hour and the boy hit the side of the car and rolled across the pavement. My heart was thundering in my chest. I didn't know what Cory had gotten into, but it wasn't good. I couldn't stay in Alabama long. It was just too sad.

A week after I returned to Nashville, Uncle Kelly called me and said, "You've got to get down here. Your mom has gone nuts."

When I asked him what she did, he said, "She called me this morning going bat shit about one of those birds. When I got to the house to pick her up to take her to the vet, she was standing in the front yard in a housecoat covered in ice cream stains and she was holding that limp little bird. She was high as a damn kite.

When we got to the vet, she burst through the door yelling, 'My bird, my bird! My little bird! You've got to save my bird.' Oh, my God, Aimee, I was about to die. The waiting room was packed and I just wish you could have seen her trying to give that little dead parakeet mouth to mouth resuscitation. She had its little beak open, blowing into it, and she was pressing it's tiny chest with her fingers. She looked down and pouted like she was gonna cry and said, 'My chicken died.'"

We knew we had to do something. She was eating oxycontin like Skittles.

Blue Mustang

BACK IN NASHVILLE, MY DREAMS were coming true, but as usual, life was gearing me up for the big ride: the roller coaster from bliss to black in a blink. I had the title track of Sara Evan's debut album, "Three Chords and the Truth," and her first single, and Bill and I had the title cut and first single of another new artist, Shona Patron, with "Something Real." Plus, Mila Mason's "Closer to Heaven" was about to come out.

When I got the incredible news that the song "Me," which I wrote with Marv Green, had made it onto Faith Hill's record, I was ecstatic. I ran outside, jumping up and down, doing cartwheels in the backyard. I couldn't wait to tell someone. I had never had a song recorded by a real star, a real established star like Faith. The first person I called was Mom and I screamed, "I got a Faith Hill cut! I got a Faith Hill cut! My song's on her new record."

"I got a new bird," Mom mumbled back at me. When I told Marv, he wrote a song called "My New Bird" and sang it to me, trying to cheer me up. "I always wanted a bir-ir-ird, a bird that loved only me. I always wanted a bird that was mine and could be my very best friend."

I got my first, big BMI royalty check for the song "Places I've Never Been" for $12,800. It went to number three on the charts. When you write a hit song, it takes about nine months before you start getting paid. You get paid in a few bursts, then the checks start to dwindle down until you have another hit song. BMI collects the royalties from the radio, then the checks come every few months.

I had never had any real money. I deposited the check at SunTrust Bank, then drove straight to Bill Henderson's Chevrolet on Broadway. I paid cash for a cobalt blue Mustang convertible with a white ragtop. It was a few years old, but it was the most beautiful car I had ever seen. I couldn't believe it was mine as I drove it off the lot.

I was so used to scraping by, digging for change in the ashtray for three dollars' worth of gas, and praying I didn't break down on the way to work. I knew more about transmissions, radiator belts, and charging cables than most of the guys I knew. That night I went straight to Fanfare, a massive outdoor music festival with around 20,000 people in the audience. I listened to Mark Wills sing my song and watched strangers sing along. It was surreal.

The following night I showed off my new car. After too many beers and a shot of tequila, there were seven people piled inside with my friend, Regina, driving, and Keith Urban and a few strangers, screaming the words to "Don't Do Me Like That" by Tom Petty. I was twenty-seven years old and loving every minute of it, except for when I was lonely back at my apartment all by myself.

A couple of nights a week I went out with my two closest girlfriends, Melissa and Regina. They were both publicists for record labels, and we went to all the industry events and awards shows. Every year we went to the Country Radio Seminar where the new, upcoming artists played live with their bands for the radio programmers, and every year somebody left with a crown: Kenny Chesney, Keith Urban, Blake Shelton, the Dixie Chicks, Shania Twain, Taylor Swift. You know when you see a big star being born.

You can never really get to know someone once they're famous because everybody has an agenda and they learn to guard themselves. But when you meet people before they're famous, that's a different story. If you come up struggling together, and believe in each other from the get-go, before anybody knows how the cards are going to fall, then that's something entirely different.

Land Cruiser

CHRIS HAD ALWAYS BEEN right by my side my entire relationship with Max. They knew each other and had mutual friends. Every time I confided in him about how Max was still seeing Jen, Chris always said things like, "I can't believe he doesn't know how lucky he is."

Chris was the only person who I confided in about how bad Mom's addiction to pain killers had gotten and Dad's mental illness. He listened to me in a way no one ever had. Chris had been married for about a year when we met. His wife wasn't that supportive of him being a songwriter, so she didn't come to most of the songwriter shows. When she went out of town for six weeks to work, Chris was at my apartment almost every night. Sometimes we wrote and sometimes we just talked.

One night we went to Mojo Grill, an outdoor bar and restaurant right off of Music Row. We stayed for over four hours talking about our dreams, about our pasts, about everything. Chris' hair was sticking up everywhere like it usually did.

It was October and there was a tropical breeze. I could feel the chill of an early fall in the air. I had a little bit of a buzz from drinking two Coors Lights, and Chris had a couple of Red Stripe beers. It was the first time we had ever been out alone drinking. Later that night, we sat on the tailgate of his white, vintage Land Cruiser in the gravel parking lot of my apartment.

He reached out to help get me down, then pulled me into his arms and hugged me. I wanted to melt into his leather jacket. He leaned down and tried to kiss me. "Oh, my God, you're married," I said, and pushed him away. I was shocked, but I shouldn't have been. I knew that he had feelings for me. I saw it in his eyes every time he looked at me, but I always pushed that thought out of my mind because he was off-limits. It went against every moral fiber in my being to have an affair with a married man.

After that night, he didn't call me for four days and it was torture. I broke down and called him. I could not imagine my life without him in it.

"I'm sorry and I'm embarrassed. I feel so bad," Chris said.

"Well, we can never do that again," I told him and he agreed. We continued writing and I tried to force myself to stop thinking about him constantly and to stop calling him when I just needed to talk.

Book of Bad Ideas

I MET JAY THAT JANUARY and we started dating. He was twenty-four years old to my twenty-seven years. He played electric guitar in a band that was on tour for most of the year. I went weeks at a time without seeing him, and when I did, he usually, in some subtle way, made me feel bad about myself. Being with Jay, my insecurities spiked. After he commented on my butt looking wide in a pair of blue jeans, I started losing more weight and got down to 110 pounds.

Having dinner with Jay's family was like walking into a 1960s sitcom. His mom wore an apron and filled her husband's iced tea when he rattled the glass. Everything was so proper and normal. I felt like a catch; divorced with scars up both wrists with a mom struggling with addiction and a dad who was in and out of the mental hospital. I hid the shitshow going on in my family. I never told Jay when my dad went back to the psych ward or had electroshock therapy, or about how bad my mom's addiction had gotten. Jay never went back to Alabama with me and he didn't really care about getting to know my family.

Chris was the only guy I had ever talked to about my family who didn't judge me. He felt for me. He wanted to help me and he understood what I was going through because he had a sister who had struggled with a lot of the same issues. We continued to write a couple of times a week and I pushed my feelings down.

One day, Chris and I were eating lunch at an Indian buffet close to Music Row, when he said his wife wanted to have a baby. I could tell that he was searching my eyes to see how I felt. They had been married for two and a half years and she was in her mid-thirties. I encouraged him, "You'll be the best dad. Oh, I bet your baby will be so cute." If he had a baby, that would seal the deal and stop my feelings for him and his for me. I thought a baby would make them closer.

About six months later, we were sitting in the lobby of County Q Studio eating Chinese food when Chris said, "I'm gonna be a dad." It was like someone punched a hole in my stomach, but I told myself that it was meant to be this way. Marv and Bill were both congratulating Chris. I was happy for him too, but something inside me was sinking. I continued to date Jay, but Chris and I spent as much time together as possible. We were spending too much time together.

After I had a couple of hit songs, I was able to buy a house. Chris helped me tour different homes. Thankfully, he talked me out of buying a little, rock house in the middle of nowhere that was in a flood zone. I didn't know what I was doing. When I saw a yellow Victorian house with a wrap-around porch that was built in the late 1800s, I fell in love with it. I had a great idea. If I buy this house two streets over from where Chris lives, he won't be able to spend so much time at my house because his wife would pass by every day and know that he was there. But that turned into a damn disaster.

That December, they had the baby that was supposed to fix their marriage and change my feelings. I went out of town to L.A. and stayed with a friend from high school. I forced myself to stay away from Chris for a couple of months, but we still talked on the phone constantly. I filled my diaries, trying to convince myself that Jay was the one for me, praying that we would get more serious and someday get married, but deep down, I knew that it was never going to work. Every time I tried to imagine being his wife and having kids with him, I couldn't see it in my mind.

I bought my house so impulsively that I didn't realize the pipes and the wiring had problems. It only had one closet and no dishwasher. I had complained about washing dishes a couple of times, and then Chris showed up wearing his construction overalls and said, "Let's go to Home Depot and get you a dishwasher."

Later that night, Chris stood in my kitchen with splinters of wood in his hair, a chainsaw, and crazy construction goggles. He was wiping his sweat on his forearm. I hugged him. I absolutely loved the smell of his skin. Something kept tugging at me like a magnet pulling me to him. It was a primal urge. I wanted to kiss him and I hated myself for it. That night, when he said goodbye, he stood a little closer than usual and looked into my eyes a little longer. Chris didn't want to go home, and I didn't want him to.

Diary Entries:

June 6, 1998

I miss Chris so much it makes me sick. I could just go around vomiting. Everything seems wrong without him. No one makes me laugh the way he does. No one has ever looked at me the way he does. I can see how much he loves me. My heart is exhausted. I can't make my mind stop thinking about him. Last night Chris demoed a new song, "Albuquerque." Hearing him sing it, I knew the words were about me. "I can't get her out of my head to save my life."

June 8, 1998, 3:20 am

I've done a lot of stupid things in my life and most of them happened last week. I bought a house two streets over from Chris, thinking if I'm his neighbor, he won't be able to stay over here all the time because his wife would see his car at my house. Now we don't have anywhere to go, so we spend hours sitting in my car in the MAPCO parking lot. I'm in love with someone who's taken and I am trying

to do the right thing and stay away from him, but I struggle with
moments of weakness.

One night we wrote a song in the basement of DreamWorks Publishing called "Desire." When we finished, Chris came across the room, cradled my face in his hands and pushed me against the back wall. Then he gave me the best kiss I had ever had in my life. I felt it straight in my heart to my core. I kissed him back. "I gotta go. I gotta go right now," I said, and left. I needed to get as far away from him as possible.

I went to the gas station to fill up my tank to drive to Gadsden, but I was so shaken that I drove off with the gas nozzle still in the car and gas was shooting everywhere. I drove through the night thinking about how unfair it was that I finally met my soulmate, but I couldn't be with him.

Genetic Lottery

THE SUMMER OF 1998, MY PARENTS had been divorced for over a decade when within two weeks, they both decided to end it all. Mom went first. She had been taking about forty to fifty oxycontin per day, but when she overdosed, Mom swallowed a whole bottle of Excedrin PM. I got the call and went to Gadsden. Uncle Kelly, Mike, Cory, and I had an intervention with her at the hospital. We told her how much we loved her and how much we needed her and asked her to go to rehab.

I stayed with her at the hospital for a couple of days, but she slept most of the time. Mike took Mom to all of her doctor appointments. He stayed with her at the hospital, picked up her prescriptions, and cooked for her. After visiting with my mom for a while, I drove back to Nashville because I had a writing appointment with Kenny Chesney and Bill. Kenny was the one person I knew while I was married to Dustin, so he never let me live that down.

I was too wrecked to write and had to cancel my demo session that week. It cost over two grand to pay all of the players for the studio when I didn't have the songs. It was a good thing I canceled my session, though, because the next day my Aunt Beth called. I knew when I saw her name on the caller ID that it wasn't good.

"Aimee, your daddy's overdosed. He's alive. He's in an ambulance on the way to the hospital," she said.

"What happened?" I asked.

"I just had a weird feeling and went into his bedroom to check on him. He was passed out on the bed with empty prescription bottles everywhere," she said. "I'm so glad Mother didn't find him." She kept talking and I drifted from the conversation. "Aimee, are you okay?" Beth asked. She was caught off guard by how emotionless I was. I started laughing, which I think freaked her out a little more. I wanted to scream, *I'm as okay as anybody could be who had both their parents in separate psych wards for trying to kill themselves ten days apart!*

"Yeah, I'm okay," I said, and I drove back to Alabama that night. The next day I drove to the psychiatric hospital to see Dad. When I walked into his room, I was expecting him to be out of it like he had been for the last year, so medicated that he would sound like a zombie. But he was sitting up in his hospital bed in a gown that was half open in the back, aggravating the nurse.

"Baby doll, I'm feeling so much better. They got my medicine straightened out and I'm moving back to Nashville. I got another writing deal and I'm gonna buy a house and some horses." He was pretty manic, but I would take that any day of the week.

I drove to Birmingham again to see Mom at the psychiatric hospital and hung out there all day. Mom wanted to play Scattergories with two female patients in their early twenties and she barely talked to me except for wanting to introduce me to Lucy and Shelly, her brand new best friends. It made me sick. She hadn't been my Mom in over a year. It made me wish that I hadn't driven almost four hours from Nashville to come here first.

They had a circle share session with the family. It got so fucked up it was like I was in the room with people shooting up their problems, addicted to them, their new drug to revel in. "I can't do this anymore," I said, and kicked my metal folding chair. It smashed loud against the gym floor.

I drove from Birmingham the sixty miles to Sardis City, Alabama, where Cory was living in a backwoods religious rehab called Mecca. I wanted to talk to him about what was going on with Mom and Dad. The place was about ten miles down a dirt road in the middle of nowhere. There were four or five trailers and a log chapel. Trying to talk to Cory was like trying to have a conversation with an audiobook of the Bible. He kept spurting bible verses at me.

Cory was the first one who knew that I was falling for Chris, and he had the whole place praying for me that I would not live in sin. A man with scary eyes came out of one of the trailers and got right in my face and told me, "If you repent right now, Satan will set you free. You're living in a house of snakes."

That night I was driving back to Nashville. I didn't know whether to laugh or cry or both. I felt like my emotional circuits had all been fried. Lately, when something sad happened, I laughed. When my friend told me her dog died, I started laughing. I couldn't control my emotions anymore. I couldn't cry, no matter what happened. Watching my mom over the last five years have surgery after surgery and become so addicted to oxycontin, along with watching my dad losing his mind, it broke my heart over and over like the intricate layers of an onion, until at my core I felt nothing. I would say numb, but that's a feeling.

Amazed

I CALLED CHRIS FROM A TRUCK STOP on the way home. He said he would be working late at DreamWorks and wanted me to listen to a new song he had written. Chris was in his song pluggers office in a big, leather executive chair. I walked over to him, and he reached out his arms for me to sit in his lap. Something inside me broke. It was like the Hoover Dam. I was crying so hard I didn't know if I would ever stop. I was madly in love with him. He was my best friend and when anything good, bad, or funny happened, he was the first person I called. I couldn't imagine my life without him, and I don't think I would have survived the shock and horror that was waiting for me right around the corner without him.

The night that I wrote the biggest hit song of my career, "Amazed," I had a demo session the next morning and needed one more song. Chris and Marv came over around 6:00 pm and we sat in the back room of my house. I told them, "I want to write a love song," and they were down. I lit about thirty candles, which always set the mood for me. I didn't have a title, but I had a few opening lines.

> *Every time our eyes meet*
> *This feeling inside me*
> *Is almost more than I can take*
> *Baby, when you touch me*
> *I can feel how much you love me*
> *And it just blows me away*

And then Chris and Marv came up with the opening of the chorus:

> *I don't know how you do what you do*
> *I'm so in love with you*
> *It just keeps getting better*
> *I want to spend the rest of my life with you by my side*
> *Forever and ever*
> *Every little thing that you do,*
> *Baby I'm amazed by you.*

There was magic in the song from the very first line. Marv and his girlfriend, Tasha, were getting serious, Chris and I were falling in love, and the energy and emotional charge that was in the room that night got inside the song. Every time it comes on, that feeling comes with it.

The next morning, we were back in the studio with five musicians recording the demo. Usually the demo is the record, but with a different singer. When an artist takes the song, sometimes they copy it exactly, even with the same musicians playing the exact same parts. But "Amazed" took on a life of its own in the studio. We were all arguing in the vocal booth because I was convinced that the song didn't have a title.

"What are we gonna call this?" I asked Chris and Marv. "I love this song. I'm just worried about what we're gonna call it," I told them.

"Let's just call it 'I'm Amazed by You' for now," Marv said.

When we turned it in, our publishers didn't really jump up and down over the song. I don't know if anyone commented, but somewhere along the way one of the publishers, or someone in A&R at the record label, changed the title to just the word "Amazed."

That song changed my life. It went on to be one of the most played love songs of all time. It paid for the dream house I had been drawing all my life with the turret, the red tile roof, and the little stream running along the right side of the house. It was just like I had always drawn it. Even though the song went on to be an eight-week number one and spent eleven weeks on the Adult Contemporary chart at number one, and was the first country song in decades to cross over to the Billboard Hot 100 and take the number one spot on the Pop chart. The funny thing is that people still don't know the song by the title. But, if you sing a couple of lines of the chorus, they can usually sing along.

Chris and I were so in love and we poured all of those feelings into that song and dozens of others. We sang everything we couldn't say, so in the summer of 1999, our love songs were all over the radio. "You're Everything" is a song that Chris wrote for me that was recorded by Keith Urban. We also wrote another song, "Let's Make Love," with Bill and Marv that became a hit song for Faith Hill and Tim McGraw.

I got together with Bill Luther and wrote a song for Chris called, "My Best Friend." The song went on to be a three-week number one hit for Tim McGraw and made the bad grammar hall of fame.

> *You're more than a lover*
> *There could never be another*
> *To make me feel the way you do*
> *Oh, we just get closer*
> *I fall in love all over*
> *Every time I look at you*
> *I don't know where I'd be*
> *Without you here with me*
> *Life with you makes perfect sense*
> *You're my best friend.*

Chris came over one night and told me, "Whether you and me get together or not, I'm not supposed to be in that marriage. I know I'm not." He was crying and said, "I'm so sorry I drug you into this. I should have been stronger."

I hated myself for loving him and I hated him for loving me. He said that he was getting divorced and that he was afraid that if he waited, he would be trapped and only stay because of their son, who was now nine months old. We tried to stay apart, but that lasted about two days.

Chris got an apartment close to Music Row, and I lived in my house two streets away from his ex-wife. She ran by my house every day, pushing her jogging stroller back and forth up my street. I would look out the window and race to my car, so scared that I would run into her. I had met her a few times, but I didn't really know her. I have a master's degree in guilt and torturing myself. I kept waiting for her to drive her Camry through the front of my house, or to knock on my door and ask me to stay away from Chris, but she never did. She just ran by my house every day. I wrote her a letter telling her that I was sorry and I hoped that one day she could forgive me.

Out of everything that I had been through, Mom and Dad's suicide attempts, my own suicide attempt, the abuse I endured as a child, and being married to Dustin, falling in love with Chris landed me in therapy for the first time. It was the most painful thing I had ever been through. Nothing hurts as much as hurting somebody else. Without Chris, I don't know if I would have made it through the blow that was coming my way that knocked my world off its axis.

I knew that Chris would take care of me, no matter what, for the rest of my life. You have to believe that something's out there for it to exist. You have to believe that you can find it or you never will. Chris and I got engaged on August 21, 1999. He wrote a song for me for our wedding called, "You're Everything." It was one of Keith Urban's first hits and the lyrics said:

The first time I looked in your eyes I knew
That I would do anything for you
The first time you touched my face I felt

What I'd never felt with anyone else

I want to give back, what you've given to me
And I want to witness all of your dreams
Now that you've shown me who I really am
I want to be more than just your man

I want to be the wind that fills your sails
And be the hand that lifts your veil
And be the moon that moves your tide
The sun coming up in your eyes
Be the wheel that never rusts
And be the spark that lights you up
All that you've been dreaming of and more, so much more
I want to be your everything

When Chris played me the song, I told him that I loved it, but I didn't know about the line about the wheel rusting. Keith Urban always loved the story and told everybody at his fan club parties, "Who writes a song for somebody like that and then hears them say they want to rewrite it?"

Dad moved back to Nashville and rented a room at the Ramada Inn on Trinity Lane. It was run-down, but it was attached to the Broken Spoke Saloon, the bar where Tim McGraw and many others played before they were famous. It was where legendary songwriters hung out. There was live music, and lots of it, seven nights a week. And Dad was always right in the middle of it. Chris and I picked him up on the weekends and took him to a movie or out to dinner or just to check up on him. It was heartbreaking to see him technically homeless.

I had watched him have a fleet of Mercedes, make millions and mingle with celebrities. I had seen him win awards on TV and be a guest on *The Oprah Winfrey Show*. Now he couldn't afford a coat and drove a $500 car that he said was like driving a fucking oven because the windows wouldn't roll down. Dad told us that he had been working for this thing called Manpower, where they send men out on jobs. He said he worked at the county fair when it was in town. "They had us out there shoveling chicken shit, but I wasn't embarrassed because I was kind of the boss."

One of the last times I saw my dad was the day that Chris and I got engaged. We picked him up and drove to Alabama for Opal's wedding. Dad was upset that Opal was getting married again, and the whole way there he complained. "I can't believe that Mother's not going to be a Mayo anymore."

When we arrived, we were standing in Opal's kitchen and Dad put on gray dress pants that wouldn't zip that she had laid out for him. "Aimee, get in here and look at what Mother laid out for me to wear," he said like he was ten years old and it was her duty to take care of him. "You're my witness when she gets all upset that I'm wearing blue jeans."

It took everything inside of him to sit still for the twenty minute service. No one at the reception knew that they were never going to see him again. He didn't want to stay long at the reception. On the drive back to Nashville, Dad was telling stories and laughing so hard that we were laughing, too. He was leaned over the front seat with a Dr. Pepper in one hand and a Moon Pie in the other. He just kept telling stories nonstop the whole three-hour drive. He told Chris, "I wish you could have met my father." He leaned in closer, "If there were two pieces of fried chicken left, he would take the wing just so somebody else could have the leg. That's just the kind of man he was."

Dad had been so worked up about Opal marrying Tom that I waited until the drive back to Nashville to tell him that Chris and I were engaged. I showed him my ring and he said, "That's pretty, baby doll. I know he'll take good care of you."

When we pulled into the parking lot of the Ramada Inn, Dad jumped out of the car and said, "Wait a minute. Don't go anywhere. I got something for you."

He walked over to that beat-up car and came back with a stack of newspapers the size of a microwave. "Hey, look at this, I bought every one the guy had." It was the *Tennessean* from a couple of weeks earlier when I was the featured songwriter in the Songwriter's Showcase. Dad had turned into my biggest fan.

"I love you, baby doll," he said, then he hugged me and kissed me on the top of my head. Then he shocked me by saying, "I love you too, buddy," to Chris. The sun was going down and Chris and I watched as he walked around the corner to go into the Broken Spoke Saloon.

"I feel bad that he lives here," I said.

"He seems happy," Chris said. "He's got a place to sleep, someone to clean his room every day, and he loves hanging out and listening to live music at the Broken Spoke. Your daddy don't care nothing about money."

"Well, I know that," I said, and laughed.

Chapter Eleven

—

TALKING TO THE SKY

Happy Birthday

THAT SEPTEMBER DAD STARTED PLANNING a big birthday bash for himself. I don't know why it didn't strike me as weird. During my whole life, I had never seen him celebrate his birthday. He usually cussed people out for getting him a gift. Also, he was turning 49. Why not wait for the milestone, the BIG 5-0? He called me ten times a day for weeks, asking for phone numbers, telling me who all was going to be there. "Okay, here's who's playing; Buzz Cason, he's gonna get up first and open the party with a prayer, then he's gonna play that song he wrote 'Endless Love.'"

"Okay, that sounds good," I told Dad.

"And Don McLean's supposed to be there, but he probably won't play 'American Pie.' He doesn't like to play that song, baby doll. But he might play 'Vincent' if you ask him. You know that song, 'Starry, starry night. Paint your palette blue and gray. Look out on a summer's day with eyes that know the darkness in my soul'."

"Yeah, I love that song, but I ain't gonna ask him to sing nothing. I don't know him, Dad."

"Well, Dobie Gray's gonna be there and Joel Sonia's coming over after he plays the Opry, but what I'm most excited about is Cory's gonna play a new song that he said he wrote for me." As soon as we got off the phone, Dad called me right back. "I lost Bob Riggins' number have you got it?" I looked it up and gave it to him.

"I love you Dad, but I'm writing," I said.

"Well, I'll see you tomorrow night. Don't be late."

"I'll be there." Me, Chris, Uncle Kelly. and his boyfriend, Free, all got ready and rode to Dad's birthday party together. When we arrived at the Broken Spoke Saloon, the first person I saw was my brother. I couldn't believe how good Cory looked. He had been clean for five months and he had even quit smoking. So that was one good thing that came out of that crazy rehab in the woods. The last time I had seen him, he had cornrows and a pierced lip. Now his blue eyes were crystal clear.

"Where's Dad?" Cory asked.

"I don't know. I can't believe he's not here."

"Me neither," Cory said. "He called me ten times yesterday, making me promise I'd be here. I've been on a Greyhound bus all day."

Dad's friend, Bob, came up to me to introduce me to his new girlfriend, and then he asked, "Where's your daddy at?"

"I don't know. I'm about to go find him."

Every guest echoed Bob as I walked through the room: "Where's Danny?" "Where's your Daddy?" "Hey, Aimee, is your dad here?"

There was an uneasy fear in the air. A bad feeling. I told Cory, "Maybe he took some sleeping pills and he's in his room asleep." Even to me, my voice sounded unconvincing.

"Yeah," Cory said, but I could see in his eyes that he was as scared as I was. Uncle Kelly said that he and Cory would walk across the street to the parking lot of Gabe's Lounge. Dad had spent a lot of time there and he said that the after-party was going to be there.

"Okay, well Chris and I will go to Dad's room," I said.

Dad had been living in that run-down Ramada Inn for a few months in room 171. Standing at the door, I knocked then pounded with my fist until I hurt my hand. Dad's car was there and I could see that the lights were off through the crack in the curtain. "Let's go get somebody to unlock this door," I told Chris. More guests were beginning to show up, wandering around, not sure where to go or what was going on.

I tried to smile, but I felt hysterical. My mind replayed over and over the conversation that we had the previous morning. "Baby doll, wait until you see who all's coming to this party. This is gonna be a party that nobody ever forgets." Songwriters were crowded in the smoky bar with their guitar cases. Cory and Uncle Kelly said that Dad wasn't at Gabe's Lounge across the street. We walked back around to room 171 and my heart jumped with joy when I saw that the light in Dad's room was now on and the 'Do Not Disturb' sign was stuck in the door.

"Okay, he's awake. Thank God, I was getting worried," I said to Chris.

"So was I," Uncle Kelly said.

"I guess let's just go wait for him."

Walking back into the bar, I was standing next to a cigarette machine when I saw a wild-eyed woman who worked at the hotel. She grabbed Chris' arm and began tugging at his six foot, five inch frame. She was pulling him toward the Coke machines at the end of the walkway, whispering something into his ear, trying to walk him back outside. I followed them.

"What's going on?"

"I don't know," Chris said, "I'm trying to figure that out."

I raised my voice, "Somebody tell me what's happening!" Police cars were pulling into the parking lot. A buzz of panic was now palpable in every person I saw. The 'let's pretend everything is okay' game was over.

Four police cars pulled into the parking lot, followed by an ambulance. Everyone was emptying out from the Broken Spoke Saloon and Gabe's Lounge. There was a crowd of around a hundred people standing in the parking lot. I watched the glowing lights from the police cars spinning blue triangles across the faces of legendary songwriters, celebrities, and all of the motel guests who had wandered out of their rooms into the middle of the chaos, driven by morbid curiosity.

I saw Cory walk across the parking lot and sit down on a concrete curb. He was bent over, holding his knees, rocking back and forth. When I sat down next to him, he grabbed my hand and said, "Let's pray."

At that moment, something happened to me that I had never experienced before. I couldn't pray. Every time I tried, all my words and thoughts seemed to be locked in a black box that I couldn't open. I have an OCD with praying. Every time I pass a church, I pray. I prayed about songs, sunny days, and stuff that shouldn't even be prayed about. My eyes were closed and my heart was ready, but I couldn't pray. My soul refused.

I held Cory's hand and his voice broke my heart. He was begging God, "Please, please, please," through broken sobs. I sat staring at room 171, watching the police officers. They were swirling and twirling yellow police tape around the stairway, unrolling it like they were putting up streamers at a party. Three more cops were huddled on the walkway in front of Daddy's room.

Every time they opened the door, everyone tried to get a glimpse inside. People were coming at me, mouths moving, earrings jiggling, but I couldn't hear a word. I watched another fire truck arrive. Chris was walking toward me, crying. He was crying hard. He hugged me so tightly that I didn't want him to ever let me go. I wanted him to make me disappear, to take me out of there.

"The police want to talk to you," he said. He was having trouble getting the words out.

"No, I don't want to go. This is just a joke. Daddy's trying to shock everybody."

"Aimee, you gotta go talk to them." I held his hand, and he put his arms around me and shielded me from the crowd, but I could feel their whispers and stares crawling all over me like tiny white spiders. I walked into the center of the three officers, their radios spurting static and voices. They were standing in front of Daddy's room, talking to each other as casually as if they were standing at a concession stand at a football game.

A detective walked up to me. "Is there anything we should know?"

"About what?" I asked.

"About Mr. Mayo,"

"I don't know what you mean," I said.

"Well, does your father have enemies?"

"What are they talking about?" I asked Chris.

"Is there anything we should know about your father?"

"Well, he's bipolar and he struggles with depression, but he's been doing way better." The detective walked away and another officer stepped toward me. He had no face, no age, no name. He was just a voice that would echo through me forever. "Ma'am, you do know your father's deceased?"

The cold, emotionless tone of his voice was like he was telling me my dad was dead and calling me a dumbass in the same breath. I heard a primal howl and didn't even realize that it had came from me. I went limp and Chris caught me. The police wouldn't let me inside his room and I didn't know what was waiting on the other side of that door.

"Please let me go in there," I pleaded with the detective.

"We don't think you should. Your dad's been dead for at least twenty-four hours, maybe longer."

That made me think that he didn't do it. I pleaded again with one of the cops until he finally let me go inside Dad's room. "Okay, but I don't think you should," he said, and opened the door. I didn't have a choice. I had to go in that room. I had to see it with my own eyes to make it real.

Walking into Dad's hotel room, the smell hit me first. It was foreign and familiar. I recognized it instantly even though I had never smelled it before. It caught me in the back of the throat, and I could feel it absorbing into my skin. Staring down at my daddy, I saw that he was lying between two double beds. He was on a stretcher that sat on the dirty, burgundy carpet. I fell to my knees beside him. His face was swollen, he had a dot of blood in the corner of his mouth, and one of his eyes looked like it was almost open.

I watched his chest and I saw it rise. I tried to convince myself that he was breathing. I saw a flash of him jumping up, grabbing me, and scaring me like he loved to do. "I got you this time, baby. I got all of y'all. Let's go have fun!"

Daddy was right in front of me, but I was alone in the room. I couldn't feel his essence, his energy, his body seemed hollow. The part of him that laughed and loved, the magic, the music, what made my dad my dad, was gone. Looking at his hands, they mirrored my own. That was the first hand to ever hold mine. A thousand memories flooded my mind; how he taught me to ride my bike, pulling my first tooth, taking me to my first movie. His mischievous brown eyes that won my mother's heart had closed for the last time.

Cory came into the room and walked over to me. He was still crying hard. As he knelt down to hold my hand, we said a prayer over Dad, hoping that he was at peace and that he was in Heaven with Jesus. I told Daddy that I loved him, and as we left the room, I knew that I couldn't watch them roll him out in a body bag with all of those people looking at me. Walking back out into the night, nothing felt real. It was like someone had pulled the breaker on reality like someone had let a monster out and it was coming for us all.

"Is he dead?" Bob asked one of the cops. The officer nodded and Bob started punching a brick wall over and over. His knuckles were dripping blood.

"How did he die?" Chris asked one of the detectives.

"You'll have to wait for the autopsy. It will probably be three to six weeks."

I looked up at the gray clouds moving through the sky, and then at the agony on my little brother's face. "Please God, please tell me he didn't kill himself. Please tell me he wouldn't do that to Cory and me."

Life's Last Parade

THE POLICE SAID WE HAD TO WAIT three to six weeks to find out what caused Dad's death. I was consumed with the question. How did he die? There were no prescription bottles around him and there weren't any in the bathroom either. He would have left a suicide note. He was a writer. My mind kept going over how happy Dad had been the last time I had talked to him. He was writing songs again and excited about the future.

I prayed nonstop that he didn't kill himself. He wouldn't gather all of those people together, then kill himself and leave Cory and me broken in the aftermath with an audience to watch us go into shock. He was crazy, but he wouldn't do that to us. My heart wouldn't let me believe it.

Later that night, I heard Chris arguing with someone on the phone in the kitchen. "I am begging you not to print that," he said. A reporter we both knew who covered all of the country music awards and wrote for the *Tennessean* had called to give us a heads up about an article that they were writing about my dad. Chris tried to stay calm, but the anger was coming through his voice. "We don't even know what happened. You can't put a story like that in the paper when we don't even know what happened yet. I'm begging you to wait." Then I heard him yelling, "Yeah, I guess the truth doesn't sell papers."

The next morning, it was right there in black and white on the front page of the paper: "Songwriter Danny Mayo Found Dead in Hotel Room."

Later that day we went back to Daddy's hotel room to go through all his things. All that was left of the millions of dollars he made were a few pairs of tennis shoes and some thrift store clothes. In the brown minifridge, he had two, little, microwave meals; a country fried steak with mashed potatoes and a chicken pot pie. They both had orange clearance stickers on them. This made me burst into tears.

Sitting on his nightstand was a wad of two-dollar bills and the paperback book, *How to Win Friends and Influence People*. Between the rumors from what had happened at the Ramada Inn and the story on the front page of the paper, most people thought he had gathered us all together to go out with a bang.

***

WE DROVE TO ALABAMA FOR THE FUNERAL. Dad had been dead for five days, so it was a closed casket, but I insisted that I see my dad one more time. The funeral director took me into his office. He shut the door and said, "I strongly suggest that you don't see your father. It's been too long and you don't need to see him like this."

"I've got to see him. Somebody has to see him," I said.

My grandmother wanted to remember him the way he was. So did my Aunt Beth, but someone had to see my dad before they sealed the casket. Someone had to bear witness to make sure he was in there and that they put him in a suit. I stared down at my daddy in the casket. He was dressed in a gray suit, which didn't feel right. Even at black-tie events, he would go wearing blue jeans, a leather vest, and rhinestones, or even feathers. It was always something crazy.

This was the first man who ever loved me. The first hand that ever held mine. My daddy. He taught me how to swim. He taught me how to make the perfect fried chicken. He bought me my first camera and took me to see Cyndi Lauper. He was the biggest dreamer I knew.

Sitting in the funeral service, I felt numb. A preacher I had never seen read bible verses that sounded more like fortune cookie fortunes. He was the preacher at Opal's church, but he didn't know my dad or his wild reputation and his struggles. We played Sarah McLachlan's song "Angel," and I ached from the lyrics. We played a hymn for Opal and a song that Daddy had written years before for his own funeral, "Life's Last Parade." I couldn't look at Cory, Opal, or my Mom during the service.

Afterward, I stood with my grandmother as a line of people came by to pay their respects. I felt like a statue, cold and numb, while distant relatives I didn't know tried to hold me, cry with me and comfort me. All I remember is the powdery perfume of the older women and their warm breath in my face as they talked about the Lord and that time would make it better. Everyone talked about time. But time just seemed like a rowboat to nowhere.

Beyond and Beyond and Beyond

TWO WEEKS AFTER THE FUNERAL, the medical examiner finally called and said, "Mr. Mayo had a massive heart attack." He started talking about interior arteries and medical words, but I was too busy rejoicing in my head to hear anything else he said. None of that mattered. Dad died of natural causes. I asked if there were any drugs in his system and the examiner said, "All the toxicology report showed was a trace of antihistamine."

***

THE NEXT DAY I FOUND OUT THAT I WAS PREGNANT.
My emotions were everywhere. There was life growing inside me
and my dreams were coming true, but my heart was breaking at
the same time.

Chris and I kept our original wedding date, so on November
11, 1999, we were married in Sedona, Arizona. Twenty two of our
closest family and friends met us there. The night before our wedding, we all went to dinner and had Italian food, then we went
back to the hotel and took over the lobby playing Charades. Mom
had been clean for over six months. She sat behind me, laughing
so hard that everyone was laughing with her.

Our wedding was at the Tlaquepaque Chapel. Everything
about it felt right; the gorgeous, green vines that covered the stuc-
co walls, the cobblestone walkways, the giant sycamore trees, and
the red and purple flowers in the courtyard.

The chapel was tiny and seemed timeless with its hand-
carved, leather pews, whitewashed adobe walls and the sun shining through the stained-glass windows. Everything about the day
felt right; the warm desert breeze, the smell of jasmine. Mom did
my hair and put it up in a swirly bun with little pearls pinned
throughout. She looked beautiful, her dark hair blowing in the
wind. She was back to her good, time-loving, loud, laughing self.
All of my friends adored her. When she felt good, there was no
one in this world who was more fun. Cory was as bright-eyed as
I had ever seen him.

I stood there, with morning sickness, in my wedding dress as
Chris read the most achingly romantic vows to me. He held my
hands, looked into my eyes, and promised, "I will always take
care of you, always." And I knew that he would.

Throughout the service in the windowsill, a mountain bluebird sat and watched the whole ceremony. Everyone noticed and
took photos. It was even on the wedding video. "I know it's crazy,
but I think that little bluebird was Daddy," I told Chris. I had
tears in my eyes. I was so happy and sad at the same time.

On that trip, Mom and I, along with Cory, Uncle Kelly, and
Chris, drove out to see the wonder of the Grand Canyon. "Aimee,
I've never seen anything like this in my life. And I never thought
I would, baby," Mom said, and put her arm around my waist. I

292 | AIMEE MAYO

looked at her, soaking up the glory of the Grand Canyon, and I was filled with love for her.

The day after the wedding most of the guests met at sunrise to go on a hot air balloon ride. High into the heavens, we were floating in the unbelievably blue sky. Cory, Uncle Kelly, and Free, were on the hot air balloon across from us. Almost everyone who came to the wedding was now in two, rainbow-colored hot air balloons, soaring over the glorious red rocks. It was magical, spiritual, and unforgettable.

***

WE WERE NOMINATED FOR A GRAMMY for our song "Amazed." I was five months pregnant and looked like I had a beer belly in my black and sequined dress. I felt our son kick for the first time on Sunset Boulevard on the way to the awards. Chris, Marv, and I were starstruck at the Grammys. "Holy shit, I just saw Prince when I went to the bathroom," Marv said.

Jennifer Lopez walked past me, looking for her seat. "You have got to see her dress," I told Chris. It was the green one that was cut down to her navel that was on the cover of every magazine a few days later.

My emotions were zooming. I told Chris and Marv, "I'm so scared they're gonna call out another song and I'm gonna stand up." They were too nervous to talk. The presenters announced the nominees for 'Country Song of the Year.' "And the winner is, 'Come on Over' by Shania Twain."

We sat in our seats, staring at the stage and took the blow. They called out for Shania to come to the stage. Everyone waited, but she wasn't even there.

A few months later, we were nominated for, and won, 'Song of the Year' at the Academy of Country Music Awards. Once again, I sat in the auditorium with my ears ringing, trying to listen to the announcers. When they opened the envelope and read our names, it didn't feel real. When we went on stage to get our award, I was barefoot, eight months pregnant, and jumping up and down. Dolly Parton said, "You'd better settle down, or you're gonna have that baby right here."

Cory wrote a song about losing Dad and it became a giant hit for George Strait. Cory could have been famous. He still could. He's like a modern-day Kris Kristofferson. It doesn't get any more raw or real. He's so much like my dad.

When we went to the grocery store and some guy behind us had a whole buggy full of lettuce, everybody was wondering why, but Cory couldn't stand it. He turned around and asked the guy, "What are you, a fucking rabbit?" Then the guy laughed and said he worked at a salad bar and they were out of lettuce. If you got in the car with Cory, you could end up anywhere, just like with Dad.

When he was waiting for his first royalty check, he was living with Mom and Mike. He had a pregnant girlfriend, Toby, and didn't have a car.

"I know what I'm getting when I get that royalty check." He said.

"What?"

"A boat."

The next year, I became one of the few women in the company of Taylor Swift and Dolly Parton to ever win BMI's 'Song of the Year' and 'Songwriter of the Year.' I wished so badly that Dad could have been there to see it.

***

SUDDEN DEATH, AND THE SHOCK OF IT, broke my heart and my mind. Death is the most final word in the world. I couldn't believe that I could blink and someone would just be gone. The empty ache of loss sat on the shoulders of every bad day. Grief is a soul breaker and a sanity shaker. It will carve you clean.

We think our parents are immortal. Losing a parent is losing your childhood, your teenage years, and the past. It's losing the world you shared. It's losing their love and the volumes of memories that are now yours and yours alone.

I prayed for a dream for God to give me closure on losing my dad. I kept having the same recurring nightmare that I was in a hotel room fighting with Dad. "Everybody thinks you're dead. What are you doing' hiding' in here?"

This went on for years. But I finally had my dream when Chris and I were in Denver, staying downtown at the Oxford Hotel. We were writing with Ryan Tedder of OneRepublic. When I saw Dad in my dream, he was as blissful and animated as ever, and he said, "Baby doll, it's just beyond and beyond and beyond..."

Talking to the Sky

SEVEN YEARS LATER, Chris and I were writing a new song. Our first son, Levi, was born with one eye open and he looked just like my dad. We named him Levi Daniel Lindsey, his middle name after my father. We brought him home from the hospital nine months to the day that Dad died. I joked to Chris, "What if I just had my dad?"

Twenty-two months later, Oscar was born. He was my side-kick and our little spiritual guru. In 2007 my sweetest surprise, our daughter, Lola, was born.

The following summer, in 2008, we were on the top deck of a Mediterranean cruise ship. Chris and our seven-year-old, Levi, were lying side by side on plastic, strappy lounge chairs. They both had their hands locked behind their heads, looking up, gazing at the universe. Our younger son, Oscar, was running a Hot Wheel up and down the lounge chairs, and our ten-month-old, Lola, sat in her stroller, smiling up at everybody with her two little Tic Tac teeth. She had on a ruffled, pastel pink and green bonnet, and every time I looked at her, she burst into a fit of giggles, which caused us all to laugh.

"We're floating in an ocean of stars," Levi said.

"It's crazy to think the earth is spinning almost a thousand miles an hour right now," Chris said.

"I know," Levi said, his eyes getting big.

We were solving the mysteries of the universe. What is God? Where did we come from? If God made everything, who made God?

"Why do you think everyone thinks Heaven's in the sky?" I asked Levi.

"I don't know why," he said, and shrugged his shoulders.

Oscar, our five-year-old mystic, marched over to us. "I need to tell you one important thing about the sky," he said.

The wind was blowing his golden curls into his face, and he brushed his hair out of his mouth.

"Okay, what is it?" I asked.

"Everybody thinks that Heaven is in the sky, or in the clouds in the daytime, but when someone dies, they go somewhere they love best, wherever they want to go, whatever they imagine."

"That's a beautiful thought," I said.

"I'm the one that thought of it," Levi said.

Oscar jumped on him, saying, "No. You. Did. Not." Then he said, "I'm a vampire, and there's bats, and they're sucking blood!"

"Somebody's gonna be crying in about three minutes," Chris said, watching them wrestling around. Lola had been rocked to sleep by the waves, and she looked like an angel.

"Are you ready to go back?" Chris asked.

"Can I meet y'all in the room in about fifteen minutes?"

"Yeah, baby," he said, and leaned down to kiss me on the top of my head. I watched him pushing the stroller and the boys started dancing to the weird foreign disco music blasting from the nightclub just inside the door. My heart was so full that I could barely contain it.

Mom and my Aunt Debbie were in their cabin on the cruise ship. I had always wanted to take them on a cruise. Mom was doing great. She lived in Nashville now, just down the road from our house. The house with the turret, the red tile roof, and a stream running right alongside the right side of the yard. In the last week, we had gone to the Vatican, the Eiffel Tower, and the Coliseum in Rome. We had spent that day in Croatia and heard "Amazed" at an outdoor restaurant where we had lunch.

I walked over to the edge of the cruise ship. The water looked like black, liquid glitter. The ocean was a mirror of the sky. The stars were everywhere. I could taste the salt on my lips and the wind was whipping through my hair. I felt the rhythm of the water and the harmony of the universe. As I stood there on the bow of that ship, I could see the Milky Way for the first time since I was a child. Staring up at the magic we call the sky, I realized that something up there, something somewhere, had heard my prayers all along. I was living the life that I had imagined. The life that I had written and dreamed about in my diaries for all those years. It had come true. I had met my poet, we fell in love, and the world sang along. I had a fun, crazy house full of kids, music, laughter, and love.

I looked up at the sky with a smile on my face and tears in my eyes, and asked, "How is this my life?"

The End

Kenny Chesney
Jamey Johnson
Dee Downey Pruett
Dallas Davidson
Keith Urban
Uncle Kelly
Angela Bostelman
Jerry Bostleman
Kelly Harwood
Craig and KK Wiseman
Sarah Buxton
Tom Bukovac
Marv and Tasha Green
Todd DiBenedetto
Karen Conrad
Demming Bass
Brantley Gilbert
Mike Cronin
Rhett Akins
Clint Higham
Deric Ruttan
Ron Kitchener
Amy Price Neff
Jim & Molly Cantino
Connie Harrington
Ben Vaughn
Lisa Boullt
Ross Ellis Lipsey
Lorraine McKenna
Karyn Rochelle
Julian King
Caitlyn Smith
Laurie Armstrong Ford
John Danielson
Chris Craddock
Laura at Island Kids
Carolyn Dawn Johnson
Scott and Teri Hendricks
Josh and Carly Kear

Dana Tredway
Steve Zalla
Tom Douglas
Gina Cross
Shane Caudle
Andrew Rollins
MJJC 1987
Troy Tomlinsom
Brad Warren
Brett Warren
Steven McEdwan
Caroline Haney
Ron Harbin
Charles Gambino
Marvin Baker
Lana Carden McCay
Kathi Regas
Keith Cargal
Ddbies 247
Louis Glaser
Jimmie Wetzel
Brett James
Beth Ann Kessler
Erin Pauling
Barry Dean
Kristi Akridge Mertel
Matt Maher
Eric Holijes
Gary Allan
Shane Stevens
Gary Burr
Monet Maddux
JT Corenflos
Kelly Clague
Stephen Gage
Tobi Vos
Shawn Cole
Jerald Barrett
Beth Laird

John Wilson
Cassie Petty
Stephen Gage
Diana Taub
Nathan Chapman
Troy Verges
Ralston Wells
Drew Russell
Phillip Noe
Vanessa Royal
Denise Wilson
Korie Bernard
Ang Bryant
Scott and Sandi Borchetta
Meri Fernandes
Kent Earls
John I
Lindsey Hinkle
Kerri Edwards
Mike Dungan
Deana Carter
Shannan Hammer
Jeff Royal
Clay Myers
Travis Hill
Kristen Robinette
Kirstie Smith
Michelle Luther
Marilyn Jennings
Dann Huff
Cynthia Chloewinski
Eugene N Lisa Vaughn
Christian Barker
Gay Verges
Alison Junker
Kelly Herring Elrod
Mark Nesler
Karen Lowery
Leslie Dabrowiak
Cary Barlowe

Hillary Lindsey
Teresa Forbes
Dan Hampton
Denton Fllms
Catherine Thornhill Teat
Kathy Lindsey
Liz Morin
Melissa Lagrandeur
Nate Lowery
Renee Allen
Lynn Allen
Dana Wilson
Emily Bennetti
Chuck Weaver
Melissa Stevens
Phil May
Whitney Jones Fisher
Darlene Hutcheson Greer
Clinton Bishop
Renee Rancourt
Brad Warren
JT Harding
Winter Pavone
Amy Beck-Cody
Nena L. Kobayashi
Elaina Karras
Alison Lagarde
Bob Regan
Marc & Krista Oswald
Keisha Chapman
Ryan Lafferty
Dl Restivo
Karen Mundy
Jim McReynolds
Kendi Onnen
Grace Schoper
Chris Garner
Rhonda Campbell
Craig Campbell
Jen Miller

Tracy Slezak
Mary Teague
Alicia Witt
Carla Houser
Missi Gallimore
Cassie Rea
Leslie Mendelson
Beth Snead
Tiffany Bratcher
LeRoy Falcon
Kelly Carr
Suzie Chism
Christy Bobo
L.A. Ballard
Tim Miller
Chuck Cargal
Christine Droney
Mark Irwin
Kathryn Sprayberry Wins-
lett
Tommy Lee James
Wendy Christiansen
Kelly Archer
Sharon Kinter
Gary Jenkins
Bonnie J Castillo
Jaimie Jones Schilken
Jill Bow
BJ Hill
Craft Services
Emily Landis
Julie at Global Changes
Kris Vedder
Sherman Allen
Cari Tilley
Carlette Scarbrough
Bobby Pinson
Ira Shivitz
Shannon Forrest
Sarah Eisner

Ruth Greenwood
Rusty Gaston
Bryan Simpson
Patti Watson
Tim McFadden
Shea Fowler
David Hall
Andrea Hall
Chris Spintzyk
Tom Pate
Dale Bobo
Jonathan Yudkin
Gary McCorkle
Jake Orlowitz
Sam Baratta
Kristi Akridge Mertel
Lynn Allen
Renee Allen
Sherman Allen
Rhett Akins
Kelly Archer
Marvin Baker
L.B. Ballard
Sam Baratta
Christian Barker
Jerald Barrett
Demming Bass
Danny Bear
Amy Beck-Cody
Emily Bennetti
Korie Bernard
Beth
Clinton Bishop
Christy Bobo
Dale Bobo
Bonnie
Lisa Boullt
Angela Bostelman
Jerry Bostleman
Tiffany Bratcher

Ang Bryant
Gary Burr
Craig Campbell
Rhonda Campbell
Lana Carden McCay
Chuck Cargal
Keith Cargal
Carolyn
Kelly Carr
Deana Carter
Shane Caudle
Nathan Chapman
Suzie Chism
Cynthia Cholewinski
Shawn Cole
Karen Conrad
JT Corenflos
Craft Services
Craig
Gina Cross
Leslie Dabrowiak
John Danielson
Deston Films
Todd DiBenedetto
Christine Droney
Kent Earls
Kent and Martha Earls
Kerri Edwards
Sarah Eisner
Meri Fernandes
Teresa Forbes
Shannon Forrest
Shea Fowler
Stephen Gage
Charles Gambino
Chris Garner
Rusty Gaston
Louis Glaser

Tasha Green
Ruth Greenwood
David H
Andrea Hall
Shannan Hammer
Dan Hampton
Caroline Haney
Ron Harbin
Connie Harrington
Maw Maw and Paw Paw
Harwood
Scott Hendricks
Kelly Herring Elrod
Clint Higham
BJ Hill
Faith Hill
Lindsey Hinkle
Eric Holljes
Carla Houser
Dann Huff
Darlene Hutcheson Greer
John I.
Mark Irwin
Brett James
Gary Jenkins
Marilyn Jennings
Jill
Jaymie Jones Schilken
Julie
Alison Junker
Elaina Karras
Carly Kear
Keisha
Kelly
Kendi
Beth Ann Kessler
Julian King
Sharon Kinter

Ron Kitchener
Ryan Lafferty
Alison Lagarde
Melissa Lagrandeur
Emily Landis
Kathy Lindsey
Ross Ellis Lipsey
Karen Lowery
Nate Lowery
Michelle Luther
Monet Maddux
Matt Maher
Marc
Phil May
Gary McCorkle
Steven McEwan
Lori McKenna
Leslie Mendelson
Michael
Jen Miller
Tim Miller
Missi
Liz Morin
Clay Myers
Eugene N.
Phillip Noe
Jake Orlowitz
Erin Pauling
Winter Pavone
Cassie Petty
Bobby Pinson
Cassie Rea
Kristen Robinette
Karyn Rochelle
Andrew Rollins
Jeff Royal
Vanessa Royal
Drew Russell

Carlette Scarbrough
Christopher Schelling
Grace Schoper
Ira Shivitz
Bryan Simpson
Tracy Slezak
Kristie Smith
Beth Snead
Chris Spintzyk
Kathryn Sprayberry Winslett
Stephen
Melissa Stevens
Shane Stevens
Diana Taub
Mary Teague
The Creative Fund
Catherine Thornhill Teat
Cari Tilley
Troy Tomlinson
Dana Tredway
K.U.
Ben Vaughn
Lisa Vaughn
Kris Vedder
Gay Verges
Troy Verges
Tobi Vox
Patti Watson
Chuck Weaver
Ralston Wells
Jimmie Wetzel
Dana Wilson
Denise Wilson
John Wilson
Alicia Witt
Jonathan Yudkin
Steve Zalla

Made in the USA
Las Vegas, NV
10 March 2021